working with **parents** of **AGGRESSIVE CHILDREN**

TIMOTHY A. CAVELL

working **with** parents of **AGGRESSIVE CHILDREN**

A Practitioner's Guide

American Psychological Association
Washington, DC

Published by
American Psychological Association
750 First Street, NE
Washington, DC 20002

Copies may be ordered from
APA Order Department
P.O. Box 92984
Washington, DC 20090-2984

In the U.K., Europe, Africa, and the Middle East, copies may be ordered from
American Psychological Association
3 Henrietta Street
Covent Garden, London
WC2E 8LU England

Typeset in Century Schoolbook by EPS Group Inc., Easton, MD

Printer: Automated Graphic Systems, White Plains, MD
Cover Designer: Watermark Design Office, Alexandria, VA
Technical/Production Editor: Allison L. Risko

The opinions and statements published are the responsibility of the authors, and such opinions and statements do not necessarily represent the policies of the APA.

Library of Congress Cataloging-in-Publication Data
Cavell, Timothy A.
    Working with parents of aggressive children: a practitioner's guide / Timothy A. Cavell.—1st ed.
        p. cm.
    Includes bibliographical references and index.
    ISBN 1-55798-637-1 (cloth: acid-free paper)
        1. Aggressiveness (Psychology) in children.   2. Violence in children.
    3. Parent and child.   4. Parent-child interaction therapy.   I. Title.

RJ506.A35 C38 2000
155.4'8232—dc21

                                                                99-045997

British Library Cataloguing-in-Publication Data
A CIP record is available from the British Library.

Printed in the United States of America
First Edition

For Ed and Erin

Contents

Preface

The workshop of character is everyday life.
— Maltbie D. Babcock

The joys of parents are secret, and so are their grieves and fears.
— Francis Bacon

Like most people in this country, I was shaken by news of the high school shootings in Littleton, Colorado. Many others in my community were shaken too. A local television station held a public forum so concerned citizens could offer their ideas and ask questions. A panel of local experts was formed to answer their questions. As a member of that panel, I thought we did an okay job even though none of us could answer the questions looming largest in everyone's mind: "Why?" and "Where next?"

I believed we faltered, however, on some other important questions. These questions were not about controversial topics such as gun control, school prayer, or media violence. Instead, these questions were from worried mothers who were seeing signs of antisocial behavior in their own children. The mothers wanted a reason to believe that their children would not resort one day to excessive violence. I liked hearing their questions because too often the phrase "We need to help these parents" is shot out like a fireworks display—always a crowd pleaser but nothing of lasting value. I was excited about the possibility of discussing in a public forum these real questions from real parents about their aggressive children.

The mothers offered up their questions and listened eagerly as experts in law enforcement, education, and mental health gave their answers. What followed was often a frustrating experience, both for me and for these mothers. Panel members who fielded their questions spoke in vague generalities and with little appreciation for the challenges these mothers face. One of the better responses came from a school superintendent who admitted that school was an unlikely place for one mother to get the help she needed. In the end, I was saddened by what amounted to a missed opportunity. For many viewing this forum, the complexities of working with parents of aggressive children were left undiscovered, and simplistic notions about what these parents need were allowed to persist.

Hopefully, those who read this book will be able to discover what was not addressed in that televised forum. This is a book for practitioners who treat aggressive, school-age children and have the opportunity to work with the parents of these children. Some would say this is a book about parent training.

I view it more as a guide to parent therapy or parent work, as in marital therapy or couples work. For me, the term *parent therapy* does a better job of capturing the type of intensive therapeutic work that is needed if practitioners are to help families with severely aggressive school-age children. The term *parent training* tends to connote a specific and perhaps exclusive focus on skills training. I have often felt the term is a liability because it fails to convey the complexity of the work and invites the perception that parents need only participate in order to benefit.

This book goes beyond the kind of parent training program that focuses on young, preschool children who are mildly oppositional; its focus is the type of parent therapy required if one is working with highly aggressive, school-age children. Examples of the former are well known and widely available. Examples of the latter are less common, apparently hidden somewhere between prevention for preschoolers and treatment for teenagers. A second, related gap addressed in this book is the difference between clinic-based parent training programs and parent intervention conducted in the schools or with school-based populations. The former provides a service to parents who seek help; the latter is an attempt to serve parents who need help but may not seek it.

Before discussing the specifics of parent therapy, I begin in chapter 1 with a brief overview of the research literature on childhood aggression. Included here are general empirical findings on the etiology, behavioral correlates, and prognosis for children who are aggressive. A brief discussion on the assessment and treatment of aggressive children and their parents is also contained in chapter 1. Chapter 2 is a general introduction to parent training. I describe parent training from both a historical and a theoretical perspective. More specifically, I highlight the overlap and the distinctions between the two major models of parent training—behavior management and relationship enhancement. The chapter concludes with a summary of research on the efficacy of these two models. Chapter 3 introduces a conceptual model designed to help practitioners gain a better appreciation of the tasks involved in helping parents of aggressive children. In this integrated model, which I have termed *responsive parent therapy* (RPT), I blend aspects of structural family, relationship enhancement, and behavior management therapies with recent work in the area of attachment and children's socialization. The RPT model represents my attempt to provide an up-to-date and integrated model of parent therapy. Chapter 3 explores both the essential elements of this model, which reflect a relationship-based theory of socialization, and its specific features. RPT features a supportive, working alliance with parents, combined with therapy and training across six areas of parenting: acceptance, containment, prosocial values, parenting goals, family structure, and parental self-care. Finally, Chapter 3 discusses issues related to the depth of coverage and the possible sequencing of the different intervention components.

The next six chapters are devoted to each of the components of the RPT model. Chapter 4 focuses on techniques for fostering a cooperative and working alliance between trainers and parents. Parents' resistance to training and effective response to such resistance are addressed. The topics of identifying realistic parenting goals and educating parents about possible child effects that can adversely affect the quality of the parent–child relationship are also addressed here. Not only are these topics important in their own right, they are also useful topics to cover when forming an alliance with parents who feel defeated and discouraged.

Chapter 5 describes methods for teaching parents the skills needed to convey accurate understanding and emotional acceptance of their child. Specific acceptance skills include nondirective play skills and active listening skills. In chapter 6, the critical area of behavior containment is addressed. Drawing from a large body of research in the area of behavior-management parent training, I discuss commonly used techniques such as response cost and "time-out." However, I also address other issues that have received less attention, including techniques for coping with the costs of containment, methods for enhancing both the short- and long-term effects of discipline, and the importance of constructing containment scripts. Chapter 7 is a brief look at the issue of promoting parents' endorsement of prosocial beliefs and values. Some parents need assistance in making their values explicit to their aggressive children. I discuss possible reasons why parents may fail to do this on their own, and I offer specific suggestions for how parents can lead and guide children in prosocial ways. Chapter 8 is devoted to the topic of family structure. I propose in this chapter that structure and organization can buffer parenting practices from the impact of stressful events. I review what I call the *4 Rs* of family structure —roles, rules, rituals, and routines—and give examples of how practitioners can help parents enhance each of these structures. In chapter 9, I address the critical issue of parental self-care. I begin by reviewing a series of empirical studies that attempted to alter various aspects of parental self-care and then offer an expanded view of self-care strategies that can be used to increase parents' energy, strength, and commitment. This chapter presents several strategies that may be helpful to parents with the recognition that parents can vary widely in their self-care choices.

I conclude the book with a discussion of school-based parent intervention (chapter 10) and a brief epilogue. I point out that school-based parent interventions can refer to parent training conducted in schools and to parent work that targets school-based samples of aggressive children. I suggest that the latter is a more challenging task for practitioners. Therefore, I share several tips and tactics learned from my own involvement in PrimeTime, an ongoing school-based prevention project that uses parent consultation conducted in the home. In the epilogue, I discuss service delivery and parent involvement in light of the relationship-based model of socialization that guides RPT.

Whenever possible, I present guidelines that are based on empirically validated principles. Less emphasis is given in this book to specific parenting techniques. By emphasizing principles over techniques, I create a fair amount of ambiguity for practitioners who are just beginning to work with parents of aggressive children. Therefore, inexperienced parent therapists would benefit by combining the guidelines in this book with supportive supervision. For more experienced practitioners, this text offers a model of parent therapy that has clear, practical applications for working with parents of severely aggressive, school-age children.

Acknowledgments

I want to thank Jan Hughes, the series editor, for her invaluable assistance and unceasing support in the writing of this book. I also want to thank Eric Johnson, Susie Snyder, and Mary Lou Kelley. Whatever clinical skills I may possess in working with parents of aggressive children are due in large measure to these individuals. The William C. Hogg Foundation has been a generous supporter of my research on interventions for aggressive children. I am especially grateful to Wayne Holtzman and Reymundo Rodriguez for their support and encouragement. I also want to thank my graduate students, in particular Lisette Constantin, Jennifer Welch, and Chandra Kinnee, for their contributions to the Responsive Parent Training Project. Thanks also to the many parents of aggressive children with whom I have worked and who have entrusted me with their parenting concerns. I have probably learned more from them than they have learned from me.

I credit Allison Risko, the technical editor, for making the final version of my manuscript a book of which I can be proud. Thanks also to Joy Montgomery and Kim Cozzi for their valuable assistance in typing portions of this book and to Miriam Aune, Ryan Loss, Joni Wilson, and Jill Womack for their assistance with copyediting and working on references. I am also grateful to the good folks at Deluxe Diner who tolerated my "academic loitering" as I worked on this book.

I am also indebted to Cheryl Bodiford McNeil and Jean Dumas for their excellent reviews of an earlier draft of this book, and to Greg Pettit for his comments and his encouragement.

I wish to acknowledge my own parents, Ed and Erin, for their models of parenting: They taught me that parenting is about cherishing and trusting in yourself, your values, and your children. Thanks to my own children (Hannah Jeanne, Caroline Hope, and Timothy Graham), who educate me daily about the many ways in which children can show their needs and their gifts. Finally, I want to thank my wife and coparent, Lauri Percy, for the many insights she has given me about the challenges of parenting three young children. Her candor and passion remind me that parenting —although neither simple nor easy—is an opportunity for creating a lifetime of shared rewards.

working **with** parents
of **AGGRESSIVE CHILDREN**

1

First Things to Know (and Learn) About Aggressive Children and Their Parents

This book is about how to work with parents of aggressive, school-age children. The essence of this book is contained in three premises. The first premise is that practitioners must be responsive to the needs of parents if parents are to be more responsive to the needs of children. To be responsive, practitioners must learn to combine skill and motivation with an accurate understanding of the problems and opportunities that face parents of aggressive children. Practitioners may be tempted, when working with these parents, to make some rather naive assumptions. One is to question parents' level of concern and their moral fiber. Such questions are not completely unfounded given research indicating that parents of aggressive children can be harsh and critical in their discipline (Patterson, Reid, & Dishion, 1992). Some of these parents may even show signs of antisocial personality disorder (e.g., Frick & Jackson, 1993; Lahey, Russo, Walker, & Piacentini, 1989). However, when practitioners question parents' character and approach them with a strong negative bias, they miss seeing the real strengths that most of these parents possess. The second outlook to guard against is that of being Pollyannaish about the likelihood of "turning parents around." There exists considerable empirical support for the use of parent training as an intervention for aggressive children (Kazdin, 1993, 1997). However, it is naive to believe that every family with an aggressive child will be transformed and made indistinguishable from other families. Therefore, the first lesson of this book is that helping parents of aggressive, school-age children requires a clear understanding of their plight. A narrow vision of what parents need will not suffice. By fully understanding the challenges that confront parents of aggressive children, practitioners are less apt to be frustrated by them.

For readers who want more information about aggressive children, there are a number of excellent sources. These include special journal series on children's conduct disorder (Richters & Cicchetti, 1993; Tolan, Guerra, & Kendall, 1995) as well as published chapters and books. Hinshaw (1992), Loeber, Farrington, Stouthamer-Loeber, and Van Kammen (1998); and Patterson et al. (1992) all provide excellent overviews.

The second premise of this book is that current models of parent training are outdated and are in need of revision if practitioners are to work effectively with parents of aggressive, school-age children. Current approaches to parent training focus primarily on the defiant preschooler and not on the older, school-age child whose conduct problems are more antisocial in nature. The core curricula in these programs have changed little in the 30-plus years since their development, and the underlying conceptual models have been rather impervious to the influence of more recent empirical and theoretical research. In this book, current models of parent training serve as the foundation for a broader and more up-to-date framework for how to work with parents of aggressive children—a framework that draws from both applied and nonapplied areas of psychology.

The third premise of this book addresses the question of what aggressive, school-age children need in order to be socialized. That is, what should parents do to help aggressive children abide by the rules against hurtful behavior at home, at school, and in the community? Guiding this book is the view that socializing aggressive children requires their long-term participation in relationships that provide emotional acceptance, behavioral containment, and prosocial guidance and modeling. This premise has important implications for how to work with parents of aggressive children. First, effective intervention for parents of aggressive children is not simply a matter of teaching a set of techniques that parents then impose on their children. Rather, it is an attempt to right a relationship that is going badly. In other words, working with parents of aggressive children is more like marital therapy than parent education or individual child therapy. Second, parenting strategies that promote a child's long-term socialization warrant greater emphasis than strategies that promote a child's immediate compliance. Most parent training programs have emphasized the latter while assuming the former. Third, acceptance, containment, and prosocial guidance and modeling are difficult skills to maintain when parents feel overwhelmed and their children are hard to manage. Therefore, the chief task for practitioners is to help find that combination of acceptance, containment, and prosocial guidance that is most realistic and sustainable given both the parent and the child. This book is an attempt to articulate and illustrate the strategies for doing that kind of parent intervention.

Three Kinds of Information

Practitioners need three kinds of information if they are to gain a clear understanding of the dilemma facing parents of an aggressive child. The first is accurate information about what is *normative* for aggressive children. The bulk of this chapter is devoted to reviewing normative information about aggressive children. The source of this information here is empirical research documenting the characteristics and tendencies of aggressive children in general or on average. The second type of information that practitioners need is *idiographic* data regarding the child in question.

Shirk and Russell (1996) suggested that a lack of attention to idiographic information and an overreliance on nomothetic data (and vice versa) can mislead the practitioner. They argued that in the nomothetic approach to clinical practice

> characteristics of the individual case tend to be equated with characteristics of the group as a whole. Consequently, it becomes tempting to move directly from diagnosis to intervention without an adequate assessment of the individual characteristics of the specific case. The logic goes something like this: If aggressive children have been shown to be deficient in problem-solving skills, and a child is identified as aggressive, problem-solving therapy is often judged to be the treatment of choice. (p. 266)

In the case of childhood aggression, idiographic questions address the specifics of problem onset, severity, and duration as well as the presence of various risk and protective factors that can function to exacerbate or ameliorate a child's subsequent adjustment. For example, one might ask, what unique set of factors conspired to produce severe aggression in *this child*? What factors are now maintaining the aggression? Is aggression evident in multiple domains, and is it a long-standing problem or a recent development? Is aggressive behavior the only type of antisocial behavior being exhibited, or is aggression part of a mix that also includes authority defiance and covert acts (e.g., stealing)? Are there additional diagnostic concerns (e.g., learning problems, hyperactivity)? What positive attributes (e.g., intelligence, athletic ability, attractiveness) does the child possess? How healthy and how skilled are the child's parents? Is the home well organized and safe or is it prone to chaos and conflict? Have parents, teachers, or peers begun to reject the child interpersonally and emotionally? How does this child see herself? Is there recognition of and distress over how she affects others, or is this child more apt to blame others and inflate her own view of self? One must ask questions of this sort to gain an understanding of the child in question and to plan any intervention that follows.

The third type of information one needs has to do with the relationship within which aggressive children and their parents operate. This kind of information is similar to the data that a marital therapist would gather when assessing and treating adult couples. As is the case for marital therapists working with spouses, parent trainers must have an appreciation for how parents and children are experiencing and interacting with each other. How a child or a parent thinks, feels, and acts within the parent–child relationship can be distinct from how they might function in other domains or in other relationships (Dumas & LaFreniere, 1993). Therefore, the nature of that relationship, its history, and the subjective experience and meaning it holds for its participants are all important pieces of information in their own right.

These three types of information—normative, idiographic, and relational—all have bearing on how one works with parents of aggressive children. Practitioners who are well acquainted with normative information may know a lot about the "typical" aggressive child, but they do not know about a specific aggressive child until they obtain additional, idiographic information. On the other hand, normative data about aggressive children helps to determine which issues to consider when conducting an individualized assessment. Idiographic information about a given child's diagnosis, etiology, and prognosis should also be combined with an appreciation for the parent–child relationship, which is the primary context for socialization. Practitioners must learn how each member of this dyad experiences and coordinates his or her interaction with each other.

Things to Know About Aggressive Children

The remaining sections of this chapter are for those readers who want to update their working knowledge of that which is known generally about aggressive children. The goal here is to place the work of "parent helping" in its proper nomothetic context. I begin by discussing the value of adopting a developmental psychopathology perspective when working to understand the history and future trajectory of at-risk children. I then address issues of definition, diagnosis, and temporal stability before reviewing the rather large literature on the causes and correlates of childhood aggression. I also discuss variability within samples of aggressive children and current trends in assessment and treatment. Readers who are familiar with this literature would do well to move on to chapter 2.

Developmental Psychopathology

One cannot adequately discuss childhood aggression without reference to its developmental context. For one thing, behaviors that are thought to typify aggression are not uniform across the life span. Instead, aggression is marked by heterotypic continuity as children's tendency toward hostile actions and rule violations is transformed with each shift in development: Strong-willed toddlers who are easily frustrated and difficult to soothe may grow into oppositional preschoolers who taunt their siblings and defy their parents; hard-to-manage 2nd graders who disobey class rules and often fight with their peers may become socially rejected 4th graders who are academically behind and in the habit of lying and swearing and then grow into troubled 7th graders whose identified peer group is known for skipping classes, vandalizing property, and shoplifting. Viewing aggression only in terms of very specific behaviors can lead to an oversimplification of how it originates, why it persists, and how it evolves over time. Across developmental periods, aggression changes not only in its topography, but also in its significance. For example, a young child's display of aggression in the home becomes a more serious concern when similar behaviors are used to influence others at school or in the neighborhood. Children who are continually aggressive at school run the risk of being rejected by their peers. Peer rejection, in turn, can lead to greater contact with deviant peers and to a disdain for school values, thereby setting the stage for later antisocial behavior and delinquency (Dishion, Patterson, Stoolmiller, & Skinner, 1991; Patterson, Capaldi, & Bank, 1991; Patterson, DeBaryshe, & Ramsey, 1989). Over time and with repeated episodes, aggressive behavior thus becomes a more deeply rooted aspect of children's personalities and a more pervasive feature of their social ecology (Eron, 1987; Loeber, 1990). This fact has profound implications for the design and success of any treatment program that targets aggressive children (Kazdin, 1987).

To understand how the consequences of aggressive behavior at one point in time can contribute to later forms of antisocial behavior requires the comprehensive framework offered by the developmental psychopathology perspective (e.g., Richters & Cicchetti, 1993). This model, which lies at the intersection between human development and psychopathology, focuses on the transactional nature of children's interactions with the environment and emphasizes the processes by which these transactions promote or disrupt a child's developmental organization (Cicchetti, Cummings, Greenberg, & Marvin, 1990). An organizational approach to understanding children's development makes the following assumptions (Mash & Dozois, 1996):

1. The individual child plays an active role in his or her own developmental organization.
2. Self-regulation occurs at multiple levels, and the quality of integration within and among the child's biological, cognitive, emotional, and social systems needs to be considered.
3. There is a dialectical relation between the canalization (or crystallization) of developmental processes and the changes experienced through the life process.
4. Developmental outcomes are best predicted through consideration of prior experience and recent adaptations examined in concert.
5. Individual choice and self-organization play important roles in determining the course of development.
6. Transitional turning points or sensitive periods in developmental processes are most susceptible to positive and/or negative self-organizational efforts. (p. 36)

The developmental psychopathology model, although at times unwieldy, can be a useful heuristic for understanding a number of complex developmental issues that are important to the assessment and treatment of childhood aggression. For example, as is the case with other forms of human behavior, aggression in children is associated with a number of dispositional (e.g., difficult temperament) and environmental (e.g., harsh parenting) variables that do not operate in a simple, unidirectional fashion. Instead, these factors interact reciprocally and recurrently. This presents both a burden and a potential benefit to practitioners: Cause and consequence are irretrievably tangled, but therapeutic gains are less likely to have an isolated impact. Therapeutic gains may be short-lived, however, if the scope of the impact is limited.

Defining Aggression

Perhaps the most straightforward way to define *aggression* is as a class of behaviors that have in common an intrusive, demanding, and aversive effect on others (Olweus, 1979). Note that the impact of the behaviors and not their intent is what is emphasized in this definition. Eron (1987) has noted the difficulties of trying to measure one's intent to be aggressive, particularly with children. He defined aggression as "simply an act that injures or irritates another person" (p. 435). Aggressive acts include physically and verbally aggressive behaviors (e.g., threatening others, purposefully disturbing others, being verbally combative, making derogatory remarks, hitting, shoving) as well as the destruction of property. This class of behavior has also been described as *antisocial, coercive,* or *agonistic* (Patterson, 1982; Scott, 1992). These more general terms have use in that they speak more to the behaviors' impact than to their topography or surface-level appearance.

In line with other researchers, I make little attempt to separate aggression from antisocial behavior in general in this book. Aggression covaries with other norm-violating acts and therefore can be viewed as part of the larger construct of antisocial behavior. However, because some researchers make a distinction between overt (e.g., verbal and physical aggression) and covert (e.g., stealing, truancy) forms of antisocial behavior (e.g., Hinshaw & Anderson, 1996; Loeber, 1990), I eschew studies and findings relating solely to covert antisocial acts.

Diagnosing Aggressive Children

Highly aggressive children typically meet *Diagnostic and Statistical Manual of Mental Disorders* (4th ed. [*DSM–IV*]; American Psychiatric Association [APA], 1994) criteria for a diagnosis of conduct disorder (CD). In this disorder, one finds "a repetitive and persistent pattern of behavior in which the basic rights of others or major age-appropriate societal norms or rules are violated" (APA, 1994, p. 90). To meet diagnostic criteria, the child must manifest at least 3 such violations in the past 12 months, with one being within the past 6 months. Violations are grouped into four categories: (a) aggression to people and animals, (b) destruction of property, (c) deceitfulness or theft, and (d) serious violations of rules (e.g., truancy, running away). Young children whose level of aggression and antisocial behavior are not severe enough to meet criteria for CD usually fit a diagnosis of oppositional defiant disorder (ODD). In fact, a diagnosis of ODD is often seen as a developmental precursor to a CD diagnosis (Moffitt, 1993). Comorbid diagnoses are also common for aggressive children, with perhaps the most common being attention-deficit/hyperactivy disorder or ADHD (Milich, Widiger, & Landau, 1987). Kazdin (1993) estimated that 45 to 70% of children with CD also evidence ADHD. Childhood aggression is frequently associated with learning difficulties also. Rutter, Tizard, and Whitmore (1970) found that one quarter of slow readers showed antisocial behavior and one third of children with CD had reading disabilities.

An important addition to the *DSM–IV* criteria for CD is the inclusion of a subtype indicator. Extensive research (summarized by Moffitt, 1993) supports a distinction between childhood-onset and adolescent-onset CD. Children who evince early symptoms of CD differ from their late-onset counterparts in a number of significant ways. As a group, they tend to have a higher incidence of comorbid problems with hyperactivity, impulsivity, and inattention. They are also more likely to suffer deficits in verbal intelligence and executive functioning. There is also evidence to suggest they are more likely to have a family history that is positive for substance abuse and criminality. Moffitt (1993) refers to early-onset CD as life-course persistent reflecting the fact that the prognosis is much worse when CD begins in childhood.

The Stability of Childhood Aggression

Besides being a salient and aversive pattern of behavior, aggression manifested early in life tends also to be fairly stable. In fact, it would appear that early aggression is more durable than changeable and that the likelihood of change diminishes over time (Loeber, 1990). Eron and his colleagues have likened the stability of aggressive behavior to the stability of intellectual functioning (Eron, 1987; Huesman, Eron, Lefkowitz, & Walder, 1984, p. 1120). In a longitudinal study that used structural modeling techniques, Huesman et al. (1984) found stability coefficients for aggression of .50 for boys and .35 for girls. Olweus (1979) estimated that bivariate correlations between measures of aggression collected over time average around .75.

Longitudinal research by Campbell and her colleagues (Campbell, Pierce, March, Ewing, & Szumowski, 1994; Pierce, Ewing, & Campbell, 1999) has been particularly helpful in understanding the stability of childhood aggression. Her work begins tracing the development of disruptive behavior from when children are 3 years of age. A recent article in this unique body of work examined the likelihood that hard-to-manage preschool children would receive a disruptive behavior diagnosis at age 9 or 13 (Pierce et al., 1999). When the researchers assessed the first cohort of children at age 13, they found that 41% of those in the hard-to-manage group received a diagnosis of ODD or CD compared to only 8% of control children. In a second cohort of hard-to-manage boys, 28% received ODD or CD diagnoses at age 9 compared to 8% of control children.

The Pierce et al. (1999) study also provided informative analyses examining the persistence of problem behavior among hard-to-manage preschoolers. In the first cohort, 50% of hard-to-manage children exhibited significant levels of problem behavior when assessed at age 6 and at age 9. The remaining 50% failed to show a persistent pattern of problem behavior across these two assessment points. Of those children who showed persistent problems, 65% received an ODD or CD diagnosis at age 13 compared to only 18% in the nonpersistent group. When any disruptive behavior diagnosis was considered (ODD, CD, or ADHD), children in the persistent problem group were 52 times more likely to meet diagnostic criteria than hard-to-manage children with inconsistent problems. In the second cohort, 27% of hard-to-manage preschool boys showed a persistent pattern of problem behavior, and 73% improved when reassessed at age 6. When these boys were evaluated again at age 9, 59% of the persistent group met criteria for an externalizing disorder diagnosis (ADHD, ODD, or CD) compared to only 24% in the improved group.

The findings from this study indicate that children whose early problems persist past school entry are very likely to meet diagnostic criteria for ODD or CD. This study also offers strong support for programs that assist parents and teachers of hard-to-manage preschool children so later problems can be averted. Interventions targeting preschool children with severe levels of problem behavior, or who show a combination of ADHD and ODD symptoms, are especially justified. The work of these researchers also suggests that interventions for aggressive preschoolers may yield greater gains than treatments targeting aggressive school-age children simply because a significant percentage of hard-to-manage preschoolers (50–73%) do not persist in problem behavior past the ages of 6 or 9.

Discussions on the stability of childhood aggression commonly cite the "50% rule" (Lahey et al., 1995). The 50% rule suggests that roughly half of the children diagnosed as CD will improve over time, no longer showing signs of aggressive or antisocial behavior. Two studies have challenged this "rule," however, suggesting that aggression that begins in childhood is more persistent than formerly thought (Fergusson, Horwood, & Lynskey, 1995; Lahey et al., 1995). The Fergusson et al. study examined children whose behavior-problem scores were in the top 10%; the Lahey et al. study looked at boys meeting *DSM–III–R* criteria for CD. Both studies involved children at least 7 years of age, and both studies replicated the 50% rule: Approximately half of the cases no longer met criteria when assessed 1 to 4 years later. However, when Fergusson et al. (1995) used a latent Markov model to correct for error in measurement at a given point in time, they found that 86.4% of cases were likely to remain cases 2 years later. Similarly, Lahey et al. (1995) found that 88% of boys who were diagnosed as CD in Year 1 met criteria for CD again at least once during the ensuing 3 years. Moreover, approximately half of the boys who did not meet criteria for CD in subsequent years were only one symptom below the diagnostic threshold. These researchers also found that one fourth of the boys diagnosed as CD in Year 1 met criteria in all 3 subsequent years. Thus, whereas extreme levels of aggression may not be highly stable over time, persistent aggression does appear to be associated with more extreme levels of aggression (Moffitt, 1993).

As noted previously, the stability of childhood aggression is sometimes hidden by developmental changes in the manifestation of antisocial behavior. Many adults who commit violent and criminal acts have a history of early childhood aggression (Eron, 1987). In fact, aggression that begins early in childhood is the single best predictor of later criminal behavior (Loeber, 1990; Patterson et al., 1992). Eron (1987) reported that children who were rated as aggressive by peers at age 8 were 3 times more likely to have been entered on police records by age 19 than those not so rated. That is not to say that all aggressive children become juvenile delinquents and adult criminals. When official court records are examined, 50% to 70% of the youths arrested during childhood or adolescence were arrested later as adults. Childhood aggression also predicts other forms of adult maladjustment, including substance abuse, employment difficulties, and marital dysfunction (Loeber, 1990).

Another way to view the stability of aggressive behavior is in its tendency to be repeated from one generation to the next. Huesman et al. (1984) measured parents' aggression when child participants were 8 years of age and later measured participants' aggression when they were 30. The path coefficient between parents' aggression (severity of punishing the child participant) and participants' own aggression at age 30 was .58. Likewise, the path coefficient between participants' level of aggression at age 30 and level of aggression in their own children was .55. Other researchers have found support for the view that aggression is a multigenerational phenomenon. These researchers find that antisocial or aggressive children are more likely to have parents who display signs of antisocial behavior or deviant tendencies as measured by arrest history, MMPI scores, and the like (Frick et al., 1992; Patterson et al., 1992).

The Causes and Correlates of Childhood Aggression

Borrowing from Hughes and Cavell (1994), I have organized the variables that are most often implicated as causes and correlates of aggression into the following categories: (a) biological, (b) family, (c) social–cognitive, (d) peer, (e) academic, (f) teacher–school, and (g) neighborhood–community. The precise role these factors play in either determining or maintaining aggression is not presently clear. Nevertheless, for many of the variables, the temporal relation and the strength of the relation with aggression suggest an important functional linkage.

Biological Factors

Genetic factors (e.g., temperament), perinatal events (e.g., low birth weight), and other biological mechanisms (e.g., lead poisoning) are all biological factors that may dispose children to react to their environment in negative ways. For example, persistent demands from a temperamentally difficult child can precipitate a cycle of interaction whereby a parent's attempts to gain control over the child's behavior lead to even more intense oppositional reactions. Other putative biological factors contributing to childhood aggression include (a) a lack of autonomic nervous system responsiveness to punishing stimuli, (b) the action of certain biochemicals, such as testosterone, and (c) the presence of symptoms commonly associated with ADHD (Loeber, 1990; Lytton, 1990a).

The primary symptoms of ADHD—impulsivity, inattention, and hyperactivity—place a child at risk for a host of problems that can set the stage for later aggression. For example, untreated ADHD symptoms often make it difficult for parents to manage a child's behavior, thus potentiating the occurrence of increasingly negative and coercive interactions that can directly foster aggressive behavior (Loeber, 1990; Patterson, 1986a). Similarly, disciplinary conflicts involving teachers and ADHD children may impede a child's academic progress; these conflicts may even lead peers to form a negative reputation concerning the disruptive child (Morrison, Forness, & MacMillan, 1983). Impulsive responding and overactivity may also interfere with children's play interactions and thus their acceptance among peers. Difficulty sustaining attention can interfere with the acquisition of fundamental academic skills, thus leading the aggression-prone child to increased risk of school failure, peer rejection, and subsequent involvement with deviant peers (Dishion et al., 1991; Loeber, 1990; Patterson et al., 1991). Another way to view the interaction between ADHD and aggression is to recognize that hyperactivity without co-occurring aggression, while still predictive of some adjustment difficulties (e.g., academic difficulties), is far more benign than when it is accompanied by aggressive behavior (Hinshaw & Anderson, 1996; Walker, Lahey, Hynd, & Frame, 1987).

Family Factors

Family demographics. Several demographic variables have been implicated in the search for causes of childhood aggression. These include level of economic deprivation, single-parent status, family size, and ethnicity. These factors are often strongly correlated with one another, thus making it difficult to tease apart the separate effects of each (Cohn, Patterson, & Christopoulos, 1991). Of these, socioeconomic status (SES) factors have shown the strongest and most consistent links to antisocial behavior (Loeber, 1990). However, it also appears that low SES is primarily linked to the more severe forms of antisocial behavior and to the emergence of aggression prior to adolescence (Loeber, Stouthamer-Loeber, Van Kammen, & Farrington, 1991; Patterson et al., 1991). Also, economic deprivation and other demographic risk factors are thought to operate primarily through the disruption of essential parenting practices (Patterson et al., 1989). Lykken (1995), for example, has argued that single, low SES, often ethnic minority group mothers who have constitutionally difficult sons often struggle to perform the necessary socializing functions of parenting.

The tendency among researchers to ignore issues of ethnicity when studying childhood aggression has severely limited any discussion on the role of family demographics. For example, there has long been an over-reliance in this field on samples that contain few minority children. When mixed-ethnic samples are used, researchers are quick to disentangle the confounding effects of SES and ethnicity but are less apt to test the generalizability of findings across ethnic groups. The notion that commonly assumed etiological factors (e.g., poor discipline) can operate differently for ethnic minority children and families and those of the dominant culture is only now being given serious attention by researchers (e.g., Deater-Deckard & Dodge, 1997). Until researchers study this question more thoroughly, assumptions about the causes, the consequences, and the treatments for childhood aggression in ethnic minority families will remain tenuous.

Parenting practices. One of the strongest findings to emerge from the study of childhood aggression is the significant role that parents play in the development of aggressive behavior (Eron, 1987; Loeber, 1990; Maccoby & Martin, 1983; Patterson, 1986). Several parenting variables have been examined. Parents' effectiveness as disciplinarians, their tendency to be overly punitive or emotionally rejecting of children, their level of warmth and positive involvement, their ability to monitor children's whereabouts, and the level of stability and organization they create in their homes are among these variables. Although it is often difficult to separate parent effects (e.g., overly punitive discipline) from child effects (e.g., difficult temperament), most researchers agree that these two factors operate in a transactional manner to produce the aggressively behaving child (Lytton, 1990a; Shaw et al., 1998).

Perhaps the most influential model detailing the relation between parenting practices and children's conduct problems is the social learning model put forth by Patterson and his colleagues (Forgatch, 1991; Patterson, 1986; Patterson et al., 1991; Patterson et al., 1992). The cornerstone of Patterson's interactional model is the premise that parents inadvertently train children to engage in aggressive behavior by mismanaging early misbehaviors. For Patterson, ineffective discipline and monitoring constitute the "basic training" of antisocial children. Although modeling and positive reinforcement are involved in this process, the training of aggressive behavior is thought to rely primarily on negative reinforcement and escape conditioning. Children who successfully use coercive behavior to escape situations in which their parents were attempting to exert control are likely to repeat such acts. Empirically, Patterson's coercion model has proven to be quite robust (Patterson, 1986; Patterson et al., 1992); conceptually, it has had a tremendous impact on how researchers and practitioners understand parents and their aggressive children.

Patterson's model has emphasized parents' failure to control their children's behavior, but it also acknowledges the damaging effects of overly harsh and explosive discipline. This aspect of parenting is sometimes cast as parental rejection or the lack of warmth, nurturance, or positive parental involvement. As is true for parental control, the role of affectively positive parenting in the development of childhood aggression is also fairly well established (e.g., Eron, 1987; Greenberg & Speltz, 1988; Loeber, 1990; Parke & Slaby, 1983). There have been several hypotheses put forth to explain the relation between factors such as parental warmth and children's aggression. From an operant learning perspective, emotionally rejecting parents are thought to have less value as reinforcing agents than parents who are warm and attentive. Other researchers view the lack of parental warmth or emotional rejection as an instigating factor, prompting children to respond to parents more defiantly and aggressively than they would otherwise (Eron, 1987; Putallaz & Heflin, 1990). Others have interpreted the significance of parental warmth in terms of Bowlby's (1982) theory of attachment: Children whose sense of felt security is threatened by insensitive parenting will often respond angrily in an effort to signal parents of their distress. Also, children's early experiences with a rejecting parent–child relationship are carried forward in the form of internal working models that can negatively influence future interactions with peers, teachers, and others (Greenberg & Speltz, 1988).

Another key aspect of parenting is family stability or organization. Here I refer to parents' ability to maintain a sense of order and predictability in the home (Radke-Yarrow, Richters, Wilson, 1988) as well as their use of appropriate generational boundaries (Minuchin, 1974; Sroufe & Fleeson, 1988). Parents who do not distinguish between adult roles and child roles and who live in homes marked by frequent chaos will generally find their capacity to perform other aspects of parenting (e.g., discipline, emotionally positive interactions) greatly diminished (Maccoby & Martin, 1983).

Family disruptions. Family disruptions are those transitional events and stressful circumstances that can have a significant and deleterious impact on family functioning. Marital dissatisfaction, separation, divorce, and parental alcoholism are common examples of family disruption. Although numerous studies find an association between disruptive events and behavior problems in general, few researchers have examined the mechanisms by which aggression in particular is linked to family turmoil (cf. Capaldi & Patterson, 1991). Current findings, however, suggest that stressful events and disruptive circumstances rarely act directly to affect children; rather, the impact of these events are generally mediated by other factors. For example, children whose parents engage in frequent conflict—especially conflict that goes unresolved—may develop maladaptive ways of coping with emotional displays in others and with emotional arousal in themselves (Cummings, Ballard, El-Sheikh, & Lake, 1991). Also, family disruptions, particularly when severe and prolonged, are believed to interfere with essential parenting practices, which in turn leads to negative child outcomes such as aggressive behavior (Emery, 1989; Patterson et al., 1989; Seilhamer & Jacob, 1990). An important implication of these findings is that children are not fated to suffer from events such as divorce, parental alcoholism, and the like; children whose parents continue to respond firmly and warmly may be relatively unaffected by family disruptions.

Parental traits. Certain traits in parents have been shown to be related to children's level of antisocial behavior (Loeber et al., 1991; Patterson et al., 1991). For example, tendencies toward criminality, antisocial personality, and substance abuse are often evident in the parents of aggressive children. Similarly, maternal depression is frequently found to be associated with children's conduct problems. Although the association between childhood aggression and parental traits, particularly those of an antisocial nature, may be a function of genetic endowment, other processes may also be working. For example, recent studies suggest that parents' antisocial personality traits are predictive of family disruptions (e.g., marital dissatisfaction, divorce, remarriage) that can interfere with essential parenting practices (Capaldi & Patterson, 1991; Lahey et al., 1988).

Social–Cognitive Factors

Several empirical studies support the view that aggressive children exhibit social–cognitive deficits and distorted thinking that can lead to aggressive behavior (Crick & Dodge, 1994; Dodge, 1986). These deficits and distortions are usually described as gaps in a particular stage of social information processing. Commonly studied stages include (a) encoding, (b) interpretation, (c) response search, (d) response decision, and (e) enactment. Socially competent responses are those in which an individual attends to the relevant aspects of the social situation, accurately interprets social cues, generates appropriate social responses, selects a response, and effectively implements the selected response in that situation. Skills used at these stages are interdependent such that performance at earlier stages affects performance at later stages. An aggressive response, therefore, is the final outcome of the social information processing that preceded it. Recently, some researchers have expanded on the skill-based approach to social cognition by addressing the role of general beliefs, motivations, and goals (Crick & Dodge, 1994). Both social information-processing skills and underlying beliefs appear to be important determinants of children's use of aggressive or nonaggressive response tendencies.

Encoding. Aggressive children tend to have a bias in how they attend to and recall aggressive cues (Dodge & Frame, 1982; Dodge & Newman, 1981). Specifically, aggressive children and adolescents are apt to respond quickly to social situations without taking advantage of all the available social cues (Dodge & Newman, 1981; Slaby & Guerra, 1988). They are also more likely to selectively recall hostile cues. Additionally, the tendency for aggressive children to overattribute hostile intent to peers' actions (see below) is most evident when they make such decisions quickly and when they selectively retrieve threatening cues.

Interpretation. Aggressive children will often demonstrate a tendency to infer hostile intent when the level of threat or provocation in the situation is ambiguous (Asarnow & Callan, 1985; Dodge, Murphy, & Buchsbaum, 1984; Steinberg & Dodge, 1983). Steinberg and Dodge (1983) had pairs of same-sex children compete in a block-building task. Each participant discovered that some of his or her blocks had fallen before the prize was awarded. The cause of the blocks falling was ambiguous. Aggressive subjects were more likely to attribute their misfortune to the hostile behavior of peers than were nonaggressive participants. Aggressive children are more likely to demonstrate attributional biases in situations of high personal salience in which preexisting expectancies that others will respond to them with hostile intent influence the processing of social cues (Dodge & Somberg, 1987). These expectancies are probably rooted in the child's early socialization experiences and are thought to operate at an unconscious level (Dodge, Pettit, & Bates, 1994). Thus, the child may not be aware of them and may not question their validity.

Response search and response decision. Aggressive children and adolescents exhibit deficiencies in generating effective, nonaggressive solutions to conflict situations. It is the content of the solutions generated rather than the number of solutions generated that consistently differentiates aggressive and nonaggressive children. Specifically, aggressive children generate less effective and more aggressive solutions to interpersonal problems (Guerra & Slaby, 1989; Richard & Dodge, 1982; Slaby & Guerra, 1988). Aggressive children's first solutions to social problems may not differ from that of nonaggressive children, but their subsequent solutions are less effective, even when controlling for differences in verbal reasoning ability (Evans & Short, 1991).

The evaluation of a response depends on one's goals and one's beliefs about the legitimacy and value of using aggressive versus nonaggressive solutions. Aggressive and nonaggressive children tend to bring different goals to social situations and tend to evaluate aggressive responses differently (Guerra & Slaby, 1989; Perry, Perry, & Rasmussen, 1986; Slaby & Guerra, 1988). When aggressive children are frustrated, they tend to define the problem in terms of a hostilely motivated adversary and thus see the goal as one of retaliation. Aggressive children tend to believe that aggression will produce tangible rewards and reduce aversive treatment by others (Perry et al., 1986). They are more likely to report that aggression will increase self-esteem and enhance their reputation but not lead to excessive suffering in others (Guerra & Slaby, 1989; Slaby & Guerra, 1988). Furthermore, aggressive children report that it is relatively easy to perform aggressive acts and difficult to inhibit aggressive impulses (Perry et al., 1986).

Enactment. Aggressive children often show deficits in their ability to enact a given social skill such as making an assertive (as opposed to hostile) request, listening to another's point of view, and issuing an apology. However, these deficits can result both from an inability to perform certain overt behaviors and from errors and distortions in the social reasoning that preceded a behavioral response. Ineffective social performance can also reflect emotional interference or insufficient motivation to perform competently. Studies on the behavioral enactment of children's social skills often involve behavioral role plays rather than making use of naturalistic observation in order to tease out these other factors (Bornstein, Bellack, & Hersen, 1980; Feldman & Dodge, 1987).

Beliefs and emotions. The application of social–cognitive skills at different stages in information processing in specific situations occurs in the context of an individual's general beliefs and affective reactions. These beliefs and strategies for managing emotions are likely to operate across a wide range of situations and guide the processing of social information. For example, both children's attention to hostile cues and their attributional biases may reflect a general belief that other people are hostile adversaries (Guerra & Slaby, 1989). Similarly, children's goals in social situations may direct their attention to certain types of cues and lead them to evaluate certain solutions as more positive. Aggressive children's belief that aggression is a legitimate response to a wide range of situations may be tied to a view of the world as a place where they need to defend themselves in order to survive. These beliefs may in fact be adaptive in some communities, especially those described as "urban war zones" (Youngstrom, 1992).

Aggressive children are generally less bothered by the negative effect their aggressive behavior has on others. Aggressive adolescents minimize the amount of suffering experienced by victims of aggression (Slaby & Guerra, 1988), perhaps because they are deficient in their ability to vicariously experience the emotional reactions of others (Miller & Eisenberg, 1988). Aggressive children also tend to evaluate their own affective reaction to self-generated consequences of aggression as "wouldn't care" or as not "unhappy" even when they experience the negative consequences (e.g., being suspended from school; Guerra & Slaby, 1989).

Self-views. A topic that is gaining more attention from researchers is how aggressive children view themselves, both apart from and in relation to others. Preliminary studies suggest that aggressive children have a tendency both to idealize and to inflate their self-views (Edens, Cavell, & Hughes, 1999; Hughes, Cavell, & Grossman, 1997; Zakriski & Coie, 1996). In the Hughes et al. (1997) study, *idealization* was defined as a perfect score on measures of perceived competence and support from others. *Inflation* referred to discrepancies between a child's self-ratings and the ratings of others (e.g., teachers, parents, peers). This is an important area of research that has implications both for assessment and treatment of aggressive children.

Peer Factors

Peer rejection. Social rejection—as measured by negative peer nominations—has been shown to be a robust predictor of children's later adjustment (Parker & Asher, 1987). A consistent finding to emerge from studies of this topic is that aggressive behavior can lead directly and quickly to rejected peer status (Coie & Kupersmidt, 1983; Dodge, 1983). In fact, most researchers estimate that nearly half of all rejected children are also behaviorally aggressive (Coie, 1990). But what proportion of aggressive children are rejected by their peers? Although less data exist on this issue, some studies indicate that only about one third of all aggressive children escape the plight of peer rejection (Bierman & Smoot, 1991; Coie, Underwood, & Lochman, 1991). Cole and Carpentieri (1990), however, found that only about one third of the children identified in their study who had CD or CD-plus-depression were rejected by peers. Discrepancies among studies may be a function of whether aggression is measured via teacher or peer report.

Peer rejection and aggressive behavior are both fairly stable phenomena (Bierman & Wargo, 1995; Coie & Dodge, 1983; Eron, 1987). This co-stability is not coincidental but a reflection of the reciprocal influence each has on the other (Coie, Dodge, & Kupersmidt, 1990; Price & Dodge, 1989). To the extent aggressive behavior leads to peer rejection, subsequent interactions with peers—even if predominantly prosocial in nature—will likely be perceived in a way that maintains this negative reputation (Hymel, 1986). Prosocial acts by rejected children are likely to be seen as uncharacteristic and as due to external factors, and mild or infrequent displays of aggression can be enough to maintain a negative reputation. The net effect of these circumstances is that aggressive–rejected children may encounter little incentive for changing the aggressive manner in which they interact with peers.

Friendships. Although peer rejection implies a lack of friends, some researchers argue that children's ability to form friendships should be viewed separately from their level of overall peer acceptance (Bukowski & Hoza, 1989; Parker & Asher, 1993). Researchers have only recently begun to study the relation between friendship and aggression. Boys often engage in rough-and-tumble play with their friends (Hartup, 1989), which is distinct from aggression, and children who are aggressive tend to have friends who are also aggressive (Cairns, Cairns, Neckerman, Gest, & Gariepy, 1988). Researchers know very little, however, about the nature of these friendships. Do these friendships last long enough to be construed as significant? What is the quality of these relationships? Do friendships enjoyed by aggressive children reduce the risk associated with their aggressive behavior?

Two studies that examined the relation between friendship quality and aggressive behavior involved laboratory observations of adolescents with CD interacting with a friend (Dishion, Andrews, & Crosby, 1995; Panella & Henggeler, 1986). Both studies cast doubt on the notion that aggressive children are likely to enjoy positive and stable friendships. Panella and Henggeler (1986) found that adolescents with CD showed less interpersonal skill and less positive affect than well-adjusted adolescents. Anecdotally, the authors also reported that several participants with CD had difficulty thinking of a friend who might participate with them in the study.

In the study by Dishion et al. (1995), antisocial boys (ages 13–14 years) and their close friends were interviewed and observed interacting in a problem-solving task. The close friends of antisocial boys tended to share their demographic and delinquent characteristics. These investigators also found that "relationships of antisocial dyads were somewhat low in quality, of relatively short duration, were perceived by the boys as marginally satisfactory, and tended to end acrimoniously" (p. 148). Another interesting aspect of this study was that coders' global impressions of the boys' bossy and coercive style were more highly correlated with their antisocial behavior than were more "objective" (e.g., command, verbal attack) behavior counts. It would follow, therefore, that other individuals who interact with these antisocial boys might also find offense in their behavior.

The specific factors that determine if the friendships of aggressive children constitute a *protective factor* (e.g., an emotionally supportive relationship) or a *risk factor* (e.g., involvement with deviant peers) remains to be answered. It would seem, however, that children whose friends are also aggressive and antisocial are less likely to benefit from the socioemotional aspects of these relationships. Deviant adolescents interacting with deviant friends have been found to reinforce (via contingent laughter) each others' talk of rule-breaking behavior (Dishion, Spracklen, Andrews, & Patterson, 1996). This same process was not found when deviant youth interacted with a nondeviant friend. Unfortunately, aggressive children as a group are less likely to have prosocial friends.

Academic Factors

Aggression and poor academic performance often co-occur. A lively and ongoing debate has surrounded the question of whether aggression is a cause or a consequence of academic difficulties. Some studies suggest that aggression and associated conduct problems are best predicted by earlier cognitive deficits (Schoenfield, Shaffer, O'Connor, & Portnoy, 1988). Other investigations, however, indicate that aggressive and antisocial behavior antedate school failure (e.g., Dishion et al., 1991; Patterson et al., 1991). Still others view aggressive, externalizing behaviors and academic deficiencies as the result of a common set of underlying factors such as attentional difficulties and neurodevelopmental delay (Hinshaw, 1992). Whatever the connection, it is clear that academic difficulty is a frequent concomitant of childhood aggression.

Teacher–School Factors

Reactions from individual teachers can be an important factor in understanding a child's aggression. Although too little research has addressed this issue, teachers—like parents—can vary widely in their ability to discipline firmly and relate warmly to aggressive children (Hughes, Cavell, & Jackson, 1999). One reason for assessing variability in teacher behavior is that children's social judgments about peers are often based on how teachers react to misbehavior and poor academic performance (Morrison et al., 1983; Retish, 1973).

How schools as a whole respond to aggressive children is another important although understudied question. To the extent schools insist on compliance, cooperation, and academic engagement, children who act aggressively are likely to falter socially and academically, leading eventually to peer rejection and a sense of disaffection. On the other hand, if school is a place where academic expectations are low, where supervision is lacking, and where victimizing weaker peers goes unchecked, then aggressive children may enjoy school, but school will not be promoting their prosocial development. Little is known about how to structure schools in ways that are most likely to benefit children at risk for antisocial behavior (Dodge, 1993). Strongly enforced school policies against bullying behavior is one example of how school-wide practices may benefit individual children. Based on a nationwide survey of Norwegian schools, Olweus (1991) found that 1 in 7 children was involved in bully–victim relationships. The percentage of children who were victims fell from grades 2 to 9, but the percentage of children who bullied remained fairly stable.

Neighborhood and Community Factors

In some situations, a child's aggression may be an adaptive response to the local environment. In some neighborhoods and communities in which extreme acts of violence are not uncommon, physical and verbal aggression may be construed as necessary strategy for one's survival (Garbarino, 1995; Richters & Martinez, 1993). Exchanging verbal insults and threats —a type of verbal repartee—may even serve the function of establishing a cohesive peer group (Prinz & Miller, 1991). The interventionist is often faced, therefore, with the dilemma of viewing aggression as a "natural manifestation of normal peer group socialization in specific cultural groups or as problem behaviors with adverse consequences" (Prinz & Miller, 1991, p. 380). Indications that intervention is justified include (a) physical (versus verbal) aggression; (b) behaviors that bring the individual into contact with juvenile authorities; and (c) uncontrolled, *reactive aggressive behaviors* (i.e., defensive reactions to a perceived threat accompanied by visible anger) that lead to peer rejection within the child's own peer group.

Summary

A number of key points emerged in this discussion of the factors associated with childhood aggression: First, children who begin to use aggressive and antisocial behavior at a young age (e.g., before age 12) are at greater risk for adult criminality than late starters (Loeber et al., 1991; Moffitt, 1993; Patterson et al., 1991). Second, the strength of the association between aggression and other factors (e.g., positive parental involvement) can vary across ages (Loeber et al., 1991). Some factors decrease over time in their association with aggression (e.g., socioeconomic status), others show an increasing association (e.g., low school motivation), and still others seem to be important no matter what the child's age (e.g., single parenthood). Finally, practitioners must recognize that childhood aggression can be a serious and pernicious pattern of maladjustment. Not only is it quite stable over time, but it is also a factor in the emergence of other problem behaviors (e.g., academic failure, peer rejection, delinquency). Loeber

(1990) refers to this phenomenon as the "stacking" of problematic behaviors one atop the other. As Stattin and Magnusson (1989) noted

> it is rare to find a highly aggressive boy who is not educationally or socially handicapped in many ways. They often are restless and exhibit concentration difficulties, they show low school motivation and underachieve, and they tend to have poor peer relations. (p. 717)

Unfortunately, as aggression becomes intertwined with other facets of a child's life, incentives for the continued use of aggression only increase while the incentives to desist become more remote.

Differences Among Aggressive Children

Discussing the characteristics that apply generally to aggressive children can hide the fact that as a group they can be fairly heterogeneous. Aggressive children vary greatly in their interpersonal skills, in their style of aggressing, and in their underlying motives and beliefs. Rather than lumping together all aggressive children, it is important to recognize that diverse forms of aggression can have contrasting etiologies and treatment needs. In fact, one reason for the limited success of past skills-training programs with aggressive children is that interventionists have often failed to verify that treated children are deficient in the skills to be taught (Hughes & Sullivan, 1988).

Dodge and Coie (1987) have distinguished between two types of aggression that may have implications for intervention planning. *Reactive aggression*, as defined earlier, refers to a defensive reaction to a perceived threat and is accompanied by visible displays of anger. Children identified as high in reactive aggression are more likely to misperceive peers' actions as hostile and are deficient in generating nonaggressive solutions to social problems. Reactively aggressive boys tend to be socially withdrawn, are seen by peers as both unpopular and rejected, lack prosocial skills, and are inattentive and poorly self-controlled (Dodge & Coie, 1987; Dodge & Crick, 1990). *Proactive aggression* refers to aggressive acts that are intended to achieve some instrumental goal, such as retrieval or possession of an object or domination over others. Children identified as engaging in high levels of proactive aggression and not high levels of reactive aggression have average social–cognitive skills, are perceived by their peers as leaders, and are both popular and disliked (i.e., have a controversial peer status). Because most aggressive children display high levels of both reactive and proactive aggression, practitioners will generally need to gain an understanding of both types of aggression. For some children, however, a more focused treatment approach is indicated. For example, treatments that teach self-control skills should benefit the reactive aggressive child more than the proactive aggressive child.

There are other ways in which meaningful subtypes of aggressive children may be formed. Empirical support exists for distinguishing among aggressive children based on the following features: (a) their use of physical aggression or *relational aggression* (e.g., gossiping, excluding others from groups; Crick & Grotpeter, 1995); (b) level of callous and unemotional traits (Christian, Frick, Hill, Tyler, & Frazer, 1997; Wootton, Frick, Shelton, & Silverthorn, 1997); and (c) inflated views of self and others (Edens et al., 1999). More research is needed to test the robustness of these findings and to determine what effect the findings will have on the assessment and treatment of aggressive children.

Assessing Aggressive Children and Their Parents

Because of the externalizing nature of childhood aggression, it happens to be one of the easier behavioral problems to identify. Unlike many of the features of anxiety and depression, aggressive behavior is unlikely to escape the attention of parents, teachers, and peers. Therefore, the assessment of aggressive children is typically conducted for purposes other than identification. For example, the severity, chronicity, and pervasiveness of children's aggression are important parameters to assess. Standardized paper-and-pencil measures such as the Child Behavior Checklist (Achenbach, 1991) and structured diagnostic interviews are commonly used to assess the severity of childhood aggression. Attention is usually given to children who exceed a certain cutoff (e.g., 2 *SD*s above the mean) or who reach a diagnostic threshold. Information regarding the chronicity of aggression is usually obtained from parent interviews and archival records (e.g., school, medical). Assessing the scope or pervasiveness of children's antisocial behavior requires the reports of multiple informants (e.g., parents and teachers).

Researchers are likely to add a peer-rated measure of aggression to their assessment profile given its predictive usefulness and the tendency for teachers and peers to have different views of children's school behavior. An even more labor-intensive strategy is to observe directly the behavior of children identified as being aggressive. Researchers have conducted observations in the home, in the classroom, and on the playground. Observational data serve a number of important functions, although most do not justify the added costs to practitioners. By obtaining samples of actual behavior, researchers can assess (a) interactional processes between children and others, (b) possible treatment gains, and (c) the mechanisms by which successful treatment had its effect. Observations conducted in therapy and daily telephone interviews with parents about the occurrence of specific behaviors during the preceding 24 hours are less costly to use than direct, in vivo observations.

Other child-focused assessments are related to issues of comorbidity, risk, and protection. For example, assessing for symptoms of ADHD when working with aggressive children is an important task for practitioners. Childhood aggression and ADHD frequently co-occur, the symptoms of hyperactivity and impulsivity have been implicated in the etiology of aggression, and parents and teachers often fail to appreciate the distinction between ADHD and childhood aggression. This is particularly true in the case of children who are oppositional or aggressive but who do not necessarily have ADHD (Abikoff, Courtney, Pelham, & Koplewicz, 1993). Abikoff et al. (1993) found that teacher ratings of oppositional and conduct problems were accurate regardless of whether children displayed symptoms of ADHD. However, teacher ratings of ADHD symptoms were accurate only when ADHD-like behaviors occurred in the absence of oppositional and conduct problems. When these coercive behaviors were present, teacher ratings of ADHD symptoms were often inaccurate and spuriously inflated.

Practitioners who fail to consider alternative and comorbid diagnoses or who do a poor job of assessing idiographic factors that can protect or threaten a given child are courting treatment failure (Shirk & Russell, 1996). A thorough discussion of the assessment of such factors is beyond the scope of this text (see Mash & Terdal, 1988), as is a discussion of the methods and instruments available for assessing various parenting and family factors (see D. K. Snyder, Cavell, Heffer, & Mangrum, 1995). Regardless of which assessment tools are used, there are certain parent variables that should not be overlooked. These variables can be grouped roughly into the following categories:

1. Sociodemographics (e.g., SES, education level, ethnicity)
2. Psychopathology (e.g., depression)
3. Stressors (e.g., chronic illness, abusive partner)
4. Criminality and substance abuse (e.g., arrest history)
5. Attachment history (e.g., perceptions of primary caregivers)
6. Parenting practices (e.g., permissiveness, overly harsh)
7. Parent-related cognitions (e.g., blaming attributions)

Practitioners attending to the first five areas listed will have a fuller and more accurate picture of the parent as an individual—apart from their role as caregiver to an aggressive child. By appreciating parents as individuals, practitioners can more readily make sense of and assist with parents' child-rearing practices and cognitions.

Treating Aggressive Children

Currently, the prognosis for aggressive children is poor. Services provided by mental health, education, and juvenile justice agencies often have little impact on the downward trajectory of aggressive children. Researchers have been more successful in identifying the correlates and causes of aggression than in identifying effective interventions. Kazdin (1987) summarized the inadequacy of existing interventions for antisocial children when he concluded, "to date, little in the way of effective and empirically established treatments is available" (p. 200). Kazdin (1987) and others (e.g., Loeber, 1990) have noted that as aggressive children get older, they are increasingly less responsive to therapeutic interventions. Therefore, newly developed treatment programs tend to target younger children in order to take advantage of this window of relative opportunity (Conduct Problems Prevention Research Group [CPPRG], 1992; Webster-Stratton, 1990). Two commonly used treatments that Kazdin (1993) described as "promising" are social–cognitive skills training for children and behavior-management training for their parents.

Social–Cognitive Skills Training

Aggressive children are more likely to attend to hostile cues, infer hostile intent, endorse ineffective and aggressive solutions, believe that aggression leads to positive consequences, and lack empathy for victims of aggression. With some exceptions, interventions designed to rectify these deficits and distortions have yielded positive effects on measures of problem solving but only limited gains on measures of social adjustment (Beelmann, Pfingsten, & Losel, 1994). Kazdin and his colleagues (Kazdin, Bass, Siegel, & Thomas, 1989) found that individually administered problem-solving skills training (with considerable involvement from parents) led to significant behavioral improvement in highly aggressive children lasting up to 1-year posttreatment. However, a majority of treated children continued to exhibit clinically significant levels of aggressive and disruptive behavior. Tremblay, Pagani-Kurtz, Masse, Vitaro, and Pihl (1995) reported that disruptive kindergarten children receiving problem-solving skills training plus home-based parent training for a 2-year period were less likely to be placed in special classes at ages 10–13, but this effect was lost after age 13. Also, no Group × Time effects were found for teacher-rated disruptiveness or for court-reported offenses in midadolescence. Lochman and Curry (1986) found that children provided with self-control and problem-solving skills interventions showed decreased levels of disruptive classroom behavior and parent-rated aggression relative to untreated control participants. Three years after treatment, treated boys exhibited less substance use and behavioral deviance than control children but did not differ with respect to classroom behavior (Lochman, 1992). Finally, Prinz, Blechman, and Dumas (1994) found reductions in teacher-rated aggression 6 months after aggressive children completed a 9-month, coping-competence intervention that included socially competent peers. However, treated children were still within the clinical range on measures of aggression and did not improve on sociometric measures.

Parent Training

Parent training as a treatment for aggressive children is designed to increase parents' use of effective and noncoercive behavior management practices (e.g., time-out). Reviews of the parent-training outcome literature are generally supportive, but nagging questions about the long-term stability and generalizability of treatment gains still exist. The next chapter offers a thorough look at the existing parent-training literature.

Summary

The outcome literature on social–cognitive skills training and parent training points to three conclusions. First, the efficacy of each treatment approach is supported empirically. Second, questions about the effectiveness of each approach remain given the paucity of follow-up data and the substantial proportion of aggressive children who fail to respond. And third, the most effective interventions may be those that combine social–cognitive skills training for children and parent training for parents.

As practitioners, we can no longer be naive about the task of intervening with aggressive, school-age children. Altering the long-term trajectory of these at-risk children requires an intervention that is both potent and sustained. Universal programs such as parent education classes or class-wide social skills curricula are, at best, weak approximations of the targeted interventions indicated for aggressive, school-age children. These children and their families need treatment programs that are more intense and that reflect the stubborn nature of childhood aggression and its environmental context. Effective interventions will also be comprehensive, coordinating the efforts of multiple stakeholders (parents, teachers, and children) over time. In short, treatment programs for aggressive, school-age children must combine an accurate model of childhood aggression with a pragmatic model of how to treat it (Cavell & Hughes, in press). It is not enough to know how aggression develops and how it is maintained; practitioners working with these children and their parents also need to know which variables to target and how best to change them.

2

Parent Training for Families With Aggressive Children: A Tale of Two Models

The vast majority of parent training programs used to treat aggressive children are based on a single conceptual model. Behaviorally based parent training programs that concentrate on parents' use of effective discipline dominate the field. Chapters appearing in Dangel and Polster's (1984) and Schaefer and Breismeister's (1989) edited texts on parent training support the contention that seemingly diverse training approaches tend to follow the same behavior management theme. The near-synonymous use of the terms *parent training* and *behavior-management parent training* (BMPT) is attributable in part to the large body of empirical work that has shaped and supported this approach over the past 30 years (Dangel & Polster, 1984; Milne, 1986). The lack of empirical studies that have examined other models of parent training also contributes to BMPT's status as the dominant approach to parent training. One review of parent-training research revealed that 89% of the studies emphasized a behavioral approach to parent training (Rogers Wiese, 1992).

Few alternatives to the behavioral model of parent training exist. Indeed, Schaefer and Breismeister (1989) suggested that there is only one alternative to the behavioral approach:

> No matter what training techniques, variations of procedures, or combinations of strategies the professional employs, most formats used to train parents as co-therapists can be subsumed under one of two main methodological categories: the behavior modification approach and the relationship enhancement approach. (p. 2)

The *relationship-enhancement approach*, also known as *child relationship enhancement family therapy* (CREFT), is most readily distinguished from the behavioral management approach by its heavy emphasis on parents' use of child-centered play. Like BMPT, CREFT began more than 30 years ago and for some practitioners continues to be an attractive alternative to BMPT (Ginsberg, 1989). Yet, BMPT is widely known and accepted (Calvert & McMahon, 1987), whereas little is known about this alternative model, including its potential to withstand empirical scrutiny.

BMPT Versus CREFT

This review of the parent-training literature highlights the differences between BMPT and CREFT, focusing on (a) history and conceptual underpinnings, (b) focus of training, and (c) empirical support. The two approaches represent radically different views on how to work with the parents of aggressive children. I argue that neither approach is sufficient to meet the needs of families with aggressive children; instead, both approaches are regarded as outdated and in need of revision and expansion. I juxtapose the two models so that readers can appreciate the figural aspects of one approach against the backdrop of the other. This review is neither definitive nor exhaustive. Comprehensive reviews of the literature covering one or the other model are available elsewhere (Dumas, 1989; Forehand & McMahon, 1984; Ginsberg, 1989; L. F. Guerney & B. G. Guerney, 1985).

History and Conceptualization

BMPT

BMPT began as an attempt to train parents to use the same behavior modification techniques (e.g., social reinforcement, extinction, token economy) that child behavior therapists were using in their efforts to reprogram the social environment (Hawkins, Peterson, Schweid, & Bijou, 1966; Patterson & Gullion, 1968; Wahler, Winkle, Peterson, & Morrison, 1965). The promise of these early treatment programs soon led to greatly expanded research efforts. The work of Gerald Patterson and his colleagues at the Oregon Social Learning Center was influential among these research programs.

For nearly three decades, Patterson and his team have systematically pursued the twin goals of understanding the development of antisocial behavior in children and devising family-based intervention programs for youth with conduct disorders (Patterson, 1986). Using advanced methods of observational assessment and guided by the principles of operant and social learning theory, Patterson's research team painstakingly recorded moment-to-moment interactions among family members in the home. Patterson (1982) found that a child's level of aversive behavior could be predicted from interactions with other family members. These and other findings led Patterson to speculate that parents were essentially "training" their children to become aggressive. As he put it, "Failure by parents to effectively punish garden variety, coercive behaviors sets into motion interaction sequences that are the basis for training in aggression" (Patterson, 1986, p. 436).

Patterson's (1982) *coercion hypothesis*, as it is called, posits that children's natural tendencies to engage in coercive behaviors (e.g., whining, noncompliance)—whether in an effort to assert autonomy or to elicit specific caregiving behaviors—are inadvertently and negatively reinforced by parents who yield to these demands. The basic training for aggressive behavior is also characterized by parents who escalate their own level of coercion via intermittent "explosive" discipline or more chronic "nattering" (parental nagging) of children. Aversive parental behaviors, in turn, occasion increasingly coercive behavior from children and function to establish extended chains of mutually aversive behaviors. As the frequency and duration of these mutually aversive interactions increase, the likelihood that aggression and other more serious forms of coercion will occur is also increased. Therefore, Patterson (1982; Patterson et al., 1992) has continually stressed that a primary goal of parent training should be to eliminate or to reduce coercive chains of behavior that occur between aggressive children and other family members.

Partial support for Patterson's coercion hypothesis was found in the reports of other researchers who conducted similar microanalytic studies of the interactions of children with conduct problems and their families (e.g., Forehand, King, Peed, & Yoder, 1975; Johnson & Lobitz, 1974; J. J. Snyder, 1977). As was true for Patterson and his colleagues, these researchers were guided by an enthusiastic blend of operant and social learning theory, and it was this theoretical perspective that has had the strongest influence on the nature of BMPT. The picture that emerged from this campaign of research was one that viewed parents of aggressive children as having a deficit in the kinds of behavior management skills that a trained behavior modifier might use.

Importantly, several early studies (e.g., Greist, Forehand, Wells, & McMahon, 1980; Patterson, 1982) failed to support the notion that parents inadvertently reinforce childhood aggression. As Snyder and Patterson (1995) noted, studies of clinic-referred and nonreferred families generally find very small differences in the rates at which aggression is reinforced. Other studies fail to support the kind of parent–child interactions (e.g., compliance followed by praise) that would be predicted by social learning theory (Greist et al., 1980; Roberts, 1985; Westerman, 1990). The BMPT model proliferated even though it lacked support for some of its basic tenets. In fact, it was originally thought that training parents to extinguish (i.e., ignore) inappropriate behavior and to reinforce desirable behavior was sufficient to eliminate children's coercive pattern of interacting. Researchers soon discovered, however, that punishment techniques such as time-out were also needed if BMPT was to be an effective intervention for aggressive children (Patterson & Fleischman, 1979). As these programs have evolved, teaching parents to punish their child's noncompliance has taken on increasing importance (Forehand & McMahon, 1981).

CREFT

The term *relationship enhancement* was used originally by Bernard Guerney (1977) to describe a number of intervention programs that trained family members to use client-centered therapeutic skills (Levant, 1983).

One program in particular was designed to treat children between the ages of 3 and 10 years who had a variety of emotional or behavioral difficulties. This program, originally termed *filial therapy* (B. Guerney, 1964), was designed to teach parents the skills of child-centered play therapists (Ginsberg, 1989; L. F. Guerney, 1983). Child-centered play therapy is essentially a downward extension of adult Rogerian or client-centered therapy (Axline, 1969). As such, *filial therapy* assumes that children have the capacity to solve many of their emotional and behavioral difficulties if given an atmosphere in which they feel accepted and valued, where their feelings are acknowledged, and where limits are placed on their behavior sparingly but firmly. For Axline (1969), child-centered play was the most feasible way to create such an atmosphere. B. Guerney (1964), however, considered individual play sessions a rather inefficient approach to meeting the mental health needs of children. He thought it more practical to train parents to use these play therapy skills with their own children. Early success with filial therapy led him to believe that parents can be taught to use these skills. He also believed the therapeutic value of these skills were enhanced when practiced by parents: "Every bit of success the parent achieves in successfully filling the prescribed role should have an effect many times more powerful than that of a therapist doing the same thing" (B. Guerney, 1964, p. 308).

Besides renaming their approach as CREFT, the originators of filial therapy also tried to broaden its focus (L. F. Guerney, 1983; L. F. Guerney & B. Guerney, 1987). L. F. Guerney and B. Guerney (1987) recognized that problems experienced outside of play will often surface during play sessions. Therefore, the play session can serve as a "learning laboratory" that brings into focus salient issues about the dynamics of the parent–child relationship (L. F. Guerney, 1983, p. 28). In this way, CREFT directly targets the affective quality of the parent–child relationship rather than a specific problem behavior exhibited by the child. There are other parent training programs that are conceptually similar to CREFT (e.g., Coufal & Brock, 1979; Jernbeg, 1989; Lieberman, Weston, & Pawl, 1991; Speltz, 1990; Stollack, 1981). However, filial therapy and CREFT remain the most visible examples of the relationship-enhancement approach. Programs described by Coufal and Brock (1979) and Stollack (1981) are direct offshoots of filial therapy, whereas Jernbeg's (1989) program is one in which parents observe their child's participation in therapist-conducted play therapy.

Focus of Training

BMPT

Although differences exist among various BMPT programs (Barkley, 1987; Eyberg, 1988; Forehand & McMahon, 1981; Patterson, Reid, Jones, & Conger, 1975; Webster-Stratton & Herbert, 1994), most follow a common format of initial instruction in techniques designed to increase desirable behaviors followed by instruction in techniques designed to decrease undesirable behaviors. This two-stage model was derived from the work of Constance Hanf (1969; Hanf & Kling, 1973). Her original program targeted mothers whose young (ages 2 to 7 years) children with physical disabilities were engaging in a variety of disruptive and noncompliant behaviors. One of the most widely disseminated BMPT programs is that of Forehand and McMahon (1981). In it, parents participate in both a differential-attention phase (Phase 1) and a compliance-training phase (Phase 2). As is typical with the BMPT model, Forehand and McMahon's (1981) program is designed to increase parents' control over their child's behavior. The program emphasizes five skills: giving attends, giving rewards, ignoring, issuing commands, and implementing time-out (p. 50).

Phase 1 training teaches parents to attend in a positive manner to their child's appropriate behavior and to describe it in a way that is free of questions, commands, and criticism. Parents are taught to avoid structuring their child's play and to follow along by providing running commentary of the child's play activity. Parents next learn to reward their child for specific behaviors they wish to increase. Parents learn how to use three types of rewards: physical rewards (e.g., hug, kiss), unlabeled praise (e.g., "great!"), and labeled praise (e.g., "I like the way you are playing with those colors"). In the last part of Phase 1, parents are trained to extinguish negative behaviors by actively ignoring those behaviors they wish to decrease. To enhance the effectiveness of this extinction procedure, parents are taught to avoid eye contact and physical contact with their child and to refrain from communicating verbally or nonverbally. Parents are told they may need to turn 90 to 180 degrees away, to stand up, or to leave the room to ignore in this manner. Play sessions are the typical context for training parents in these differential attention skills. Parents are typically told to rehearse these skills at home in daily 10-minute practice sessions. The primary goal of Phase 1 is to teach parents to interact contingently with their child so they can be "more effective reinforcing agent[s]" (McMahon & Forehand, 1984, p. 300). Recent variants of BMPT, however, also recognize that parent–child play sessions have value for promoting positive interactions between parents and children (e.g., Eyberg, 1988; Webster-Stratton & Herbert, 1994).

Not all BMPT programs use a child-directed phase or place as much emphasis on these so-called positive parenting practices. For example, the program used by Patterson and his colleagues (Horne & Patterson, 1980; Patterson et al., 1975) places very little emphasis on play and attending skills. Training begins with teaching parents to use commands and to observe and record instances of compliance and noncompliance. Training then shifts to the use of positive reinforcement (praise) to increase desirable behavior and to the use of time-out to decrease negative behavior. Trainers deemphasize such techniques as playing with and listening to their children, which are not taught until much later in the program.

As with most other BMPT programs, the second half of Forehand and

McMahon's (1981) program focuses on giving effective commands and the use of time-out. Phase 2 begins with parents learning to give direct, concise commands. Trainers caution parents to give such commands judiciously and only when parents are prepared to enforce compliance with the command. Parents are given examples of poorly delivered (β) commands. These are *chain commands* (multiple commands delivered simultaneously), *vague commands* (e.g., "Be good"), *question commands* (e.g., "Do you want to help me pick up these toys?"), *"let's" commands* (e.g., "Let's go take your bath"), and commands that are obscured by rationales or other verbalizations. Parents then learn the aspects of appropriate (α) commands: direct, specific, and singular commands, followed by a 5-second pause for compliance. If their child initiates compliance within 5 seconds, parents are taught to use the reward techniques learned in Phase 1 as reinforcement.

If the child does not comply within 5 seconds, parents are trained to repeat the command and to warn the child that noncompliance will be met with a time-out consequence. The warning is of the *if . . . then* variety: "If you don't pick up these blocks, then you will have to go to time-out." If the child complies, parents praise or attend to the child; if the child does not begin to comply, parents implement time-out. In Forehand and McMahon's (1981) program, parents are trained to use a 3-minute chair time-out. Children are not to be released from time-out until they have been quiet for 15 seconds. Parents are trained to spank children twice on the bottom if they try to escape. Once time-out is over, parents are supposed to return to the situation that elicited noncompliance and repeat the original command. Parents then praise the child for initiating compliance or, if the child fails to comply, repeat the command, warning, and time-out sequence as before.

The manner in which BMPT programs are delivered can vary from group didactic instruction to intense, closely supervised individual training. For example, parents in Forehand and McMahon's (1981) program learned their skills through didactic instruction, modeling, role playing, clinic rehearsal and feedback, and home rehearsal. These parents also were trained individually by cotherapists in clinic settings equipped with one-way observation mirrors and bug-in-the-ear coaching devices. Forehand and McMahon (1981) reported nine sessions on average. Patterson and his colleagues also used an individualized training format (e.g., Patterson, Chamberlain, & Reid, 1982; Patterson et al., 1975), although the average number of sessions these investigators used was often twice that reported by Forehand and McMahon (1981). The rather costly and time-consuming nature of individualized training led Webster-Stratton (1987) to develop a program based on videotaped modeling and instruction. The videotape series contains approximately 250 vignettes that can be used in a training group or self-administered by individual parents. The skills modeled in these tapes parallel those in the Forehand and McMahon (1981) protocol, although additional emphasis is given to parent–

child play and parents' coping with potential stressors (Webster-Stratton, 1987).

CREFT

CREFT is considered appropriate for children ages 3 to 10 years experiencing a range of behavioral and emotional difficulty. Training is typically conducted in a group format with 6 to 8 parents, although CREFT can also be used with individual families. Early outcome studies were based on groups lasting 12 to 18 months (B. G. Guerney & Stover, 1971), but CREFT groups typically span anywhere from 4 to 7 months and individually administered CREFT is often completed in 2 months (L. F. Guerney & B. G. Guerney, 1985, 1987).

CREFT is composed of four phases: (a) training in play therapy, (b) home play sessions, (c) transfer and generalization, and (d) phase out. Phase 1 of CREFT begins with a program description and rationale followed by demonstration play sessions conducted by the therapist. In line with Axline's (1969) model of play therapy, parents are taught to let the child determine completely the play activities "within specified, definite limits, such as no destruction of non-play material, and no activities which would be physically painful to child or parent" (B. Guerney, 1964, p. 305). Parents are to refrain from using verbal (e.g., commands, questions) or nonverbal (e.g., disapproving expressions or gestures) means of controlling the child's play behavior. Instead, parents are to communicate genuine acceptance of the child and an awareness of feelings through the use of "traditional" techniques of Rogerian therapy. These include "structuring, restatement of content, and, with major emphasis, clarification of feeling" (p. 306). Thus, parents learn to attend to and describe their child's behavior, to parrot or paraphrase their child's statements, and to reflect their child's feelings.

Parents also learn to structure the beginning and end of play and to set limits on unacceptable behavior. At the beginning of each play session, children are told they are free to say anything and do almost anything they wish during this special play time. They will be told if they do something that is not allowed. Toward the end of each play session, children are told when play will end in 5 minutes and when it will end in 1 minute. If children become destructive or physically aggressive during play, parents are to reflect children's desire to engage in the prohibited behavior but to state clearly the limit and provide the child with an alternative structure for play. If the child repeats the act, the limit is repeated along with a warning indicating that play will end if the limit is defied again. For a third transgression, play is terminated after the limit is repeated. In subsequent play sessions, initial violations of previously set limits are met with a reminder and a warning that play will end if the limit is crossed again.

Parents are taught these skills by observing demonstration sessions from behind one-way mirrors and then discussing both the child's play behavior and specific skills used by the therapist. Parents are informed that children with emotional and behavioral problems often follow a general pattern of play that begins with aggression and issues of control, followed by regressive and immature play, and eventually ends with more reality-based play focusing on skill mastery. Parents are then given direct instruction and role-play exercises to prepare them for their own practice play sessions. Parents conducting the practice sessions, which are observed by the therapists and other parents, are praised for using appropriate play skills and are given feedback for future sessions.

Parents who are having difficulty in acquiring these skills are asked to discuss "their own feelings and other phenomenological aspects of the new behaviors they are attempting to acquire" (L. F. Guerney & B. G. Guerney, 1985, p. 510). This procedure, referred to as *dynamic processing*, is considered a critical part of CREFT. L. F. Guerney (1983) described dynamic processing as similar to the interactions between a therapy supervisor and supervisee. As such, "parental insight and growth in the affective and cognitive domains and in the parent–child relationship" (p. 38) is promoted by CREFT therapists maintaining a role of sensitive collaborator, demonstrating to parents their acceptance, empathy, and support. L. F. Guerney and B. G. Guerney (1985) cited a study by Eardley (1978) reporting that CREFT without the dynamic processing component resulted in no greater gains than that produced by a no-treatment control group. Only the CREFT group that included dynamic processing made significant improvements. Phase 1 of CREFT is designed to prepare parents for home play sessions, which were originally considered the primary mechanism of therapeutic change. However, a study by Sywulak (1977) indicated that considerable improvement in child symptomatology and parental acceptance occurs during Phase 1 prior to home play sessions. It would seem, therefore, that dynamic processing is a major factor behind any therapeutic gains realized during this first phase.

The second phase of CREFT begins after parents have had at least two practice sessions in the clinic. Parents are asked to begin conducting home play sessions once a week for about 30 to 45 minutes. Each week parents discuss home play sessions and receive supportive feedback from the group and dynamic supervision from the therapist. Home play continues until the child has begun to show improvements in behavior outside of play and is playing in a manner indicative of the final stages of play therapy. In Phase 3, parents are trained to transfer skills used during play to nonplay situations. Initially, parents are asked to relate problem situations at home that produce feelings similar to those experienced during play. Similarities and differences between play and nonplay interactions are then discussed, albeit with the understanding that the demands they routinely face as parents do not equate with the demands they face when playing with their child. In the final phase of CREFT, play sessions are faded and replaced with "special times" that lack the formality of play sessions. The child's prerogative to select the activity and the parent's role as empathic responder are retained. Meetings at this point take place every 3 to 4 weeks and continue for approximately 3 months.

Empirical Support

BMPT

In many respects, data supporting the use of BMPT are impressive. Kazdin (1987) stated that literally hundreds of outcome studies have evaluated the use of parent training with children with behavior problems of varying levels of dysfunction, with many of these studies involving BMPT programs. A recent meta-analysis by Serketich and Dumas (1996) uncovered 117 parent-training outcome studies in which the behaviors targeted for treatment included at least one of the following: aggression, temper tantrums, or noncompliance. Most reviews of the BMPT outcome literature (e.g., Dumas, 1989; Hughes & Cavell, 1994; Kazdin, 1987; G. E. Miller & Prinz, 1990; Patterson, 1985) noted that early single-case studies offered clear support for programs that trained parents in techniques based on operant and social learning principles (e.g., Patterson & Brodsky, 1966). Impressive initial results soon gave way, however, to findings from group-outcome studies that both supported (e.g., Patterson, Chamberlain, & Reid, 1982) and failed to support (e.g., Bernal, Klinnert, & Schultz, 1980) the short-term efficacy of BMPT. Patterson (1985), noting that "a number of studies ... have failed to provide support for the efficacy of parent training for families of oppositional children" (p. 1347), argued that poorly trained, novice therapists or treatment formats that were too brief (e.g., only 8 to 10 weeks) may have contributed to these negative findings. However, these assertions do not fit completely with recent findings from studies conducted by Webster-Stratton and her colleagues (e.g., Webster-Stratton, 1990; Webster-Stratton, Kolpacoff, & Hollinsworth, 1988; Webster-Stratton, Hollinsworth, & Kolpacoff, 1989).

In evaluating her videotape version of parent training, Webster-Stratton (1987) randomly assigned parents of 114, 3–8-year-old children with conduct problems to one of four conditions: individually administered videotape modeling (IVM), group discussion plus videotape modeling (GDVM), group discussion with no modeling (GD), and wait-list control. Participants in the IVM group had no contact with therapists, whereas those in the GDVM and GD groups were taught by fully trained and experienced clinicians. Participants in all three treatment conditions met weekly for 10–12 sessions, with 12 sessions being the maximum allowed. All three treatment groups showed at least some improvement relative to the control group when assessed across diverse measurement techniques: home observations of parent and child behavior (e.g., criticism, positive affect, child deviance), parent daily telephone reports, parent questionnaires, and teacher questionnaires. Although there was a tendency to find greater differences between GDVM and GD participants and control participants (than between control and IVM participants), comparisons among the three treatment groups yielded virtually no differences. These findings challenge the hypothesis that negative results from earlier BMPT outcome studies were due solely to the use of therapists who lacked experience or to treatments that were too brief. Characteristics of the children and parents participating may better explain differences in outcome across these studies (see below). If true, then the effect of therapist's experience or treatment duration may go undetected unless these variables are examined within a sample of parents who are least likely to respond to BMPT (Patterson, 1985).

The meta-analysis by Serketich and Dumas (1996) provides additional empirical support for the short-term efficacy of BMPT. Of the 117 controlled outcome studies they located, only 26 met the following criteria for inclusion:

1. Parents or caregivers were instructed in the use of differential reinforcement or time-out.
2. Children were of preschool or elementary school age.
3. BMPT was evaluated against a control group (no treatment, attention placebo, or an alternative treatment), and both groups contained children who displayed elevated levels of problem behaviors.
4. BMPT and control groups had to contain at least 5 participants each.
5. At least one outcome measure had addressed the child's behavior.

From these 26 studies were computed 36 comparisons between BMPT and control groups. Two thirds of the studies used individually administered parent training. The average number of sessions was just under 10, and the mean age of the child was 6 years. The investigators computed mean effect sizes across the 36 comparisons and found an overall mean effect size of .86 (SD = .36), indicating that children whose parents participated in BMPT were functioning better than 81% of the children in the control group. Also, the mean effect size did not differ greatly by the source of the outcome variable: parent report, .84; observer report, .85; teacher report, .73. A mean effect size of .44 was also found for measures of parents' personal adjustment (e.g., stress, depression).

These data are encouraging and provide strong support for the value of the BMPT approach. However, clinicians should be cautious when interpreting these findings. Participants in the control group received an alternative treatment in only 4 of the 36 comparisons. In fact, Serketich and Dumas (1996) found that over the past 25 years only 22% of BMPT outcome studies used adequate control groups. They concluded, therefore, that "the results of the meta-analysis largely provide support for the effectiveness of [BMPT] in comparison to no intervention" (p. 181).

The long-term benefits of BMPT have rarely been assessed, and most parent-training outcome studies fail to provide follow-up data (Serketich & Dumas, 1996). Kazdin, Mazurick, and Bass (1993) have suggested that "long-term follow-up of treatment from controlled clinical trials is largely unavailable" (p. 15). Follow-up studies do exist, and these have ranged in duration from 1 to 14 years (Baum & Forehand, 1981; Forehand & Long, 1991; Long, Forehand, Wierson, & Morgan, 1994; Patterson & Fleischman, 1979; Webster-Stratton, 1990; Webster-Stratton et al., 1989). These studies are also fairly consistent in reporting positive findings. However, the conclusions that can be drawn from these studies are limited by a lack of comparison data from participants who were left untreated or who received contrasting treatments. Existing follow-up studies also suffer from differential drop-out rates between target and comparison participants. For example, Forehand and Long (1991) found important differences between families who did and did not participate in a 7 1/2-year follow-up study. Families who participated in their follow-up had children who were more compliant at posttreatment than those who were not assessed at follow-up. In a similar study with a 14-year follow-up, participants who were located and agreed to participate in the assessment ($N = 26$) had higher SES scores than nonparticipants (Long et al., 1994). The two groups did not differ, however, in pre- or posttreatment levels of compliant or deviant behavior. Follow-up studies showing generally supportive results can also be contrasted with studies in which treatment gains were lost at follow-up (Dumas, 1989). Dumas (1989) suggested that failure to maintain significant gains in child-rearing skills at follow-up is likely due to differences in the level of *insularity* (i.e., low income, social isolation, emotional distress) experienced by the participating parents. For example, Dumas (1989) pointed out that in Baum and Forehand's (1981) follow-up study, positive results were based on a sample in which only 1 of the 34 families received public assistance.

Follow-up studies reporting the clinical significance of BMPT treatment effects generally reveal that most children benefit. However, sizeable numbers of treated children do not respond to BMPT. In Webster-Stratton's (1990) 3-year follow-up study, 53.7% of mothers and 74.5% of fathers rated their child's behavior as falling within the normal range, but 59.0% of mothers and 45.5% of fathers were still concerned about behavior problems. Teachers rated 73.5% of the children as falling within the normal range of functioning at follow-up; however, 61.0% of these children were in the normal range before treatment began. Of those in the deviant range before treatment, just over half (53.3%) were found to be clinically improved at follow-up. In comparing the findings of her 3-year follow-up study with those of other BMPT researchers, Webster-Stratton (1990) concluded that the "results are similar to other parent training studies, which have suggested that 30% to 50% of treated families fail to maintain clinically significant improvements" (p. 148).

As suggested by Dumas (1989), one reason why children may not respond to BMPT is that their parents are experiencing greater stress than parents of children who do respond positively. Several risk variables have been shown to be linked empirically with a poor response to BMPT. These include both characteristics of the child (e.g., severity of problem behavior) and characteristics of the parent (e.g., depression and antisocial traits). Maternal depression is particularly important because it has been shown to be a better predictor of mothers' ratings of child behavior than independent observations of the child's level of disruption (Greist, Forehand, Wells, & McMahon, 1980). Webster-Stratton (1990) has described the parents of nonresponding children as parents who "had themselves experienced deprived and nonnurturing childhoods with painful memories of alcoholism and drug abuse in their fathers and depression in their mothers" (p. 148). Stressful family circumstances, such as single-parent status, marital discord, poverty, and social isolation, are also implicated as predictors of a poor response to BMPT (Dumas, 1989; Webster-Stratton & Hammond, 1990). As noted in chapter 1, economic deprivation, marital discord, and other family risk factors are thought to operate primarily through the disruption of essential parenting practices (Patterson et al., 1989).

The same risk variables that predict a poor response to BMPT (and that predict continued childhood aggression generally) also predict which families are most likely to drop out of therapy. Researchers have estimated that about 28% of parents drop out of BMPT (Forehand, Middlebrook, Rogers, & Steffe, 1983). Kazdin and his colleagues (Kazdin et al., 1993) found the likelihood of families dropping out of parent training increased steadily as the number of child, parent, and family risk factors increased. There is also evidence that parents with older children (i.e., 6.5 to 12.5 years old) are more likely to drop out of treatment prematurely (Dishion & Patterson, 1992).

Given that certain risk factors predict a poor response to BMPT, researchers (e.g., Dadds, Schwartz, & Sanders, 1987; G. E. Miller & Prinz, 1990; Patterson, 1985; Patterson, 1985; Webster-Stratton, 1994) have suggested that BMPT by itself is inadequate to meet the needs of many parents with aggressive children, particularly those experiencing significant levels of psychopathology, marital conflict, social disadvantage, and isolation. These researchers often suggest that nonresponders to BMPT will need adjunctive therapies in order to reduce the level of coercion in their families. However, it would appear that more research is needed before researchers can state unequivocally why some children do not respond when parents participate in BMPT therapy. Questions remain about inconsistencies in the specific variables found to predict treatment outcome (Dumas, 1989) and in the extent to which risk factors predict outcome above and beyond parent ratings (Kazdin, 1995a). Particularly important to address is the possibility of interactions among the variables that place families at risk. For example, some risk variables (e.g., depression, low SES, lack of social support) may moderate the relation between single-parent status and treatment outcome. Another issue to explore is the relation between parent or family risk factors and variables identified as possible mechanisms of therapeutic action in parent training (e.g., Spitzer, Webster-Stratton, & Hollinsworth, 1991). Unfortunately, parent training, like child therapy in general, has been the focus of very little process research (Kazdin, 1995b).

One exception, a study by Forgatch (1991), uncovered some important reasons why a substantial number of children may not benefit from BMPT. In this study, 50 families received either individually administered parent training (35 families) or family therapy that included aspects of parent training (15 families). On average, families received 19 treatment sessions each. Posttreatment assessments were used to categorize families as either improved or unimproved on the basis of whether their parenting practices had improved at least 30% from baseline. As expected, improvement in parenting practices was associated with a decrease in child antisocial behavior. Parents' use of monitoring was more predictive of treatment gains than was their use of discipline, and neither positive reinforcement nor problem solving were related to a reduction in child antisocial behavior. Families that improved on both discipline and monitoring were expected to be the most improved. However, only 25 families (50%) improved their use of discipline, only 8 (16%) improved their monitoring skills, and only 5 (10%) improved both their discipline and monitoring. These findings raise questions about the extent to which participation in BMPT leads consistently to positive changes in targeted parenting practices.

What of the 50 to 70% of families who show improvement following BMPT? Treatment effects often involve changes in the kinds of problem behaviors (e.g., noncompliance, tantrums) that are usually exhibited by young children (Campbell et al., 1994). Greenberg and Speltz (1988) suggested that maturation alone may explain pre-to-post reductions in the frequency of deviant behaviors. Patterson (1985) recognized the possibility that "untreated control groups of preschool problem children . . . may show more 'spontaneous remission' than is obtained for comparable groups that are eight or nine years of age" (p. 1373). To address this question, Dishion (described in Patterson, Dishion, & Chamberlain, 1993) reanalyzed archival outcome data testing for differential effects by age. The outcomes of children 2.5 to 6.5 years of age versus the outcomes of children 6.5 to 12.5 years of age were compared. Dishion found that 63.2% of the younger children versus only 26.9% of the older children showed clinically significant improvement. However, when Dishion and Patterson (1992) restricted these analyses to families who actually completed treatment, they found no differences in the outcomes of younger children versus older children. They did find that parents with older children were more likely to withdraw from BMPT therapy than parents with younger children. Indeed, of the 14 families who did not participate in the termination observations, 12 were families with older children. Dishion and Patterson (1992) also found that 52% of their clinical sample improved their levels of aversive behavior from the distressed to the nondistressed range. These findings parallel those reported by Ruma, Burke, and Thompson (1996). In their study, Ruma et al. found that a child's age was not a significant predictor of treatment outcome. However, adolescent participants had higher pretreatment levels of problem behavior than younger children, and pretreatment level of problem behavior was the only consistent predictor of BMPT treatment outcome. In other words, the more severe the problems, the worse the child's outcome, and adolescents tended to have more severe levels of problem behavior. Greenberg and Speltz (1988) also suggested that parent–child dyads striving to "look good" may cause highly focused behavioral observations to overestimate the extent to which families continue to benefit from parent training. For example, over 90% of parents assessed in a 1-year follow-up study were satisfied with their BMPT program even though 49% reported the presenting problem still existed and 77% reported that their child was currently receiving services elsewhere (Charlop, Parrish, Fenton, & Cataldo, 1983).

The limited number of studies assessing the generalization effects of BMPT typically show that treatment benefits carry over to siblings (Arnold, Levine, & Patterson, 1975; Humphreys, Forehand, McMahon, & Roberts, 1978) and to untargeted problem behaviors (Wells, Forehand, & Griest, 1980). However, results concerning the generalization of treatment benefits to other settings such as classrooms have been more equivocal. Some studies report a contrast effect in which deviant behavior increased at school (Johnson, Bolstad, & Lobitz, 1976), whereas others report no effects whatsoever (Wahler, 1969). More recent studies have found significant benefits in nontreated school settings (McNeil, Eyberg, Eisenstadt, Newcomb, & Funderburk, 1991; Webster-Stratton et al., 1988). Both of these newer studies used versions of BMPT that place greater emphasis on teaching parents child-directed play skills in combination with effective discipline techniques. The extent to which BMPT's focus on specific problem behaviors creates positive ripple effects on other aspects of child and family functioning is also unclear (McMahon & Forehand, 1988). That is, are increases in child compliance and decreases in ineffective commands accompanied by wider and similarly positive changes in how family members interact and perceive each other?

Parents who participate in BMPT programs tend to rate the training experience as a positive one. Consumer satisfaction measures, completed both immediately after treatment and at follow-up, typically ask parents for their perceptions regarding the training format and the specific skills taught (McMahon & Forehand, 1984; Webster-Stratton, 1989). Findings suggest that parents may prefer performance-oriented (e.g., skill-rehearsal exercises) and group discussion formats over formats that rely solely on the use of lectures and written material or self-administered videotapes. As for specific techniques, parents typically rate rewarding good behavior and time-out as more useful than all other techniques. However, follow-up studies usually find that rewarding is perceived over time as less useful by parents and time-out as more useful, although the absolute level of satisfaction for these techniques remains high. Both of these parenting techniques represent rather salient and immediate attempts to control a child's behavior. Ignoring and attending—techniques in which parents must inhibit their urges to control their child's behavior—are seen as less useful to parents. Also, parents' ratings of child-directed play skills tend to differ for mothers and fathers in that mothers tend to report far more difficulty playing with their children in this nondirective way (Webster-Stratton, 1989). Based on these findings, Webster-Stratton (1989) suggested that "parent training programs ... perhaps should assist mothers in being more playful" (p. 113).

CREFT

Currently, empirical support for CREFT parent training is limited. Most studies that have directly evaluated the impact of CREFT are either anecdotal or quasiexperimental in nature. Also, the majority of these are unpublished doctoral dissertations supervised by the originators of CREFT. However, reviews of this circumscribed literature suggest that CREFT is a potentially viable approach to improving critical parenting skills (e.g., Ginsberg, 1989; L. F. Guerney & B. Guerney, 1987). Unfortunately, previous studies have given little attention to the type of childhood dysfunction with which CREFT is effective. A notable exception is Ginsberg's (1984) use of CREFT with parents of children with mental retardation. Whether CREFT is equally effective in helping children whose symptoms involve defiant and aggressive behavior or the internalizing problems of anxiety and depression has not been adequately addressed. Also, despite the apparent potential for using CREFT with abusive parents, empirical data on this question has not been gathered. Because the empirical literature in support of CREFT is limited in size and scope, especially when judged against the BMPT literature, direct comparisons between these two models offer few unequivocal conclusions.

Initial CREFT studies evaluated the extent to which parents, mothers in particular, could successfully acquire the skills of a play therapist. In an early study by Stover and B. Guerney (1967), judges' ratings of audiotaped interactions indicated that mothers who received training were able to adopt a more reflective role vis-à-vis their clinic-referred children than mothers in a no-contact control group. Results showed a greater tendency for CREFT-group mothers to restate the content of their child's verbalizations (Stover & B. Guerney, 1967). Statements in which mothers clarified their child's feelings—a more sophisticated reflective skill—were rather infrequent, however. These gains were assessed after 10 weeks of instruction and after two previous training–play sessions. A subsequent study (B. Guerney & Stover, 1971) corroborated these earlier findings and indicated that CREFT-trained mothers showed "recognition and acceptance of the child's behavior, and often showed acceptance of his [sic] underlying feelings as well" (p. 110).

B. Guerney and Stover (1971) also evaluated the impact of CREFT on children's behavior using parent and therapist ratings. Using a one-group pretest–posttest design, 71 clinic-referred children and their mothers (58 boys, 13 girls) began participation in CREFT. These children had been culled from an original pool of 452 referrals to one of two participating clinics. Referrals were solicited using a number of sources (e.g., newspapers, schools). Notably, most of those referred were excluded based on a telephone interview that screened out parents interested in specific academic remedial help or "where *both* health history and acting-out impulsive behaviors obviously suggested need for medical, pediatric, or neurological attention first" (p. 6). Of the 51 mothers who completed the 12- to 18-month treatment, all reportedly improved, with 18 rated as *very much improved*, 22 as *much improved*, and 11 as *somewhat improved*. Parent ratings on the Des Moines Parent Rating Scale and the Wichita Guidance Center CheckList (WGC) also indicated significant improvement posttreatment. However, pretest mean scores on all WGC subscales for this sample of 51 completers fell within 1 standard deviation of the mean scores from a normative sample of 200 children.

B. Guerney and Stover (1971) attempted to assess the extent to which children who were acting out ($n = 25$), were withdrawn ($n = 20$), or were of a mixed or indeterminate status ($n = 26$) differed in their responsiveness to filial therapy. Classification was done by staff members, and agreement among them was satisfactory. Differences among the groups in their decision to participate in filial therapy, to drop out of therapy, and to benefit because of therapy were all nonsignificant. However, families who decided not to follow through with the recommendation for filial therapy tended to have children who engaged in greater conflict with their mothers and evinced greater overall maladjustment.

To evaluate further the nature of these results, Oxman (1971) collected a similar set of ratings from a control group of mothers ($N = 77$) who were assessed at baseline and at 1-year follow-up. These dyads were matched with B. G. Guerney and Stover's (1971) CREFT participants on a number of demographic variables (e.g., SES, family size). This so-called control group was rated more favorably at pretest, but analyses controlling for initial levels of adjustment showed greater gains over a 12-month period for children of CREFT mothers. It is difficult to interpret the findings from Oxman's (1971) study, given that children were not randomly assigned to conditions.

Sywulak (1977) attempted to improve on earlier studies by having 19 parent–child dyads serve as their own controls during a 4-month waiting period prior to participating in CREFT. Parent ratings of their child's adjustment and of their own level of acceptance indicated significant improvement at posttreatment. Sensue (1981) followed a subset of these families ($N = 16$) for 3 years and found that many of the immediate treatment gains had been maintained. Sensue also found that parents reported having been quite satisfied with the CREFT training experience and that nearly all would recommend it to other parents without reservation.

Finally, Coufal (1982) compared parents in a CREFT group with those in a similar parents-only group or in a no-treatment control group. Children were 3–10-year-olds experiencing low risk and mild distress. Based on a behavioral interaction task, Coufal found that parents in the CREFT group displayed greater empathy, involvement, acceptance, and affection than other parents. These parents were also better able to allow their child self-direction. Differences in the children's behavior were not examined, however.

Responsive Parent Training

One final CREFT-related study to consider is one I conducted with the assistance of my graduate students (Cavell, 1996; Cavell, Constantin, Welch, & Kinnee, 1999). My interest in CREFT began years ago while I was a predoctoral psychology intern. I had the good fortune then of co-leading a CREFT group for parents of clinic-referred children, the majority of whom were defiant, disruptive, and somewhat aggressive. I was intrigued by this type of parent work because it seemed to produce such fundamental changes in the parent–child relationship for many of the participants. Once trained in the play skills, these caregivers (some were parents but others were stepparents, foster parents, etc.) would set aside 30 to 40 min each week to have an uninterrupted play session with their child in the home. The task of having to attend to their child's behavior, comments, and feelings without intervening (except when the child was aggressive or destructive) seemed to create for parents an option for relating with their child that had not been previously available. It also seemed to reduce children's motivation to make life difficult for their parent. Perhaps the sense of revelation that parents expressed when they recounted the past week's play session was most impressive. Each week they seemed to discover new insights about the child they thought they knew so well and about the task of parenting such a child.

I then set about the task of developing and testing empirically my own adaptation of CREFT for families with children with conduct problems. In this adapted version of CREFT, which I termed *responsive parent training* (RPT), I eschewed a Rogerian perspective in favor of a blend of attachment and family systems theories. Pilot tests conducted in our university clinic, and the lack of adequate data on the use of CREFT with children with conduct problems, suggested a need to expand beyond the typical CREFT model. I was strongly influenced by Greenberg and Speltz's (1988) chapter on the role of attachment in the ontogeny of conduct problems. Work in the area of attachment offered a much firmer theoretical and empirical basis for targeting parent–child relationships and for teaching the skills of nondirective play. Also influential was the work of Salvador Minuchin (1974) and other structural family therapists. Minuchin's emphasis on family organization and boundaries seemed to be a necessary complement to the more dyadic and affectively focused work of parent–child play that so predominates CREFT. Therefore, RPT was conceived as a program to teach parents the skills by which they could enhance the emotional quality of the parent–child relationship (e.g., freedom to express emotions, felt security, feelings of worth) while also establishing and retaining appropriate generational boundaries and family structure. This seemed a much closer approximation to the Baumrindian notion of authoritative parenting than that produced by either CREFT or BMPT alone.

Also influencing the RPT model was research suggesting that a strong therapeutic alliance is critical to working with parents whose children are difficult and aggressive (Stoolmiller, Duncan, Bank, & Patterson, 1993). Influential here was Patterson and Forgatch's (1985) early work on parent resistance, Safran's (1990a, 1990b) integration of cognitive and interpersonal therapies, and the CREFT procedure of dynamic processing (L. F. Guerney & B. G. Guerney, 1985). Patterson and Forgatch's work made it clear that practitioners cannot ignore the common therapeutic problem of parents resisting efforts to teach and confront. Safran's therapeutic recommendations and the CREFT practice of dynamic processing suggested promising options for dealing with parent resistance. The assumption that efforts to assist clients can be undermined by dysfunctional interpersonal schemas and that therapists should communicate a willingness to join with clients by "unhooking" from whatever nonproductive exchanges these schemas are likely to foster (see chapter 4) was borrowed from Safran (1990a, 1990b). Given that many parents with aggressive children appear to operate from dysfunctional interpersonal schemas (Pettit, Dodge, & Brown, 1988; Wahler & Dumas, 1989), Safran's recommendations seemed to make good sense for parent trainers. Dynamic processing (see above) can be used to help parents explore thoughts and feelings that surface as they learn skills to enhance the dynamics of the parent–child relationship. Dynamic processing allows therapists to maintain the role of sensitive collaborator, demonstrating to parents their acceptance, understanding, and support. Unhooking from parents' dysfunctional interpersonal schemas and maintaining the role of sensitive collaborator seemed useful tools for therapists working with resistant parents.

A Preliminary Trial

To test this mix of CREFT, structural family therapy, and techniques for promoting a strong working alliance, I evaluated RPT against a BMPT video modeling (BMPT-VM) condition. Parents assigned to the BMPT-VM condition (N = 23) participated in the self-administration of Webster-Stratton's (1987) videotaped training series. Webster-Stratton and her colleagues (Webster-Stratton et al., 1989) found clinically significant gains for families participating in this version of BMPT, with few differences between it and formats involving therapist-led group discussion. RPT (N = 30) was conducted in groups of 6 to 8 parents who met for about 2 hours per week, for 10 to 12 weeks. Graduate student coleaders followed a detailed manual, and I supervised them for about 2 hours each week.

Preliminary analyses were based on those children and parents who completed at least half of the training sessions (Cavell, 1996). Of these, 24 were in the RPT condition and 12 were in the comparison treatment condition. The first group of families to be assessed were randomly assigned to RPT or BMPT-VM conditions. However, logistical constraints required shifting to an assignment procedure whereby all parents in a given semester were assigned to one condition or the other, with a coin toss determining which condition was administered first in that academic year. Children ranged in age from 3 to 10 years (M = 6.41 years), and 74% were boys. Although some parents were referred by other professionals, most responded to a newspaper advertisement that announced "parent training for parents whose children are difficult and disruptive at home or school." The mean Child Behavior Checklist (CBCL) Externalizing T score was 63.83 (SD = 8.22) or just above the 90th percentile, a clinical cutoff recommended by Achenbach (1991). As is common with other clinic-based studies, this sample was lacking in minority-group member representation. Roughly two thirds of the parents were European American and married, 40% were college graduates, and the median income level was between $30,000 and $35,000.

Parents completed the CBCL (Achenbach, 1991), the Eyberg Child Behavior Inventory (Robinson, Eyberg, & Ross, 1980), the Parenting Stress Index (Abidin, 1983), and a measure of negative attributions used by Dix and Lochman (1990). Mothers' observations of their child's behavior (and their own use of spanking and parent–child play) were obtained via the Parent Daily Report (PDR; Chamberlain & Reid, 1987). The PDR is a brief telephone interview covering the previous 24-hour period conducted four times over a 2-week period. Children completed Harter and Pike's (1984) measure of self-perceived competence, and for those in school, teachers completed the teacher report form of the Achenbach scale.

Parents were visited in their home by two research assistants who briefly interviewed them and then videotaped them playing with their child for 10 minutes with a set of toys provided. Parents were also asked to direct the child to clean up the toys once the play was over. From these home visits and videotaped play sessions, my colleagues and I obtained interviewers' global impressions of parents' effectiveness, as well as judges' ratings of the level of positive affect exhibited by parents and children and the amount of control parents exerted during play. We also used the total number of toys children picked up and the latency to respond to parents' directives as measures of compliance. Families were assessed at pre- and posttreatment and at 1-year follow-up.

Major Findings

There were three main findings. First, participants were much more likely to drop out of the BMPT-VM condition: 47.8% from the BMPT-VM versus 20.0% from RPT condition. Most of the BMPT-VM dropouts occurred after being assigned to that condition but before even starting the intervention. We suspect that unmet expectations for contact with a therapist, for participation in a parent training group, or for both may have produced this high rate of attrition. Dropouts did not differ from completers (those with at least 5 sessions) on any variable except the Eyberg Inventory Problem Intensity score, which was higher for children whose families dropped out. Because of the unexpected loss of participants and the exploratory nature of the study, alpha was set at $p < .10$ for all subsequent analyses.

The second major finding was that both conditions led to gains from pre- to posttreatment and from pretreatment to follow-up on the CBCL Externalizing scale. Pre- to posttreatment gains for both conditions were also found for problem behaviors on the PDR. The third major finding was that RPT and BMPT-VM seemed to produce differential results in line with their respective emphases. From pre- to posttreatment, RPT parents were rated as less controlling during play, and their children were rated as displaying more positive affect; however, BMPT-VM parents obtained higher global ratings of effectiveness from home interviewers. At follow-up, differential effects were noted on the PDR and the Harter: RPT parents reported greater use of parent–child play, and their children showed greater gains in self-worth; BMPT-VM parents, on the other hand, observed fewer behavior problems in their children when measured via the PDR. All other analyses were nonsignificant.

The results of this preliminary study, although compromised by the small sample size and the lack of adequate external measures of improvement, suggest that RPT is a promising alternative to existing BMPT programs. Particularly noteworthy was the finding that training parents to use child-centered play skills and then processing with them their understanding of these skills can lead to superior maintenance of parent–child play was particularly noteworthy. The fact that RPT fared worse than BMPT-VM on PDR problem-behavior scores was disconcerting. However, this difference could be a reflection of the emphasis in BMPT on parents' efforts to control problem behavior. Differences in PDR problem-behavior scores were at odds with the fact that both groups of parents reported gains on the CBCL. The high attrition rate in this study, combined with the fact that few minority and disadvantaged families came to our clinic, reinforces the need to conduct similar interventions in settings (e.g., schools) that are more accessible to such families.

The pattern of findings from this study also suggest that integrating features of BMPT and RPT makes more sense than using any single approach. Consider, for example, that in responsive parent training, my colleagues and I made no efforts to train parents to use time-out. In fact, such efforts were specifically avoided, although several parents reported having tried time-out at some point in the past. Our concern at the time was that extensive training in the use of time-out could lead parents to expect that conflict itself could and should be avoided. Instead of being trained to use time-out, parents were taught to establish clear generational boundaries and greater family structure, to rely on unambiguous commands and the judicious use of parental authority, and to develop and use limit-setting scripts that would buffer parents from the cognitive and emotional obstacles they face when shifting to a position of authority. Parents could have chosen to use time-out as part of their disciplinary scripts, but efforts in that direction were not promoted by therapists. Efforts to ensure that RPT was conceptually and clinically distinct from BMPT-VM make sense given our research goals. However, avoiding time-out makes little sense for practitioners, given its documented effectiveness and given the value of scripting nonviolent forms of discipline (see chapter 6, this volume).

Conclusion

Thirty years ago, two separate approaches to parent training began to unfold. BMPT and CREFT began as interventions designed to extend to parents a set of skills originally used by therapists. Since that time, BMPT has assumed a predominant role in both research and practice, due in large measure to the vast amount of empirical work supporting its conceptual base and therapeutic efficacy. The fact that more than 50% of families fail to benefit from BMPT is a serious concern, but a lack of controlled outcome research evaluating other types of parent training has limited the options available to practitioners. CREFT, which has a past as lengthy as that of BMPT, has been ignored by most parent-training researchers. The brief review offered here virtually exhausts the empirical literature surrounding CREFT. Alhough the findings from these studies are encouraging, CREFT continues to suffer from a lack of published research documenting its efficacy. As the quintessential example of the relationship enhancement model of parent training, CREFT departs widely from the BMPT model. Well-controlled outcome studies of CREFT that incorporate reliable, valid, and commonly used dependent measures are long overdue. Without stronger empirical support for relationship-enhancement approaches to parent training, clinicians cannot afford to rely solely on CREFT to meet the needs of aggressive children and their families.

In the next chapter, I present a conceptual framework for working with parents of aggressive children that integrates the significant contributions of both the BMPT and CREFT models. Lessons learned from our preliminary investigation of RPT are reflected in this framework. This new framework is designed to combine the documented advantages of existing programs with important expansions and revisions that are needed for effective "parent therapy" with parents of aggressive, school-age children.

3

A Framework for Intervening: Responsive Parent Therapy

Without question, practitioners and the parents they serve have greatly benefited from the contributions made over the past 30 years by each of the two models of parent training discussed in chapter 2. The term *parent training* has become commonplace in American society, and this mode of intervening with families is now firmly ensconced within the mental health care armamentarium. For aggressive children, parent training is considered a key ingredient of any comprehensive treatment package (Hughes & Cavell, 1994; McCord & Tremblay, 1992; Pepler & Rubin, 1991). As one approach to parent training, BMPT appears to be an effective and acceptable intervention for many families with difficult children. Also, research linked conceptually to BMPT has greatly expanded the understanding of the processes by which aggressive behavior is made manifest. CREFT, which is a radical departure from the prevailing BMPT model, is less widely known to researchers and practitioners, and a solid body of research in support of this model does not yet exist.

In this chapter, I outline a conceptual framework that practitioners can use when working with the parents of aggressive children. This framework is my attempt to integrate and update existing models of parent training. I present the underlying assumptions of this model and describe its seven components. I then discuss important linkages among the various components and close with a discussion of how to select and sequence these components. In subsequent chapters, I provide detailed information about how to implement each treatment component.

This framework is not meant to be highly prescriptive; it is a guiding heuristic for practitioners making decisions about how best to help parents of aggressive children. I have three reasons for not casting the model in highly prescriptive terms. First, the roles practitioners play when working with parents of aggressive children can vary greatly. Some practitioners are equipped to offer school- or clinic-based parent training groups, whereas others offer only therapy for individual families. Some are the primary service providers for families, but others play a limited provider role, perhaps that of consulting with or supervising paraprofessionals who provide direct service. Limited resources and restricted access to services can also create wide variability in how much time and effort practitioners devote to working with parents of aggressive children. Because of these obstacles, it seems unreasonable to present a framework for intervention that is suitable for only one kind of therapeutic role or format (e.g., 10-week, clinic-based, group format).

A second reason for offering a therapeutic guide and not a prescriptive formula is that parents of aggressive children also differ greatly from one another. They vary not only in how much they are burdened by environmental stress (e.g., poverty), but they also differ in their resistance to treatment, in their commitment to parenting, in the types of parenting skills they find unfamiliar, and in the area they need help with first. A third reason for being more heuristic than prescriptive is that interventions tied too closely to a specific format or set of techniques can feel forced if the square peg that is a family does not fit into the round hole that is the intervention. Clinical researchers are just now recognizing the importance of distinguishing between a treatment's efficacy as assessed in a controlled outcome study under relatively ideal conditions and its effectiveness as shown by therapists implementing the same procedures in the "real world" (Weisz, Weiss, & Donenberg, 1992). Practitioners need specifics and structure, but not at the expense of knowing when and how to adapt a program if a family's case does not fit. When I describe procedures for implementing the various components of this model, I emphasize principles over techniques and general strategies over specific tactics. Specific techniques and tactics are presented, but these are meant to be illustrative or suggestive and not prescriptive.

Responsive Parent Therapy

I refer to this model of intervention as *responsive parent therapy* (RPT). The term *responsive* is meant to emphasize a focus on relationships—between the parent and the child and between the parent and the therapist. The term *therapy* is used to distinguish this kind of relationship work from what is typically connoted by the term *training*. When practitioners help adult couples with their unsatisfactory relationships, we call it *marital therapy*, not *marital training*. Similarly, to call therapeutic work with parents of aggressive, school-age children *training* is to fail to recognize the intensity and the complexity of the work required.

Responsive parent therapy is both similar to and distinct from its conceptual predecessor, responsive parent training (see chapter 2, this volume). Notable vestiges are the influence of attachment theory, structural family therapy, and recent efforts to understand and respond to parent resistance. However, RPT goes beyond a modified CREFT protocol to expand and revise existing approaches to parent training. This newly developed model of parent therapy is designed to address two issues missing from responsive parent training: parents' goals and parental self-care. This framework also blends key aspects of the BMPT model with core features of responsive parent training. Integrating these two approaches to parent training fits a recent trend among researchers to blend attachment and social learning perspectives when attempting to understand and treat childhood aggression (Cavell & Hughes, in press; Greenberg, Speltz, & DeKlyen, 1993; Kochanska, 1995; Lyons-Ruth, 1996; Richters & Waters, 1991; Shaw & Bell, 1993; Wahler, 1994, 1997). Because both perspectives are important to the study of children's socialization, retaining and integrating the two makes more sense than choosing one or the other.

Assumptions Underlying RPT

RPT is based on certain assumptions about the development of childhood aggression and its amelioration. The conceptual groundwork for some of these assumptions goes beyond the scope of this book but can be found elsewhere (Cavell, 1999a, 1999b). A list of the basic assumptions underlying the RPT model is presented in Exhibit 3.1.

Assumption 1

The RPT model assumes that childhood aggression is multiply determined by both dispositional and environmental factors. As discussed in chapter 1, dispositional factors can include a difficult temperament as well as the presence of various developmental disorders (e.g., hyperactivity). Dispositional factors are also suggested when there is a family history of criminality, substance abuse, or other psychopathology. When therapists fail to recognize the role of dispositional factors in the etiology of conduct problems and childhood aggression, they run the risk of underestimating how powerful a child's influence can be on a family system (Lytton, 1990a, 1990b). This error can impede parent training, especially if therapists overestimate parents' contribution to the development of antisocial

Exhibit 3.1

Assumptions Underlying Responsive Parent Therapy

Childhood aggression is multiply determined by dispositional and environmental factors.

Childrens' environmental experiences with parents are foremost among the environmental factors that contribute to childhood aggression.

Socializing aggressive children requires their participation in a long-term relationship with a prosocial parent or other adult who can effectively meet their containment and acceptance needs.

The behavioral demands of aggressive children often exceed parents' capacity to be accepting, containing, and prosocial.

Parents who adequately structure the family can be more accepting of, containing toward, and prosocial with their aggressive children.

Interventions with parents of aggressive children require a strong and collaborative therapeutic alliance in which therapists balance training with emotional support and understanding.

behavior. The therapeutic relationship may be jeopardized and opportunities to deal effectively with the real problem may be lost.

Assumption 2

Environmental factors, most notably parenting practices, are also contributing factors to antisocial behavior in children. Indeed, Patterson and his colleagues (Patterson et al., 1992) assert that poor parenting is the key determinant in the development of aggression, even when children are temperamentally difficult. Although other environmental factors have been implicated, Patterson et al. view these as either contextual variables (e.g., divorce, poverty), the indirect effects of which are mediated through disrupted parenting, or as products of children's "basic training" in antisocial behavior (e.g., peer rejection, deviant peers). Nevertheless, practitioners who work with aggressive children should not ignore these other environmental factors and focus only on presumed deficits in parenting.

Assumption 3

A central assumption within RPT is that effective socialization of children disposed to aggression will require their long-term participation in a relationship with an adult who is prosocial. Moreover, this relationship must be one marked by a consistent and effective blend of both acceptance and containment. The idea that acceptance and containment are complementary parenting practices is in keeping with a large body of research documenting the value of *authoritative* parenting (Baumrind, 1967, 1973; Dumas, 1996; Maccoby, 1992; Maccoby & Martin, 1983). Authoritative parents are distinguished by their ability to accept and promote their child's independent functioning while not capitulating to unreasonable demands. The notion that parents socialize children via efforts to accept, contain, and guide them prosocially is not new (Maccoby & Martin, 1983), but these efforts are usually viewed as discrete behaviors or circumscribed interactions. These parenting practices are rarely conceptualized as interlocking aspects of a single, enduring relationship, and the cumulative effect of these efforts rarely is considered the essential socializing mechanism. How parents handle a given situation is considered less important than the cumulative effect of the relationship on children's sense of being accepted or contained. As Kuczynski and Hildebrandt (1997) noted, the relationship model of children's socialization "gives a time dimension to parent–child interactions" (p. 236). I also define containment and acceptance *functionally* (see chapters 5 and 6, this volume), which means that parents may engage in behaviors that look accepting and containing, but what is critical is whether children are left with a sense of being accepted and contained. Figure 3.1 illustrates the assumptions made about socializing relationships, and it captures, more than any other depiction, the essence of the RPT model.

The implications of this assumption are far ranging for both parents

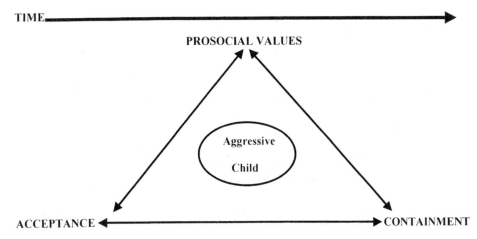

Figure 3.1. Relationship conditions for effective socialization of aggressive children.

and parent therapists. First, it suggests that effective socialization of aggressive children will be a product of a specific kind of relationship—a relationship in which children feel accepted and contained by parents who are prosocial. It also suggests that unless parents can maintain a relationship that effectively combines acceptance, containment, and prosocial values, then their aggressive child is unlikely to be socialized. Relationships that offer acceptance in the absence of containment or containment in the absence of acceptance will not suffice. For aggressive children whose parents cannot provide the necessary blend of acceptance, containment, and prosocial values, socialization may require relationships with other available adults (Cavell & Hughes, in press).

Also implicit in this assumption is the idea that discipline designed to increase a child's anxiety following a transgression or when punished is a flawed method of socialization for aggressive children. A more likely pathway is suggested by Kochanska's (1995) research on temperamentally fearless children. She found that, for fearless children, a "mutually cooperative set" between mother and child, reflected in part by an emotionally secure attachment relationship, was more likely to promote socialization than attempts to induce fear or anxiety. Increased anxiety was effective for fearful children, but it was thought to be inert or counterproductive for fearless children. Other researchers also find support for the motivational role of attachment security in promoting children's socialization (e.g., Greenberg et al., 1993; Greenberg & Speltz, 1988; Richters & Waters, 1991; Shaw & Bell, 1993). The work of these investigators suggests parents may have greater success at "pulling" aggressive children toward prosocial behavior via positive relationships than they will have "pushing out" antisocial behavior through fear-inducing discipline. Recent work by Dumas (Dumas, LaFreniere, & Serketich, 1995) and Wahler (1994, 1997) lend further credence to the notion that helping parents establish and maintain a positive relationship with aggressive children may be a more important goal than stamping out noncompliance (Cavell, 1999a, 1999b).

Figure 3.1 also suggests that successful efforts to change the social and interpersonal context of aggressive children cannot focus on only one dimension at a time. Rather, it is the effective coordination and integration of acceptance, containment, and prosocial values in the parent–child relationship that has a socializing effect on aggressive children. Therefore, the chief task for practitioners is to help parents establish and maintain a relationship that provides aggressive children with all three conditions (Cavell, 1999a, 1999b). Acceptance is necessary if parents of aggressive children are to create and maintain a mutually binding parent–child relationship (Kochanska, 1995). However, aggressive children behave in ways that are hard to understand and hard to accept. Strict limits on the child's antisocial behavior are needed to change the contingencies that shaped and maintain that behavior (Patterson et al., 1992). However, aggressive children and their acts of defiance and coercion are not easily contained. And prosocial norms are needed to counter children's emergent beliefs in the value of antisocial acts (Hawkins, Catalano, & Miller, 1994); however, aggressive children are unlikely to internalize prosocial values if their parent is more antisocial than prosocial or if their parent cannot accept and contain them.

Assumption 4

RPT also assumes that the coercive behavior of aggressive children can often disrupt parents' efforts to endorse prosocial values and exceed their capacity to be accepting and containing. Therefore, parents of aggressive children may need to acquire skills that focus on these three areas. Parents of aggressive children may also need help in understanding and appreciating the goal of this kind of socializing relationship.

Assumption 5

Parents can also benefit from efforts to structure their family and home so that the demands of continually upholding prosocial beliefs and of performing the ongoing tasks of acceptance and containment are not so burdensome. Structure in the home and family is particularly important during times of stress when parenting practices are prone to disruption. Parents of aggressive children will need help in creating the type and level of structure that is most conducive to their child's socialization.

Assumption 6

Parents of aggressive children are the primary custodians of this often-troubled relationship. For too many parents, the burden of this role can mean a recurring need for support from others and for time away from the job of parenting. Without these "refueling" opportunities (Webster-Stratton & Herbert, 1994), parents will find it difficult to sustain their efforts to be prosocial, accepting, and containing.

Assumption 7

Finally, the RPT model assumes that working effectively with parents of aggressive children requires a strong therapeutic alliance. Practitioners who work with families of aggressive children face a daunting therapeutic task that will require considerable clinical skill and effort and often the support of a supervisor or co-therapist (Patterson, 1985; Webster-Stratton & Herbert, 1994). An effective therapeutic alliance is one in which therapists are able to combine skills training with support and understanding.

The Multifaceted Nature of RPT

In my efforts to train graduate students, I often describe the challenge of working with troubled families as rather like trying to gain entry to a house that has multiple doors and windows, many of which are locked. If one can use only the front door and that door is locked, then entry is blocked. However, if one had the flexibility to try a different door or perhaps even a window, then new opportunities for entry arise. Similarly for practitioners working with troubled families, if an unforeseen obstacle (e.g., work-related stress) closes one therapeutic door (e.g., integrating acceptance skills into daily interactions), it would be useful to work from a model that offers additional strategies for change (e.g., establishing positive family rituals). The RPT model is broadly construed and multifaceted, thus allowing practitioners a fair degree of flexibility as they tailor treatment to meet the needs of their clients.

In these respects, RPT is similar to the multisystemic therapy (MST) model developed by Henggeler and Borduin (1990). These investigators have been responsible for developing perhaps the most innovative and rigorously tested approach to family therapy in the past decade (Henggeler, Schoenwald, Borduin, Rowland, & Cunningham, 1997). Like RPT, the MST model is based on the view that behavior disorders in children should be addressed through more than one level or system (e.g., individual or dyadic). In RPT, parenting goals, parenting skills, parent–child relationship issues, family system variables, and parents' overall level of health and well-being are all considered grist for the therapeutic mill. RPT differs from the MST model in that its goals are more circumscribed. In RPT, the work is primarily with parents or with parent–child dyads, whereas in MST, practitioners tend to operate across a number of systems (e.g., school, peers, community). Still, there are a number of conceptual parallels between the two approaches and RPT should dovetail nicely with MST interventions that involve direct contact with parents.

The RPT approach to working with parents of aggressive children involves seven components that are presented graphically in Figure 3.2.

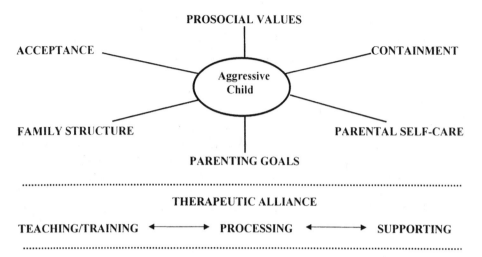

Figure 3.2. The responsive parent therapy model for working with parents of aggressive children.

Three components represent the relationship conditions considered necessary for effective socialization of aggressive children—acceptance, containment, and prosocial values. Three other components serve supportive functions for parents seeking to create and maintain this kind of parent–child relationship. These are parenting goals, family structure, and parental self-care. Collectively, these six components represent a model for understanding the task of *parenting* an aggressive child (as opposed to a task of *parent therapy*) that can be shared with parents. The last RPT component is the establishment of a strong therapeutic alliance between practitioner and parent. This component is positioned at the bottom of the figure because it represents the foundation on which all other components rest. Figure 3.3 depicts a modified version of the RPT model that can serve as point of discussion with parents and as a handout for parents.

Acceptance

In the RPT model, parents' ability to promote in children a sense of autonomy while leaving intact their sense of relationship security is considered a prerequisite to effective socialization (see chapter 5, this volume). Children who feel accepted and safe are more likely to invest in parents' system of prosocial commerce (Richters & Waters, 1991) and more likely to benefit from parents' guidance and example. Acceptance can range from tacit allowance to active endorsement depending on the degree to which parents are positive and enthusiastic about their child's behavior and the degree to which they openly and directly express their views and emotions. Child-centered play skills and the techniques of reflective listening are classic examples of skills parents can use to convey a position of acceptance.

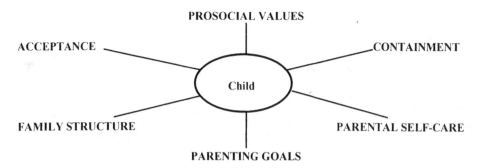

Figure 3.3. The responsive parent therapy approach to socializing children.

Containment

The term *containment* refers to parents' task in the face of childhood aggression and other forms of coercive behavior (see chapter 6). I use the term to distinguish it from the BMPT goals of gaining compliance and managing behavior (Cavell, 1999a). Like compliance training and behavior management, however, a focus on containment often involves teaching parents to use nonviolent disciplinary procedures such as time-out and the loss of privileges. But there are other aspects to containment. For example, parents must learn that disciplinary techniques will not eliminate entirely the physical and emotional "costs" of setting limits or the need to set limits in the future. Equipping parents with the skills they need to cope with these costs is an important part of containment skills training. Unless parents can learn to cope with the strain of standing firm, they are vulnerable to giving in to a child's unreasonable demands. The manner and skill by which parents demonstrate containment is not only important as a response to coercive behavior, it can also affect the overall quality of the parent–child relationship. Effective containment involves setting necessary limits and inhibiting the urge to set unnecessary limits. Parents are likely to need practice letting go of annoying behaviors just as much as they will need practice in responding with active, nonviolent forms of containment.

Prosocial Values

Presumably, the extent to which children are exposed to prosocial guidance and modeling is a function of how prosocial or antisocial their parents happen to be (see chapter 7, this volume). However, it is also likely that parents differ in the extent to which they make prosocial values explicit. Therefore, practitioners will need to assess how frequently, how consistently, and how saliently parents are endorsing prosocial values. Some parents may also need assistance in learning how to uphold prosocial beliefs and model principled behavior when overwhelmed by stress from within and outside the family.

Parenting Goals

A number of parent training programs have in their curricula a section that addresses how or what parents think. Sometimes this involves ensuring that parents have adequate knowledge about certain areas of parenting such as child development or the application of behavioral principles (Patterson et al., 1975; Webster-Stratton & Herbert, 1994). Other programs focus on parents' tendency to use faulty cognitions such as distorted beliefs or negative attributions that can damage a parent–child relationship. Still other programs focus, on adaptive cognitions such as problem-solving skills that enable parents to respond adaptively to difficult situations. In RPT, the topic of how parents think is addressed by a focus on parenting goals (see chapter 4, this volume).

The emphasis on parenting goals stems from the fact that one's goals can have a pivotal priming effect on other social information processing skills (Crick & Dodge, 1994) and on how one eventually responds in a given social situation (Cavell, 1990). Therefore, parents who are mindful of the goal of sustaining a relationship that combines acceptance, containment, and prosocial values would be expected to exercise more effective parenting than parents who pursue other goals.

Family Structure

Parents of aggressive children who have the skills needed to instill in children a sense of acceptance, containment, and prosocial values can still experience serious difficulties if their family and home are poorly organized and structured. For parents of aggressive children, responding to the often-competing demands of acceptance, containment, and prosocial guidance and modeling can be fatiguing, especially for parents who encounter recurring and unpredictable stress. Therefore, teaching parents how to structure their families and homes more effectively is an important component of the RPT model (see chapter 8, this volume). Family structures perform a number of supportive functions during times of stress and upheaval. Structuring skills can be used to establish clear roles for parents and solid boundaries between generations, to generate useful household rules, to enhance the family's sense of organization and routine, and to create positive family rituals. How families are organized and structured is a common focus in family therapy (Minuchin, 1974), but parent training programs devote less attention to these issues. Parent training proponents generally operate from a perspective that is more linear and dyadic, whereas family therapists view parenting from a perspective that is more circular and systemic. By directly addressing the issue of family structure, the RPT model creates avenues for helping that are not apparent when parents and children are viewed only as members of a dyad and not as part of a larger system or subsystem (e.g., parent or child subsystem).

Parental Self-Care

This component of the RPT model is designed to address the possibility that even with an abundance of skills and a high degree of structure, some parents will be unable to meet the socializing needs of their aggressive children. Parenting an aggressive child is almost always exhausting. If parents have experienced prolonged stress, the task of socializing an aggressive child can leave them feeling hopeless and defeated. An ugly divorce, an abusive marriage, or personal struggles with medical or mental illness can devastate parents, even those who are committed and highly skilled. Too often, however, parents of aggressive children have the double burden of lacking important parenting skills and the weight of significant stress in their life. As aggressive children become harder to accept and more difficult to contain, as they become a target of their parents' increasing resentment, and as they begin to take a greater toll on their parents' health and well-being, the importance of teaching parents to care for themselves becomes even more critical. Unfortunately, some parents fail to appreciate the value of taking time and energy away from their children to attend to their own self-care (see chapter 9, this volume). Other parents periodically abandon their duties as parents because they see no way of caring for both themselves and their children.

Therapeutic Alliance

The experience of trying to manage the behavior of an aggressive child has been described as that of having lived through a thousand defeats (Patterson et al., 1992). Spitzer et al. (1991) found that strong feelings of shame and hopelessness are common among parent training participants. When parents of aggressive children were able to struggle and work through conflict with therapists, their children were less delinquent 2 years later (Stoolmiller et al., 1993). It would seem that parent trainers who are serious about improving the relationships that parents have with their aggressive children should place primary importance on their own efforts to forge a supportive and productive alliance with parents (Webster-Stratton & Herbert, 1994). To underestimate the value of putting energy and skills into supporting and understanding these parents is, in short, a huge therapeutic mistake.

The task of joining with parents of aggressive children is often complicated, however. Many parents of antisocial children lack the kinds of interpersonal skills that would foster a smooth-working alliance (Frick & Jackson, 1993; Lytton, 1990a). Also, there is little empirical research to guide practitioners who wish to build more effective relationships with parents. Patterson and his colleagues (e.g., Patterson & Forgatch, 1985) have studied how parents resist the efforts of therapists, and Spitzer et al. (1991) have studied the process of change that parents undergo during parent training. However, there has been little systematic study of specific strategies or techniques that practitioners can use to improve their alliance with parents who feel overburdened and resistant to change (cf. L. F. Guerney & B. G. Guerney, 1985; Wahler, Cartor, Fleischman, & Lambert, 1993). In RPT, this goal is considered the cornerstone of effective parent therapy (see chapter 4, this volume).

Relations Among Various RPT Components

To implement the RPT model effectively requires an appreciation for how the various components of the model are connected conceptually and clinically. For example, as noted earlier, a strong working alliance between parent and practitioner is the foundation on which all other aspects of RPT rest. Other significant linkages among the various components are discussed below.

Parenting Goals and Other Treatment Components

In the next chapter, I discuss strategies for creating a productive working relationship with parents of aggressive children. Parenting goals are also covered in that chapter. These two aspects of the RPT model are covered in the same chapter because a strong therapeutic alliance requires a shared vision of the goals of therapy, and the goals of parent therapy should be closely linked to the goals of parenting. It makes little sense to begin a course of parent therapy that is unrelated or antithetical to parents' goals. In fact, parental resistance or outright ruptures in the therapeutic alliance can result from a perceived disconnect between parents' goals and practitioners' goals.

The importance of aligning the goals of therapy with the goals of parenting is especially critical to RPT and its use with parents of aggressive children. These parents present a variety of concerns but all want their child's behavior to be less troublesome. Some parents will be concerned about the impact of bad behavior on peers and teachers, but others simply want to reduce the bad behavior *they* have to deal with. A strong desire to curtail troubling behavior can invite some parents to see the goal of intervention as something other than their child's long-term socialization. For some parents, the goal of making bad behavior go away means (a) figuring out why their child is so angry, (b) proving they have done all they can as parents, (c) obtaining medicine that will "fix" their child's problem, or (d) blaming someone else for their child's problems (e.g., noncustodial parent). At best, the goal of wanting bad behavior to improve right away means that parents come to therapy to learn a different or better way to discipline. But even this therapeutic goal may not advance a child's socialization if it is emphasized to the neglect of other socializing aspects of the parent–child relationship. Because parent–child relationships are considered the primary means by which children are socialized, practitioners who follow the RPT model must be careful how they discuss the goals of parent therapy (see chapter 4, this volume). Parents may want to pursue goals that detract from or run counter to the socializing conditions of the parent–child relationship. To pursue such misplaced goals is to court treatment failure, but to ignore parents' stated intentions is also not productive.

Helping parents identify goals that are likely to advance their child's socialization often requires addressing the issue of child effects (Lytton, 1990a, 1990b). Parents are the primary custodians of the relationship, but aggressive school-age children are major players in the transactional mix between parent and child. Children are also active co-constructors of the meanings of their early experiences. From repeated interactions with parents and others, they form a sense of themselves, of others, and of the whys and wherefores of interpersonal relationships (Main, Kaplan, & Cassidy, 1985). The characteristics that aggressive school-age children bring to a relationship can create substantial ripple effects that influence many aspects of family functioning. The challenge of accepting and containing a coercive child can be very taxing, making the best parents look skill deficient. With such children, firm boundaries and clear rules and routines are not conveniences but necessities. With such children, parents need to be very explicit in their endorsement of prosocial beliefs. With such children, positive family rituals that reconnect parent and child, or self-care opportunities that refuel parents, are no longer nice touches but essential features of the family's daily and weekly schedule. By discussing the challenge of parenting a hard-to-manage child, parents should be more open to the goal of establishing a workable, socializing relationship.

Practitioners should also recognize that parenting goals and parenting practices are reciprocally related. Therapeutic gains in how parents understand and approach the job of parenting can greatly facilitate how they actually parent. Conversely, parents who have had little or no success implementing certain parenting practices may find it difficult to adopt a goal that seems very abstract or unattainable. Because difficulties or resistance in one area (e.g., goals) can impede therapeutic progress in the other area (e.g., practices), the task for practitioners is to shift the focus from goals to practices (or vice versa) when continued efforts in one area are met with resistance or failure.

Acceptance, Containment, and Prosocial Values

Acceptance and containment are complementary socialization processes that parents use to guide their children toward prosocial commerce. At first glance, these processes seem mutually exclusive in that children are either free to act as they choose or they are restrained in some way. Common to both, however, is that neither come at the expense of the child's relationship security (see chapters 5 and 6, this volume). Moreover, both acceptance and containment serve the larger socialization goal of sustaining a mutually binding relationship and increasing the likelihood children will invest in and commit to a prosocial system of commerce. If a child's sense of relationship security is chronically tenuous or severely disrupted or if parents are unable to create and maintain a relationship that has an overall positive tone, then prosocial guidance and modeling may go for naught (Richters & Waters, 1991). The common goals of promoting a child's commitment to and confidence in the parent–child relationship link acceptance and containment in ways that are not readily apparent.

Because acceptance and containment often involve near-opposite parenting responses, it can be a challenge shifting back and forth between the two or balancing, in a constructive way, the relative use of each. Some parents are comfortable with acceptance but avoid using containment even if children are relying on aggression to influence others. Other parents find it uncomfortable to be accepting, especially if so much of their time is spent trying to gain control over their child's behavior (Dumas et al., 1995). Participation in a relationship that provides acceptance and containment is needed before children can recognize that both are constructive acts by parents who have their best interest in mind. Without the benefit of a relationship that blends acceptance and containment, aggressive children will discount isolated efforts by parents to use one process or the other. The behavior of aggressive children can also lead to the predictable but excessive use of containment, especially when parental acceptance is neither frequent nor predictable (Wahler & Dumas, 1989). Because shifting back and forth between these twin processes is difficult and because aggressive children tend to elicit more containment than acceptance, parents often fail to see the value of being more accepting. Without parental acceptance, aggressive children will act in ways that pull for even greater containment, and parents will have less and less time, energy, and motivation to be accepting. This is essentially Patterson's (1986) view on the relation between parental control and rejection: Emotional rejection is seen not so much as a cause but as a by-product of the many disciplinary conflicts that parents and children have had. As parental acceptance recedes and parental rejection increases, children are apt to divest from the family's system of beliefs, thereby setting the stage for an even more entrenched antisocial position. Over time, parents may feel like giving up on their aggressive children, believing there are few behaviors to accept and fewer still that they can contain. Therefore, finding and maintaining the proper ratio of acceptance to containment is one of the most important goals of parenting and perhaps the only way parents can maintain a positive, stable relationship with a child who is prone to acting aggressively (Dumas et al., 1995; J. J. Snyder & Patterson, 1995).

A final point to be made about the complementary processes of acceptance and containment is that they are necessary but insufficient for effective socialization. Children also need behavioral models and clear information about prosocial standards of conduct. Figure 3.1 illustrates the important linkages among these three sources of parental influence: acceptance, containment, and prosocial values. Parental acceptance and containment sets the stage for a positively balanced parent–child relationship that engenders and promotes a child's investment into the family system (Kochanska, 1993; Richters & Waters, 1991; Wahler, 1994). However, the lessons learned from investing in that system are only as good as the examples and the information provided.

Family Structure, Self-Care, and Socializing Relationships

The challenge of accepting and containing a child while endorsing prosocial beliefs is not peculiar to the parents of aggressive children. However, parents of nonaggressive children usually perform these tasks with a lot less effort and with fewer costs emotionally and physically. For these parents, the challenge of modeling prosocial behavior and providing children with a sense of acceptance and containment does not require the family infrastructure of firm boundaries, explicit rules, regular routines, positive rituals, and frequent self-care opportunities. For parents of aggressive children, however, essential parenting tasks are impossible without that infrastructure. Parents may be very skilled at accepting and containing children, but they will be too disorganized or fatigued to sustain the effort. For parents who are not so skilled, a creative and effective organizational structure may be the only means by which aggressive children will obtain a sense of acceptance, containment, and prosocial values. Scheduled rituals for open acceptance, clear rules for containment, daily and weekly routines that affirm the family's system of beliefs, and regular opportunities for self-care sometimes prove more beneficial to parents than extensive training in dyadic skills.

Sequence of Training

Most parent training programs follow a standard sequence of one sort or another. Common among BMPT programs is to use a sequence in which the child's game or child-directed interaction sessions are followed by the parent's game or parent-directed interaction sessions (see chapter 2, this volume). There is very little research to guide practitioners as they decide how to sequence various training components. One exception is a study that examined the merits of beginning with either the child's game or the parent's game (Eisenstadt, Eyberg, McNeil, Newcomb, & Funderburk, 1993). The investigators found no support for beginning with child-directed interaction training and some evidence in support of reversing the common sequence when working with parents of young children with conduct problems (Eisenstadt et al., 1993). In Patterson et al.'s (1975) OSLC model, training begins, not with parent–child play, but with a focus on understanding behavioral principles and on the importance of tracking a child's behavior and its consequences. In CREFT, child-directed play skills are taught more or less simultaneously with limit-setting skills. As training proceeds, the focus shifts from in-session interactions to weekly home play sessions to nonplay interactions between parents and children (L. F. Guerney, 1983). The responsive parent training groups described in chapter 2 began with a brief focus on the difficulties of parenting (in an effort to build a working alliance) and then shifted to extensive training in child-directed play skills. Once home play sessions had been underway for 2 to 3 weeks, training sessions centered on establishing generational boundaries, setting limits on behavior, and enduring the costs of setting limits. Training ended with a discussion of how to optimize the structure in the family's rules, routines, and rituals.

Without more research, practitioners will have to rely on their clinical judgment when deciding how to sequence various parent training components. The issue is perhaps most relevant to practitioners who work with groups of parents as opposed to individual families. In a group format, each participant is exposed to all training components in a set sequence. When working with one family, practitioners can be much more flexible. They could, for example, begin by assessing parents' strengths in each area and then target only those where assistance is needed. However, because of the interconnectedness among these components (see above), this approach is usually not feasible. Overlap among the various RPT components also makes it difficult to train parents in one area to the exclusion of others. For example, as parents devote time and energy to learning containment skills, their use of acceptance is often diminished. Also, teaching effective containment skills is seriously hampered when the family lacks clear rules of conduct and firm generational boundaries. Therefore, parent therapists will want to attend at least briefly to each aspect of the RPT model. In this way, parents are made better aware of the various tools by which they can forge and sustain a socializing relationship with their child.

Minimal Treatment Approach

One strategy for sequencing the components of RPT, and for economizing the efforts of parents and practitioners, is to adopt what I call a *minimal treatment approach*. Under this approach, practitioners provide a highly truncated version of RPT designed to be brief, problem focused, and minimally taxing of parents. This approach is best suited for parents with relatively intact relationship skills whose child is less severely aggressive and whose family is not experiencing extreme levels of stress and chaos. Such parents need parenting assistance only because of a disruption in their life (e.g., divorce) or because their children possess characteristics that make them particularly hard to manage. Paradoxically, the minimal treatment approach can also be useful when working with parents who are difficult to engage in treatment or who are unwilling to do extensive therapeutic work (see chapter 10, this volume). By paring RPT to this minimal core, such parents may benefit despite their refusal to participate more fully.

The minimal treatment approach to RPT is made up of three steps: Therapists begin by fostering an alliance with parents based on emotional support and understanding. Second, therapists help parents to identify parent–child relationship goals that are realistic given the child's dispositional characteristics. And third, therapists assist as parents establish a clear and finite set of rules about those child behaviors that are strictly prohibited. Using this minimal treatment approach, practitioners can address a number of significant issues without pursuing extensive skills training that may not be warranted. The importance of working collaboratively (albeit briefly) with parents is retained in this truncated model of RPT (Webster-Stratton & Herbert, 1994). Attention is also given to the degree of fit between parents' goals and the type of child with whom they are trying to live and socialize (Sheeber & Johnson, 1994). Establishing an explicit set of rules about prohibited behaviors taps into several aspects of the RPT model. Insisting that certain behaviors will not be allowed is designed to augment parents' efforts at containment. However, the finite nature of the list (see chapter 5, this volume) helps parents to reduce the frequency of nattering and harsh criticism while increasing the level of acceptance in the parent–child relationship (Cavell, 1999a). Greater selectivity in containment also means less overall work by parents who are fatigued and in need of self-care, and creating and announcing explicit rules is an example of endorsing prosocial values. Finally, establishing a set of rules involves a level of planning, organization, and stability that can enhance overall family structure. If problems persist after using the minimal treatment approach, then practitioners will need to work closely with parents to reaffirm the therapeutic alliance and to reconcile any discrepancies that may exist between practitioners' and parents' goals. Once this is done, then other intervention components can be phased in as needed.

Outside-In Treatment Approach

A second approach to implementing RPT is one that assumes a need for more extensive intervention than that provided by the minimal treatment approach. For example, a more extensive regimen of parent therapy would be indicated if the target child and his or her siblings were all fairly aggressive and a young parent with a history of relationship difficulties was the sole head of the house. As in the minimal treatment approach, therapists begin the "outside-in" approach by attending to the overlapping issues of the working alliance and the goals for parenting and parent therapy. Therapists would then shift their attention to the RPT components of family structure and parental self-care. These components address issues that fall "outside" the parent–child dyad but are critical to effective parenting. Obvious gaps in these areas can be addressed in a targeted fashion. For example, psychological boundaries separating parents from children may be diffuse, daily and weekly routines may be nonexistent or unworkable, or parents may be overlooking the importance of scheduling needed self-care opportunities. Of course, helping parents develop rules about prohibited behaviors, as is done in the minimal treatment approach, should also be a part of the focus on family structure in the outside-in approach. Each of these concerns involves a systemic issue that transcends a direct focus on dyadic skills. Only after considerable work in the areas of family structure and self-care would therapists address any remaining issues related to parental acceptance and containment.

The idea here is one of working outside-in when it comes to helping parents improve the parent–child relationship. By addressing systemic issues first, practitioners do not assume automatically that parents are deficient in dyadic parenting skills (Webster-Stratton, 1994). The earlier emphasis on system changes may produce what family therapists call *second-order* or *nonlinear* changes in the parent–child relationship (Nichols & Schwartz, 1998). By restructuring the family's hierarchy, establishing clear rules and routines, or creating a periodic respite from the toils of parenting, qualitative shifts in how parents and children relate may occur. The practitioner would begin training parents in the dyadic skills of acceptance and containment only after these system-wide components are implemented. Training in these two areas requires more extensive work, and progress tends to occur in a more linear and incremental fashion than work in other, systemic areas.

Use of the outside-in approach to sequencing the components of RPT does have some disadvantages. Parents who lack critical dyadic skills must first undergo treatment components that may or may not be relevant. Of course, if practitioners were to learn that family structure and parental self-care are pockets of strength for parents, then it would be important to move quickly to dyadic skills training. Questions concerning the relation between dyadic skills training and systemic parenting issues are perhaps most important to practitioners who use a group format. Unfortunately, such questions can be answered only through further research. Practitioners who work with individual families have greater flexibility and can apply the RPT model via the minimal treatment approach,

Table 3.1. Sequencing of Responsive Parent Therapy (RPT) Treatment Components

Primary RPT component involved	Therapeutic focus
Minimal treatment approach	
Therapeutic alliance	Demonstrate support and understanding to parents
Parenting goals	Help parents identify goals in light of strong child effects
Containment, acceptance, prosocial values, self-care, family structure	Help parents construct rules about prohibited behavior
Outside-in approach	
Therapeutic alliance	Begin to establish the therapeutic alliance
Parenting goals	Begin to address differences between parenting goals and therapy goals
Family structure, parental self-care	Address family structure and parental self-care issues
Acceptance, containment	Address parents' use of acceptance and containment skills

the outside-in approach, or some other reasonable sequence. Table 3.1 summarizes the minimal treatment and outside-in approaches to sequencing the components of RPT.

Conclusion

The RPT model describes an amalgam of treatment components that collectively serve to promote a particular kind of parent–child relationship. That relationship is one in which children are accepted and contained by a prosocial parent. Over time, such relationships provide the most likely medium for socializing aggressive children. The task for practitioners is to draw from the RPT amalgam those treatment components that allow a given parent to establish and maintain a positive, transforming relationship with a given child. In the next set of chapters, I describe in detail how to implement various components of the RPT model.

4

Therapeutic Alliance and Parenting Goals

Eight-year-old Freddie was a very aggressive boy, and he was my client. His behavior had escalated to the point that he was close to being expelled from school both for aggression and for stealing. Academically, Freddie was very proficient but would often use his intellectual gifts to escape punishment or sneak out of responsibilities. He simply could not be trusted. He also had few if any real friends. He was a difficult boy to like, whether you were his classmate, his neighbor, his teacher, or his parents.

Helping Freddie meant helping his parents, thus they were also my clients. Mom and Dad were both educated white-collar professionals. They could not have children of their own, so they had adopted Freddie when he was just barely a toddler. When I first spoke by telephone with his parents, I was told they were coming to see me because they could no longer work with the previous therapist. This therapist had surmised (I believe correctly) that Freddie's parents lacked some basic parenting skills. Therefore, he had suggested a series of behaviorally based parenting techniques designed to counter these deficits. Freddie's parents were in complete agreement with this approach because they appreciated any suggestion that might give them an edge as they battled Freddie for control. What had irked them was that they felt blamed by the therapist when these interventions failed to bring Freddie's behavior under control. They felt he had never really appreciated their dilemma as parents and they eventually lost trust in him as a professional. Actually, there was distrust on both sides, for the therapist began to suspect that Freddie's parents were being emotionally abusive toward their son. The school counselor, who had been in close communication with the therapist, also held these suspicions. By the time I met Freddie and his parents, they felt that virtually every professional they had worked with—the therapist, the staff at the adoption agency, child protective services workers, the teacher, the school counselor, the principal—were all being unfairly critical of them.

Added to this messy picture was the fact that Freddie's parents were not always easy to like. Outside of the parent therapy context, they were pleasant and courteous; within this context, in which "help" did not feel at all like help, they were intensely defensive and demanding. At our first meeting I was told not to communicate with either the previous psychologist or the school counselor—two professionals they felt had been particularly deceitful. I was allowed to contact Freddie's teacher and the school principal, but these restrictions let me know these would be difficult parents with whom to work. And yet, it was clear that these parents and their son needed assistance.

Not all parents of aggressive children are as difficult to work with as Freddie's. In fact, I suspect Freddie's parents would have been more open had they not felt so betrayed by previous professionals. On the other hand, the likelihood of encountering parents who are difficult, disengaged, or resistant is fairly common in some settings. In this chapter, I discuss strategies for working with parents who may not always be open to help.

Strategies for Building a Strong Alliance With Parents

Parents of aggressive children—regardless of their contribution to the etiology or maintenance of their child's aggression—face a daunting task. They are expected by family, friends, and professionals to both love and discipline their child. Their failure to perform these twin tasks adequately can leave them tired, discouraged, and perhaps even resentful. Outsiders are often unable to appreciate the skill and effort needed to turn the tide on a developing aggressive child. Building a productive alliance with these parents is one of the more challenging tasks a practitioner will face. Unfortunately, there is a paucity of research to guide practitioners.

A useful starting point is the excellent text by Webster-Stratton and Herbert (1994). These authors make a significant contribution to the literature by describing what they call the *collaborative model* for working with parents of children with conduct problems. These authors recognize the multifaceted nature of working effectively with parents of difficult children. According to Webster-Stratton and Herbert (1994), working collaboratively with parents can involve a number of therapeutic tasks: building a supportive relationship, empowering, teaching, interpreting, leading and challenging, and prophesizing. The importance of each task is supported by qualitative research examining parents' experiences as participants in a parent training program (Spitzer et al., 1991). A clear understanding of how practitioners are to organize and sequence these multiple therapeutic tasks is lacking in the discussion of these tasks, however.

In the RPT model, the task of building a strong alliance with parents involves the use of three techniques: training, supporting, and processing. Each technique plays an important part in strengthening the partnership between parents and practitioners. It may seem odd to include training in this triad of alliance building techniques, but a strong alliance is based on more than support from a therapist. Hatcher and Barends (1996) proposed a two-factor view of the therapeutic alliance, suggesting it is a function of (a) the quality of support provided by therapists and (b) the degree to which clients and therapists are pursuing common goals in therapy. The term *working alliance* is used to reflect the fact that a strong alliance involves two parties who are collaborating on a task. For parents of aggressive children, a therapeutic alliance that does not involve the pursuit of common goals would quickly lead to a relationship that would not be therapeutic or change producing. Parents who participate in parent-focused therapy may not always be eager to change certain behaviors, but they certainly expect to get something out of the experience. Admittedly, some parents may need little more than emotional support and permission to feel tired and frustrated. However, most parents with aggressive children want to know what they can do to make things better in their troubled family. In fact, for some parents, the strength of the alliance will depend more on the skills and information they receive than on the emotional support they are provided. The tendency to value information over support is probably more characteristic of fathers than mothers and more common among parents whose attachment style is dismissing of relationships rather than secure or preoccupied (Hazan & Shaver, 1994).

As with most other forms of therapy, the supportive elements of parent intervention should serve to complement its didactic aspects. The skilled practitioner uses a dialectical give-and-take to balance change-oriented efforts with clear messages that parents are understood and accepted. To rely on one strategy to the exclusion of the other is rarely effective. However, knowing when to use one versus the other is not easy. In RPT, the technique of processing parents' internal reactions operates as a kind of shuttle between support and training. The term *processing*, borrowed from the CREFT procedure known as *dynamic processing*, involves drawing attention to and making sense of parents' cognitive and emotional reactions to issues that arise during the course of parent therapy (Constantin & Cavell, 1999b). By regularly processing parents' internal reactions, practitioners do more than enhance whatever training or supportive work they are doing. They also learn whether parents are presently in need of more training or more support.

Training

To discuss the topic of training apart from the topic of support or processing is to create artificial boundaries around these techniques that do not exist when practitioners actually do the work of establishing and maintaining a strong alliance. With that caveat in mind, there are a variety of ways to help parents acquire new skills and knowledge. *Instruction, modeling*, and *rehearsal with feedback* are the three most widely used methods of training parents. Whether the approach is BMPT, CREFT, or RPT, the task of helping parents learn new skills involves these tried-and-true approaches to training and teaching. Another important aspect of effective training is planning and organization. Practitioners who also have experience as teachers know the value of preparing before class. When teaching a skill, teachers may write whole lectures or identify specific steps to follow. A teacher who is organized and familiar with the material puts students at ease and allows them to focus on what is being taught. So it is with training parents. Practitioners who move skillfully through a curriculum at a comfortable, methodical pace will promote greater learning and less resistance than practitioners who are rushed, scattered, and disorganized. As a practitioner, there are times when I forget to use teaching techniques that I use routinely in my role as teacher. At other times, I err in the opposite direction: My well-prepared and effectively delivered training material is met with resistance by parents, who needed me to shift from being professorial to being supportive and understanding.

Instruction

What is the best way for practitioners to instruct parents? Like any new concept, parenting skills are probably best learned when placed within a meaningful context. For example, as therapists we learn to use therapeutic skills that fit a particular theoretical model. We learned that reflecting a client's comments should enhance the quality of the therapeutic relationship, which is an important determinant of client improvement. Similarly, parents need a meaningful context for understanding new information about how to interact with their child. Well explained rationales and advance organizers (e.g., outlines, labels, figures) can provide parents with the context they need to streamline the processing of incoming information. Clear rationales and advance organizers allow parents to assimilate new skills into existing cognitive schemas or, if necessary, to modify existing schemas to fit new information.

Consider the task of instructing parents to use a technique such as time-out. Parents often respond to the topic of time-out with phrases like, "Oh, I've tried that already" and "It didn't work with him." This kind of remark suggests that parents will filter any new information about time-out through the lens of their "unenthusiastic" schema. Thus in this situation, processing parents' concerns about time-out would be helpful. Processing aside, how can practitioners adequately instruct parents who come in with this sort of bias? One approach is to offer parents a broad, organizing framework that presents general ideas and assumptions before focusing on specific techniques. Parents should be more open to the specifics of training if they are given an overall plan for dealing with aggressive children that makes sense to them. A comprehensive plan explains what will be learned and why. For parents who understand the RPT model, time-out will be recognized as simply one way that parents can do the important job of containing a hard-to-manage child.

Perhaps the best way to explain the RPT model to parents is to refer to Figures 3.1 and 3.3, which illustrate the various features of the RPT model. The following is an example of how I introduce the RPT model to parents.[1]

> Let's take a look at this picture that I use to describe the job of parenting a difficult child. The place to start is right here—*parenting*

---

[1] Author's note: This example does not include occasions where I would check in and process with parents their ongoing construal of this model.

goals. It helps if parents have a clear idea of their goals when they are dealing with a demanding child. Parents can have a lot of different goals, but some goals won't work for some children, given their traits and tendencies. So much of a child's personality is either inherited from parents or is a product of how children interpret the world around them. Sometimes a child's traits and tendencies are the biggest factor in determining how hard the job of parenting will be. Some parents barely have to lift a finger or raise an eyebrow for their child to stop misbehaving; other parents can say "stop that!" 10 times, and it doesn't seem to get through. So one of the first things we'll learn is what it's like to parent your child and what might be reasonable goals for you as a parent. Once we identify a realistic set of goals, then we can begin the business of improving your relationship with your child.

This picture [see Figure 3.2, this volume] shows the kind of relationship that will allow you to enjoy your child more while also helping your child become a good "citizen"—at home, at school, and in the community. This picture says that all children need to feel accepted and loved, but they also need to be contained. In other words, they can't be free to act in dangerous, destructive ways but they also need to know they are a part of their family. Both acceptance and containment are needed if children are going to follow their parents' example and believe in parents' values.

We'll also look at whether the job of parenting requires any changes in how you structure and organize your family. Some homes are very organized, and this makes dealing with a difficult child easier. Other homes are disorganized or chaotic, which makes it that much harder to do the job of parenting, especially if parents are under a lot of stress. Ways to structure a family include setting up house rules, having a set routine each week, and using family rituals to make sure you have good times together.

Finally, we'll take a look at the job of taking care of you. Parenting a hard-to-manage child can be frustrating and tiring. To keep going, most parents have to get "refueled" on a regular basis—and not just because they deserve it but because it might be the only way they can keep at it day in and day out. Raising children can be rewarding, but at the end of a rough day or a bad week, the rewards can seem a million miles away. And if you're a parent of a difficult child, you have a lot of rough days and bad weeks ahead of you. So it's important to find some way to get refueled and ready for one more day and one more week.

Well that's the plan—these six things. I know it's a lot to keep in mind, but we'll take one part at a time, and we'll start with the kind of parenting goals that would make the most sense given who you are and who your child is.

This example illustrates how to provide parents with a general rationale for parent therapy and with advance organizers for processing more specific information. This example also shows how to elicit greater cooperation by presenting a plan that makes sense but is not so detailed as to invite early nay-saying. Those parents who seriously doubt if anyone can teach them anything new should still be open to hearing about child effects, family structure, or parental self-care. Of course, some parents may be so negative that each of the areas addressed by the RPT model is fodder for their resistance. Later in this volume is a discussion of how one can respond to such parents, but for now it should be made clear that an initial presentation like the one above will enable practitioners to identify and work with these parents before attempting further training.

What else can practitioners do to improve their manner of giving instructions? One strategy is to limit instruction to smaller and more manageable units. This point is true for any method of training, including modeling and rehearsal with feedback. I also find it useful to emphasize to parents a goal of learning new skills rather than the elimination of old habits. For example, in teaching child-directed play skills, the behaviors that parents should avoid (e.g., asking a lot of questions, directing the play) are not covered until parents have had an opportunity to master the skills they are to supposed to enact. Thus the emphasis is on building new competencies rather than on not repeating old mistakes. Focusing too soon on the things that parents should not do can leave them feeling pressure to avoid mistakes, thereby interfering with their ability to learn new skills.

Modeling

The value of demonstrating how to use a given parenting skill should not be underestimated. Modeling should be a regular part of training, and practitioners must guard against the tendency to assume that parents know what is meant by such recommendations as "follow your child's lead when playing" or "put your child in time-out when that happens." Parents may have mistaken notions about how to implement the skill, or they may not be willing to admit a lack of understanding. Even if parents are familiar with the technique in question, they can benefit from a thorough demonstration by the practitioner, especially if the demonstration involves their own child. One caveat about modeling that experienced practitioners will recognize is the possibility of intimidating parents with an "all-too-masterful" performance. Because a model who struggles with a new skill before mastering it is generally more effective than a model who easily masters the skill (Bandura, 1969), practitioners should be careful about the range of skills they model and the ease with which they use these skills. Creating an image that is too dissimilar from how parents see themselves can be threatening.

Webster-Stratton (1987), in her videotaped parent training series, includes a number of examples in which the performance is effective, is ineffective, or is of mixed effectiveness. The video consistently highlighted for parents those aspects of the models' performance that are skillful and those that are flawed. However, imperfect models may not offer the same advantage as a coping model that is generally competent. Parents may find it difficult to distinguish the skills of a flawed model from those of an effective model, and verbally discussing the flaws in a model's performance may not equate with viewing an effective coping model. These potential disadvantages are compounded by the fact that the video-modeling format was designed for parents whose verbal abilities limited their participation in other kinds of training modalities.

One analogue training study of the mixed-effectiveness approach to modeling (Constantin & Cavell, 1999b) produced evidence of the possible shortcomings associated with the approach. This study examined different ways to teach mothers child-directed play skills designed to promote greater child autonomy. Participants were 49 mothers and their 4-year-old boys. One of the comparisons made was between (a) mothers who viewed Webster-Stratton's (1987) 36-minute video *How to Play With a Child* and (b) mothers who had no training. The results were surprising in that mothers who were in the video-modeling condition did not differ from their counterparts who received no training. Moreover, boys whose mothers viewed the training video evinced less autonomy during play than boys whose mothers received no training. The findings from this one analogue study need to be considered in light of outcome studies that support the benefits of using the entire set of training tapes with parents of clinic-referred children (Webster-Stratton et al., 1988, 1989). However, the degree to which parents improved specifically in the area of parent–child play was never demonstrated in these outcome studies. Therefore, limited gains in child-directed play skills following the viewing of this mixed-effectiveness video may not be restricted to Constantin and Cavell's analogue study.

Besides using videotaped models, practitioners can also demonstrate parenting skills in sessions with target children. This live approach to modeling, like the coping-mastery model (Bandura, 1969), can serve to reduce the differences between what parents see demonstrated and what they are asked to do. Practical constraints can limit the applicability of this approach, however. Children may not be available to participate in a demonstration if there is no one to supervise them or no safe place to play when they are not part of the session. Practitioners should also be cautious about modeling punishment techniques such as time-out in situations in which the child has actually misbehaved. If the child is unaccustomed to being in time-out, the practitioner may have to choose between giving in prematurely or persisting for a long time so as to model an effective response. Therefore, it is usually wiser to model time-out when the child is not misbehaving via a "let's pretend" approach or by interacting with a younger, less difficult sibling.

Another approach to live modeling is to have parents play the part of the misbehaving child. Although awkward for some parents, this role-play strategy can be illuminating for both parents and parent trainers. Parents often gain valuable insights into their child's tendencies and motivations, and they benefit from seeing the practitioner respond to negative behaviors the child is likely to use. Practitioners benefit by learning how children are perceived by parents and by asking parents to elaborate on various aspects of the role play (e.g., particularly troubling responses given by the parent acting as child). When I use this approach to modeling, I tend to move quickly from instruction to modeling (and back again) in order to avoid a lot of preparatory fanfare. For example, I might begin by asking parents to show or tell me what their child would do in a given situation. I would then model a response to their child's behavior by saying, "If you were your child, I might respond in this way" and then modeling the response. I might even ask parents to show me how their child would react to what I had modeled. By moving directly to modeling a skill without spending a great deal of time and discussion on parents' impending "performance" as their child, practitioners avoid much of the anxiety that deters parents from doing this kind of enactment. Treating the role-play procedure as a common occurrence within parent therapy can also help practitioners who are anxious about performing in front of a parent or group of parents. In sum, the natural blending of instruction and modeling should be more comfortable for all and more useful to parents.

Another type of modeling that I use is one that might be called *selective, in vivo modeling*. The strategy here is to encourage parents to "steal" lines and scripts from other parents or adults who work well with children. Parents can often emulate what another, familiar adult would do or say more easily than they can generate a response that is wholly different from and more competent than their own typical response. If these other adults are competent caregivers, then parents should be encouraged to monitor how these individuals respond to problem situations, how they phrase their comments, and how they carry themselves during difficult situations. Parents may have access to competent caregivers (e.g., neighbors, teachers, relatives) but not appreciate the benefits of simply imitating the skills used by these models. Perhaps parents tend to view other, more competent models as having attributes that render their example as less personally relevant. On the other hand, it simply may not have occurred to parents that it is alright to study and copy what other adults do with their children. As a therapy supervisor, I often encourage my trainees to examine the work of other practitioners for new lines and scripts that are effective and worth adopting. By treating the process of modeling as a natural way to learn new skills, parents should find it easier to suspend fixed notions about how they should be parenting. In an atmosphere in which parenting skills are cast merely as tools to be used and not as extensions of one's identity or worth as a parent, a great deal of learning can take place.

Rehearsal and Feedback

Instruction and modeling, by themselves, are usually insufficient for teaching parents the skills that are covered in most parent training programs. Until parents have an opportunity to try their hand at what has been explained and demonstrated, it will be unclear to them and to the practitioner whether the skill has been successfully acquired. The purpose of using a given skill may not be clear until parents actually see it used and experience the results. How can practitioners effectively use rehearsal and feedback when working with parents of aggressive children? One of the best ways to promote the effective use of rehearsal is to focus on only one skill or small set of skills at a time. For parents who are deficient in a particular skill area, rehearsal and positive feedback are essential to the process of gradually shaping the parenting behaviors they will need. Building incrementally on parents' skill repertoire will also help them to feel less overwhelmed and more successful. This was a point made earlier in the discussion about instruction, and it applies also to modeling and rehearsal. By compartmentalizing target skills during the skill-acquisition phase and moving slowly as parents' performance dictates, the practitioner will be a more effective teacher.

As discussed earlier with role-play procedures, parents can sometimes feel awkward having someone view their performance. In a group-run format, there are often parents who are ready and willing to try a new skill. More inhibited parents have an opportunity to witness these parents practicing new skills and getting feedback. In this way, less eager parents can gradually habituate to the rehearsal task and see that it is safe to take their turn. When working with individual parents, the process of practicing a new skill should be far less formal than that used in a group setting. As noted earlier, less fanfare before parents' performance should result in less anticipatory and performance anxiety. Transitioning from rehearsal to feedback, or to additional instruction and modeling, should also be a smooth, efficient process. It should not feel like a test followed by a grading of parents' performance. To the extent that practitioners are moving at a safe, comfortable pace when they instruct, model, and give feedback, they also help parents feel more comfortable.

The value of a role-play format in which parents take on the role of the target child was mentioned previously. Role-played rehearsals in which the practitioner or some other parent acts as the child are also useful. Role-played rehearsals give parents a safe opportunity to practice a new skill. The artificial and controlled nature of this kind of rehearsal helps reduce parents' fears about making mistakes in an actual practice session. When the practitioner is in the role of the target child, the level of "difficult behavior" that parents face during rehearsals can be tightly regulated. In an actual practice session, children could become overly difficult or uncharacteristically subdued, neither of which facilitates learning. Again, such role plays should not be major productions that cause fear in the hearts of parents. For example, parents can practice certain verbal parenting skills without leaving their seat by responding to various "what-if" scenarios.

The effective delivery of feedback to parents about their performance is critical to the successful use of skill rehearsal. The process of giving feedback requires care and sensitivity on the part of practitioners. The common recommendation to "sandwich" any critical feedback between positive comments is an important rule to keep in mind. A few others should also be kept in mind: First, less feedback is generally better than more. When it is not clear whether the costs of giving more information are outweighed by the benefits, it is better to withhold feedback rather than running the risk of sounding too critical and damaging the therapeutic alliance. A second recommendation is that positive feedback should be clear and specific, but negative feedback should probably be given in a less definitive manner. For example, consider a mother who says all the right things when setting a limit with her son, but whose nonverbal messages reveal a lack of conviction about being firm. She can certainly benefit from knowing that what she said was on target. Comments such as "I was impressed with how you stated your command simply and to the point" and "I noticed that you didn't make a suggestion—you gave a direct command. That was great!" are examples of clear and direct positive feedback. However, she is likely to sense that all was not right with her performance, and a tentatively stated comment may be useful as a start to constructive feedback: "You know, it almost seemed as if you were torn between being firm and giving in. I'm not sure why I sensed that, but that's the impression I had. Does that make any sense to you?" If this mother were open to hearing this observation, the statement would do the job. However, if she were unable or unwilling to acknowledge the discrepancy between what she said and how she appeared, then the practitioner has not issued a strong challenge to her view that could disrupt the therapeutic alliance.

Another helpful way to give constructive feedback is to describe the effective techniques of an actual or hypothetical third party (e.g., "one mom I knew . . . "). Consider the mother who was not fully communicating her firmness about a limit. She may find it less critical if she were told about a mother who felt she was not being firm unless she was standing up and talking louder and lower in tone than normal, just to make sure her son was clear about who was in charge. By hearing how other parents dealt with similar struggles, parents may be more open to hearing how to improve their own skills. Parents who are particularly defensive about their parenting skills and sensitive to any criticism may require an even more cautious approach to getting feedback. Sometimes it is helpful to probe a bit after recognizing the positive aspects of parents' performance (e.g., "What did you think?" "How was that for you?" "Would you do anything differently?"). Practitioners may use another strategy in which suggestions and feedback are cast as inaccurate or unlikely to be of any help to parents. For example, the mother in our current example might be told "Your words were very clear, so it may not make much difference, but perhaps if you said the same words a little louder or with a look on your face that said 'I mean business.'" Strategic comments such as this one may be openly rebuffed by the resistant parent, but the critical information still gets through in a way that allows parents to save face and practitioners to save the alliance. Strategic questions, however, should be used sparingly and only with parents who have shown a consistent pattern of rigidly rejecting other forms of constructive feedback (Cavell, Frentz, & Kelley, 1986).

Not all feedback is given after rehearsal. Sometimes it makes more sense to offer feedback during rehearsal itself. This type of feedback, generally called *coaching*, can be a valuable teaching tool if delivered the right way. By *delivery*, I am referring to the phrasing, the pace, and the tone of the coaching. However, coaching comments can also vary in the medium used to communicate them to parents. For example, Forehand and McMahon (1981) used the *bug-in-the-ear* technology whereby parents receive radio-transmitted suggestions from the parent trainer through a receiver worn in the ear. The parent trainer typically viewed the parent–child interaction from behind a one-way mirror. Practitioners who do not have access to a bug-in-the-ear can coach by periodically delivering messages to the parent through telephone calls into the room or notes handed through the door. An even simpler way to coach is to use fairly large signs that prompt parents to try a particular skill when interacting with their child. When I use this approach to coaching, I position myself directly behind the child but facing the parent. To reduce the child's tendency to interact with me, I also announce at the outset that I am "invisible" during their play session and that I can neither be seen nor heard. This simple suggestion is almost never challenged and is usually all that is needed to keep the interaction confined to the parent and child.

As with feedback after rehearsal, coaching during rehearsal needs to be given in a way that does not disrupt the working alliance. The value of coaching is that parents can see immediately the impact of using a specific suggestion. They can also blame the practitioners if the suggestions do not work! Coaching can also be used to offer encouragement to parents whose confidence is wavering during rehearsal. Coaching ensures that the skill will be used and used in a way that is likely to produce the intended results. Care should be taken not to deliver too many coaching comments. Otherwise, parents may be rendered confused or may come to rely too heavily on the coaching. It is far better to issue a few, carefully chosen suggestions at key moments and only after it is clear the parent is unlikely to generate the response without assistance.

Before leaving the topic of rehearsal and feedback, it is important to consider here the common practice of assigning homework to parents. Homework exercises typically involve parents practicing their newly acquired skills in the home setting. This is a critical part of skills training, so practitioners should be clear about how and when parents should use home rehearsal. The practitioner will not be present and cannot applaud parents when they succeed or support them if they fail. Therefore, it is incumbent on the practitioner to prepare parents well before having them practice at home. At minimum, parents should be able to demonstrate the skills in session and report being ready and willing to try the skill at home. Practitioners often attend to the former but not the latter. One should keep in mind that written guidelines for conducting home rehearsal are helpful and should be discussed in session before parents attempt the homework. It is also key to identify beforehand any obstacles to parents completing homework.

It should go without saying that practitioners should avoid assigning homework that is not reviewed in subsequent sessions. To do so sends a message that homework is not critical to skill training, which would be a mistake. Practitioners should build into the next session's agenda ample time for parents to describe their experiences with the homework assignment. In CREFT, a major focus from the midpoint of therapy forward is on processing parents' accounts of their home play sessions. Because practitioners are not present during home rehearsal, they must rely on what parents say that they do in these sessions. In some ways, processing home practice sessions is similar to supervising someone else's therapy efforts. This point is made explicitly by the proponents of CREFT (L. F. Guerney & B. G. Guerney, 1985) and is implied in the writings of Webster-Stratton and Herbert (1994). For practitioners who do not have extensive training or experience in a supervisory role, this task can be frustrating for both parties. Readers may want to familiarize themselves with the research on effective supervision (e.g., Carifio & Hess, 1987; Hess, 1987; Worthington, 1987). Recognizing that skill acquisition is often a gradual, nonlinear process that can vary from one trainee to the next is key to effective supervision. Similarly, parents differ widely in how quickly and in what manner they learn to use a given set of parenting skills. And like therapy trainees, parents need to feel that their efforts are supported and that their strengths are recognized. But parents need more than support; they also need specific feedback. Consider a study by Henry, Schacht, Strupp, Butler, and Binder (1993) in which all therapists followed the same intervention manual. A significant treatment effect by supervisor was found in this study even though one was not expected. Therapists whose supervision included specific feedback and supportive comments outperformed therapists whose supervision lacked specificity.

In summation, home practice sessions are a critical training component, and practitioners can do much to enhance the likelihood that homework exercises will be beneficial to parents. Practitioners should not shortchange adequately preparing parents before the assignment or debriefing, and they should be supporting of parents after the assignment. In describing various methods for teaching and training parents, I have intentionally avoided addressing the topic of processing parents' reactions to new information and skills, and I have only alluded to the issue of supporting parents. In truth, effective practitioners often mix teaching and training with processing and support, going back and forth between pushing parents to try a new skill and supporting parents who feel a need to move at a slower pace. In the next section, I discuss ways in which therapists can be supportive to the parents with whom they work.

Supporting Parents

Parents of aggressive children benefit when, in our role as therapists, we recognize their efforts and accomplishments, no matter how small or seemingly inconsequential. They benefit when we strive to understand their subjective experiences as parents and communicate to them an accurate understanding of those experiences. If our understanding is not accurate, they benefit when they see our confusion and our attempts to work harder to understand them better. They benefit from our tolerance of strongly held views and strongly expressed emotions. They benefit when we regard feelings and thoughts, for which they may feel an undeserved sense of shame, as expected and natural. They benefit when we empower them to act on their own behalf, even if their actions differ from what we would suggest. And finally, they benefit when we offer them and their children a sense of acceptance.

The task of being supportive to parents differs little from the task of supporting any client in psychotherapy. Practitioners need to recognize when their relationship with parents is in jeopardy because of some external event or therapeutic action. They will also need to rely on traditional clinical skills to shore up or repair a weakened or ruptured relationship. Sometimes, efforts to support parents of aggressive children involve direct and relatively simple responses: Recognize parents' efforts and achievements, and understand and encourage them when they are down. Parents who are open to this kind of direct support reinforce therapists for making the effort. Too often, however, parents of aggressive children are less willing to change the way they parent, less able to implement new skills, and less open to advice and support from a "parenting expert." As a result, practitioners may find themselves stuck in a negative cycle of relating to parents with no clear way out. A tempting solution is to give up based on the view that parents are simply too resistant to benefit from therapy. However, there is reason to persevere. Overcoming resistance from parents and successfully repairing the therapeutic relationship appears to be one of the more significant events that can take place when working with families of antisocial children.

Patterson and Chamberlain (1994) found that outcomes for antisocial boys were related to improvements in parenting practices that were often preceded by a drop in resistance. Resistance, in turn, was predicted by a number of variables, including parents' pathology (e.g., depression, antisocial tendencies) and their level of social disadvantage. Therapist behaviors of confronting, teaching, and reframing were also predictive of resistance. The task of working with difficult parents can be quite aversive, even for experienced therapists. Indeed, Patterson and Chamberlain (1994) suggested, "the therapist must receive weekly support from staff members in order to keep going in spite of the punishment and lack of reinforcement received from these clients" (p. 68).

In a related study, Stoolmiller et al. (1993) found that when parent trainers persisted and worked through conflicts with parents, target children made significant improvements. In fact, the extent to which parents and therapists struggled and worked through resistance was more predictive of children's arrest record 2 years later than was their level of conduct problems immediately following treatment. Findings suggesting the apparent need for a struggle were also striking: Parents who never showed any resistance (i.e., were seemingly compliant throughout therapy) had children who did not fare as well as children whose parents struggled and worked through conflict with therapists. The findings of Stoolmiller et al. (1993) strongly suggest that practitioners working with parents of aggressive children should be equipped to handle the kinds of conflict that arise during parent therapy.

Conflicts that can threaten the therapeutic alliance are more common with parents who bring a history of poor relationships and antagonistic interactions to therapy. Difficult parents test the mettle of practitioners working with families of aggressive children. Unfortunately, difficult parents often have the most difficult children. Difficult parents of difficult children require a great deal of sophistication on the part of the practitioner. The odds that these parents will reject or ignore efforts to help is so great that unless practitioners can deal effectively with resistance, few gains will be made. Therapy under these circumstances can be fatiguing and frustrating, often prompting even the most well-intentioned practitioners to avoid future confrontations with parents. Practitioners need an approach to working with difficult, resistant parents that can guide practitioners through the hazards that interfere with a productive, collaborative alliance.

Chapter 2 described the integrative model of Jeremy Safran (1990a, 1990b) as particularly useful for parent therapists. Safran (1990a) sought to integrate cognitive and interpersonal models of therapy based on the view that the most significant and powerful cognitive distortions are interpersonal in nature. Drawing from the adult attachment literature, Safran also suggested that underlying self-system beliefs (i.e., about one's self, about others, and about relationships) greatly affect the manner in which individuals interact with others. Therefore, practitioners must be able to identify the recurring and dysfunctional interpersonal schemas that underlie clients' responses to relationship difficulties (Safran, 1990b). In cognitive therapy, therapists typically challenge distorted beliefs and cognitions through the use of reflection, clarification, or experimentation. In Safran's (1990b) blend of cognitive and interpersonal approaches, the approach is less threatening. Rather than openly challenge underlying interpersonal beliefs, practitioners "unhook" from the dysfunctional pattern of interaction it produces and respond in a way that disconfirms the distorted belief.

Consider, for example, a mother whose son desperately needs her to increase both the quality and the quantity of her positive, accepting interactions. In her way, however, is a mix of anger and indifference toward her son that leads her to avoid all interactions that do not involve discipline. Efforts by the therapist to discuss and counter these feelings are resisted, and she begins to withdraw affectively and cognitively from the interaction. Once she shuts down, she simply goes through the motions to avoid further discussion and conflict with the therapist. Assume, for the sake of argument, that this mother has an unstated belief that others usually fail to understand her and thus cannot help her. The critical question then is how to respond. Should one point out this underlying belief and suggest that it is not based in objective reality? Should one ask her to suspend temporarily her distrust and treat skills training as a type of "experiment" that will reveal to her the value of one's help? Both approaches may work, and both are certainly preferable to giving up on this mother. However, a less risky tactic and one that may pay more dividends is to "break set," so to speak, and respond in a way that disconfirms this parent's dysfunctional schema. Consider, for example, if this mother were told, "You seem a bit disengaged right now. That makes me think I'm missing something—that I've not got the whole picture of what it's like for you to be this child's mother day in and day out. What am I missing? What part am I clueless about?" This concerted effort to understand her dilemma and to join her where she is in her struggle as a parent is in direct contrast to what might be predicted by her biased expectations. Safran (1990b) suggested that repeated disconfirming interactions can be powerful refutations of clients' dysfunctional interpersonal schema. Moreover, they can be delivered in a way that is less likely to engender further resistance from clients who may already be defensive about the help they are getting.

In my own work with parents of aggressive children, the recommendations offered by Safran's (1990b) integrative model are frequently called to mind and applied. I suspect this is because more straightforward approaches to supporting parents are not as useful when dealing with the resistance exhibited by parents of aggressive children. When supervising students who work with resistant parents, I have been known to ask the following questions: "What does this parent need to hear from you at this time?" "What kind of interaction would move your relationship with this parent in a positive direction?" These questions emphasize the vital role played by a strong therapeutic alliance in parent therapy. It is where the energies and thoughts of practitioners should be targeted when therapy stalls or falters. The importance of attending to the alliance in parent therapy is reflected in Strupp's (1996) commentary about psychotherapy in general: "The critical feature of all successful therapy, it seems to me, is the therapist's skillful management of the patient–therapist relationship" (p. 1021). By recognizing when parents are being resistant, by identifying ways in which dysfunctional interpersonal schemas affect the alliance, by "unhooking" from their prototypical patterns of relating, and by responding in a positive manner that disconfirms pathogenic schemas, therapists can support parents in powerful and innovative ways. However, to do this kind of work requires a sustained focus on the management of the parent–therapist relationship. Practitioners cannot afford to treat the resistant parent as the exception when working with families of aggressive children. Occasional therapeutic moments and "sprinklings" of praise, encouragement, or emotional validation will not suffice. Parental support and fostering a strong alliance is not background, but figure, to the effective parent therapist. Patterson and Chamberlain (1994) reported that it was not uncommon for their parent trainers to spend only one fifth of their time teaching new parenting practices. The remainder was spent in other pursuits, most of which related to dealing with parental resistance.

The task of supporting defeated, resistant parents is complicated when parent training is conducted in a group format. The time available to practitioners working with groups of parents usually prohibits a careful, slow-paced, and supportive stance with every group member. For this reason, some group-based parent training programs are supplemented with additional individual family sessions (Patterson & Chamberlain, 1994). The responsive parent training groups (see chapter 2, this volume) used a different approach that involves writing weekly summaries and mailing these to parents before the next session. Brown used this technique, which is designed to maintain clients' connection to group therapy, in her work with alcoholic patients (Yalom, Brown, & Bloch, 1975) and adult children of alcoholics (Brown, 1988). The weekly summaries contain two parts. The first part is a paragraph or two that speaks to the entire group. A recap of the previous session, recognition of parents' gains, and acknowledgment of the difficulty of learning new skills are common elements of this group-wide message. This first part can also be used to comment on especially salient events that transpired in the last session. For example, if most members of the group were feeling particularly discouraged or defeated, then acknowledging this general mood would be justified regardless of whether it received comment in session. Another example that may warrant commentary is one in which a parent (or parents) becomes highly emotional and the mood becomes very tense, perhaps with inadequate closure. The group-oriented part of the weekly summary can also be used to remind parents of the agenda for the next session and of any homework they may have been assigned. The second part of the weekly summary is customized to fit the needs of individual parents, in particular what they need to hear now from the group therapists. Because each summary is individualized and no parent is overlooked, parents who would otherwise hide in the group setting are identified and assisted.

Writing the individualized section of the weekly summary can be a difficult clinical task. To structure the task beyond simply saying that which parents need to hear right now, practitioners should also consider parents' understanding of and connectedness to (a) the training itself, (b) the group, and (c) the group leaders. Parents may feel connected to one or two of these, but they may lack a sense of connection to all three. *Connectedness to the focus of training* can include their understanding of the program's goals, their commitment to pursuing those goals, and their degree of comfort and involvement with various kinds of training methods (e.g., rehearsal with feedback, homework exercises). *Connectedness to group members and group leaders* refers to being understood and supported by others and not feeling isolated in the group. Reviewing these three areas of connectedness offers a way to understand parents' in-session and out-of-session behavior, and these insights and observations can be incorporated into the weekly summary. Even with this added structure, the task of writing an effective weekly summary can be trying. Unlike a training session in which one can apologize for and correct misstated or misguided comments almost immediately, the content of the weekly summary sits unaltered for 2 to 3 days before group leaders can confirm the accuracy of their observations. For this reason, written comments are better stated as questions or hypotheses that parents are free to refute. One can confess confusion regarding what the parents need and how to respond to them. Written comments that describe sincere efforts to work collaboratively, even when those efforts are presently failing, can be a powerful message to parents who are used to having others give up on them or tell them what to do. This particular scenario is another example of how one can interact with parents in a way that disconfirms parents' underlying beliefs about how they will be treated (Safran, 1990b).

The following example of an individualized section of a weekly summary may help illustrate the tone and focus of these messages. This example, adapted from an actual summary, represents our efforts as therapists to repair a possible rupture in our relationship with a father. The father had been reluctant to participate in practice sessions in the clinic that addressed child-centered play skills. My colleagues and I suspected that he both feared being negatively evaluated by the group and was unconvinced about the importance and the value of such play skills. In his defense, his 10-year-old son was older than the other children and the kinds of play activities and toys used during rehearsal were somewhat youngish for his son. We sent the following summary to the father after a session that his wife attended but he did not. In it, we address our concerns that his absence may have been related to our efforts to have him practice the play skills.

> We were sorry that you were unable to attend this week's session. Your wife told us that you had a previous engagement that prevented you from coming. We want you to know that we worry that we may have pushed you too far and too fast with the play-skills training. Many parents are uncomfortable and unsure about the use of these skills. Because your son is 10 years old, these play skills might seem particularly out of place for you two. Your wife tells us that you take time to be with your son, but the activities are often not play related. She says you two run errands together or work together on various projects and chores. We find all this very impressive and see these activities as wonderful opportunities to convey to your son how valued he is in your eyes. It is this message—that he is accepted and loved by his father— that we try to teach through the play-skills training. However, as other parents with older children have told us, the play activities and toys we use may not work. For you and your son, a better fit would be the acceptance skills that focus more on listening to children as opposed to playing with them. These listening skills can be used in many of the activities you already do with your son. Again, we value your input in the group, and we look forward to your return.

In the above example, the note was sent to the father in an envelope separate from the envelope containing the summary for the mother. When two parents participate together, therapists have the option of writing one note or two. The decision is usually a clinical one. It is better to address mother and father in one note if the goal is to promote a sense of them working together as a team. It is better to address parents separately if the goal is to acknowledge that a parent is struggling individually and personally. This latter approach can be especially useful with parents who feel uncomfortable sharing messages they consider rather personal and emotionally charged. Also, although many 10-year-old boys enjoy playing with their parents and although the toys we used in training often worked well for older boys, we conceded to the father that his views were justified. By acknowledging his concerns we found a way to move forward with the larger goal of enhancing his acceptance of his son.

Brown (1988) described written weekly summaries as a mechanism for providing group members with a sense of attachment to the group and to group leaders. We did not assess specifically the benefits of this procedure in our preliminary investigation (Cavell et al., 1999). Clinically, however, the weekly summary appeared to play a pivotal role in parents' experiences in the group. Parents frequently reported that they eagerly anticipated these notes each week. Some parents even commented that they kept the notes and read them several times over. It seems that some parents found our weekly missives, particularly those written to parents whom we understand well, to be a poignant testimonial that someone truly appreciated their dilemma as parents. Again, we have no empirical data on the specific gains that may accrue from using this kind of weekly summary, but my colleagues and I suspect there are significant advantages to using it, and we feel certain that the weekly summary is not inert.

The task of supporting parents of aggressive children is a demanding, multifaceted task that operates not as background or appendage, but as figure and primary therapeutic corpus. Practitioners hoping to have success with parents of aggressive children will need to bring to bear the full weight of their clinical skills when deciding how and when to be supportive. Safran's (1990b) guidelines for blending cognitive and interpersonal approaches and our adaptation of Brown's (1988) written summary are two strategies that practitioners may want to add to their repertoire.

Processing

Many parents of aggressive children are doubly burdened: They face a difficult task with a shortage of skills. Their child is hard to contain and often hard to like. They are overwhelmed by the responsibilities of parenting, of organizing a family, and of caring for themselves. They need emotional support and better skills. Yet these parents are likely to rebuff efforts to teach them new skills, and support alone will not suffice.

The situation can be confusing and frustrating for practitioners. We can find ourselves going back and forth between teaching skills and listening to concerns and complaints. These shifts can be quick and dramatic and not always in proportion to how far the practitioner goes with one strategy or the other. For example, a mother may respond to a supportive statement about her son's misbehavior by saying, "If there was a way to make him mind, things would be a whole lot easier. But all I hear from folks is how hard it must be. I know how hard it is—tell me what I can do about it!" This same mother, when told that time-out might be beneficial, could then respond, "Time-out! Oh, don't even start with that. I'll tell you right now, that isn't going to work. I tried all that and, believe me, it won't work with him!" This shifting back and forth can cause treatment to feel uneven and disorganized, leaving both parents and practitioners bewildered. One solution to this dilemma is to transition slowly and purposefully between skills training and emotional support as needed. Navigating successfully between training and support requires that practitioners process with parents their emotional and cognitive reactions to the current focus of intervention—whether that focus is skill oriented or support oriented. By processing with parents how they feel and what they think when it comes to the events and issues of treatment, practitioners can better gauge if, when, and how to shift directions.

What does it mean to process parents' cognitive and emotional reactions during therapy? Unfortunately, few empirical studies have examined this issue. As mentioned earlier, in RPT, the term *processing* is used to distinguish it from the CREFT term *dynamic processing* (L. F. Guerney & B. G. Guerney, 1985). Proponents of CREFT suggest that dynamic processing involves the kind of probes and reflective comments that a clinical supervisor might use with a supervisee. However, there has been very little written about the specifics of conducting dynamic processing with parents. In RPT, processing is used to clarify when parents' reactions and intentions signal either a need for greater assistance or a growing level of resistance. The key to effective processing is to suspend one's assumptions about why parents do what they do in addition to one's assumptions about what parents will *say* about what they do. Preconceived notions can interfere with the task of understanding parents' phenomenology. This posture of curious ignorance is sometimes referred to as the *Columbo technique* because it is similar to the style of interviewing used by the television detective of the same name. The character Columbo was noted for his uncanny ability to gather so much information despite appearing to be rather uninformed and incompetent. For practitioners, however, the position of curious ignorance should be more real than strategic: Playing dumb, as revealed in the *Columbo* episodes, is soon recognized as an aggravating ruse. Therefore, practitioners processing with parents may need to lead with what they know or what they think they know. In this way, practitioners convey a willingness to collaborate and not deceive.

Consider the mother described in the previous example who resisted trying time-outs. How would a therapist process with her in a way that moves treatment forward? Given how strongly she expressed her views, there may be no way to accomplish this goal. Still, there may be value in learning more from this mother, and one place to begin is to tell her what one does and does not know about her:

> One thing I've learned about you is that you feel very strongly about the things you believe. You have let me know very clearly that you are tired of people telling you how hard it must be. *And*, you're tired of folks like me trotting out the same old stuff about time-out and setting limits. So I have a pretty good idea about what you don't want. What I'm not sure about is what you do want. Can you help me there? Are you clear on what you want, or is that confusing for you, too?

This example was not taken from an actual session, but if it were, I suspect a likely response from the mother would be a reiteration of her plea for a son that minds and stays out of trouble. For some practitioners, such a comment might seem straightforward and might not seem to require clarification. However, experienced practitioners who track closely what their clients say and do may suspect there is more to this comment than meets the eye.

For example, the comment, once elaborated, may reveal that the mother feels cheated and put upon by her son and his disruptive behavior, and that she often wishes someone else would do the hard work of parenting this boy. Further clarification may reveal a mother whose own dependency needs were poorly met as a child and whose current approach to coping with stressful situations is to respond in a dependent but hostile manner. She is overwhelmed by the task of parenting and can only see it as a monolithic, unsolvable burden. Although she reports knowing how hard it is to raise her son, she has not accepted that it will likely remain hard. Although she dismisses time-out as unworkable, she does not see that effective containment is an incremental process that is seldom easy but is essential if she wants her son to be socialized. Emotionally, she must come to accept the difficulty of parenting; cognitively, she must begin to see her son and her task in a less extreme manner.

Without the information generated by processing parents' cognitive and emotional reactions to the intervention, parent therapists would be left to deal with resistant parents whose "I can't" or "I won't" responses (Patterson & Chamberlain, 1994) make little sense and garner even less sympathy. The scenario I described suggests that through processing, parent trainers may gain new insights into their clients' behavior and identify potentially new treatment strategies. For instance, the mother in this example may benefit from more specific information about the relative contribution of child and parent effects on the development of childhood aggression. Accurate information about her child's prognosis that partly supports her views and partly challenges them may be a point of entry for the parent therapist. Exploring with the mother her unfulfilled "wishes" for her and her son may help her recognize that she is angry and saddened by her son's behavior, and that these emotions, although common and natural, do not have to define the nature of their relationship. Pointing out the mother's tendency to speak and think in extreme dichotomies may open her to the possibility that a one-step-at-a-time approach is worth trying.

Processing can give the practitioner more options for teaching and supporting parents because it helps clarify why current strategies are not working. Through processing, parent therapists can deliberately and smoothly transition from support to training and vice versa, thereby avoiding the "herky-jerky" feel of an intervention that is long on technique but short on understanding. Processing is an important tool by which practitioners can enhance parents' level of connectedness with the practitioner and with the intervention.

Besides serving as a way to promote greater understanding and support of parents, the second major use of processing is to enhance skill acquisition, transfer, and maintenance. When used toward this end, processing focuses more directly on parents' reactions to specific training and homework exercises. The assumption here is that many of the obstacles to parents' successful skill acquisition, transfer, and maintenance will not be immediately apparent to parents or parent trainers. The obstacles may be negative thoughts or feelings about a particular skill or technique and unless practitioners process these internal reactions with parents, these hidden obstacles will continue to influence parents' behavior. Sometimes the obstacles involve both logistical constraints and internal constraints, and processing can also help to identify these impediments. The task of processing parents' reactions to specific training or homework exercises proceeds in a fashion similar to that used to process more general issues. In this more focused form of processing, however, the practitioner's posture of curious ignorance is used to understand how parents regard a particular skill. Do they understand its purpose? Are they uncomfortable using the skill? Do they know other parents who used this skill? If not, what does that mean for parents? If so, what past impressions have they formed about this skill?

Take, for example, the technique of establishing household rules. Rules can be used to provide greater structure in the home, but it is important to set a limited number of rules that will be consistently enforced (see chapter 8, this volume). The recommendation to establish rules is ripe for misinterpretation, and practitioners should carefully monitor how parents go about doing this. Some parents may assume that if few rules work well, then many rules will work better. As a result, every disciplinary encounter becomes an opportunity to establish a new rule. Other parents may find rules unnecessary or confining. Perhaps they never liked rules, associating explicit rules with bossy teachers, for example. Practitioners should be careful when making assumptions about how parents will react when asked to try a new skill or use that skill at home and over time. Parents' unspoken thoughts and feelings need to be made explicit in an atmosphere of understanding and support.

Table 4.1 presents sample probes for processing with parents their reactions to skill acquisition, transfer, and maintenance. Among the probes are those that identify practical or logistical constraints for which parents and practitioners can brainstorm possible solutions. Practitioners should recognize, however, that external constraints could indicate internal impediments (e.g., negative beliefs, uncomfortable feelings) parents do not voice. The probes listed in Table 4.1 were those used in the analogue study by Constantin and Cavell (manuscript submitted for review, 1999b) described earlier. These probes were used in a condition that combined cognitive and emotional processing with video modeling and rehearsal with feedback. By processing mothers' reactions to child-directed play skills, additional benefits were realized over and above the gains afforded by video modeling or video modeling combined with rehearsal and feedback. Only those dyads in the processing condition showed significant improvement when compared to dyads in the no-training condition. Mothers who processed their reactions to child-directed play skills were rated as less controlling and their sons as more engaged in the play. These mothers also reported feeling more positive during play and rated themselves as better able to implement home play sessions. Training these mothers to be less controlling during play also did not lead to untoward declines in their perceptions of caregiver control beyond play. A drop in perceived control was found for control mothers, and this drop accounted for a signifi-

Table 4.1. Sample Probes for Cognitive and Emotional Processing

Probe type	Probe
Skill acquisition	How was that for you, to interact with your child in that way?
	Is it at all different from the way that you typically interact with your child? How so?
	The way your child behaved in response to you: Was it different in any way?
	What thoughts or images ran through your mind as you interacted with your child?
	Were there any changes in how you felt or thought about your child during the interaction?
	It looked [or sounded] as though you may have felt _____.
Skills transfer	Is it hard to imagine yourself using this approach?
	What's the best thing about interacting in this way? The worst thing?
	What's the easiest thing about interacting in this way? The hardest thing?
	Tell me about times in the past when you interacted with your child in this way. ·
	Do you know other parents who use this approach with their children?
Skills maintenance	Is it realistic to expect you to use this kind of approach in your home?
	Right now, what do you use instead of this particular technique?
	What would make it difficult to use this skill or technique in your home?
	How do you think your child would react if you used this skill routinely at home?

cant difference between the two groups. Mothers who were told to follow their son's lead but were not given an opportunity to process the play interaction experienced a general decline in their sense of control over the outcomes of parenting. Thus efforts to make explicit mothers' thoughts and feelings about child-directed play skills appeared to foster a more receptive attitude about this kind of parent–child interaction.

Summary

Building and maintaining an effective therapeutic alliance with parents of aggressive children requires a mix of teaching, supporting, and processing. I illustrated the distinct features of each of these strategies, but I remind readers of the need to use these strategies in coordinated and purposeful ways. When used skillfully, this triad of strategies helps to maintain a smooth and systematic flow of treatment efforts. Practitioners will cycle repeatedly through these strategies during the course of working with parents of aggressive children. Ideally, the shifts from one strategy to another will reflect parents' current readiness or stage of change at that time (Prochaska, DiClemente, & Norcross, 1992). When parents are eager to make specific changes in how they parent, practitioners can make use of methods for teaching new skills. When parents feel overwhelmed or incapable of making changes, practitioners can respond with emotional support and understanding. And when parents are unclear about what they need or they are resistant to change, practitioners can process with them their thoughts and feelings.

Parenting Goals

I imagine that few parents take the time to reflect on and list their goals as parents. Keeping children safe and healthy would almost certainly be paramount, but after that parents are likely to differ considerably in where they put their energy and effort. Even if their goals are not explicit, it seems that all parents have some implicit set of goals or rules by which they operate. Wahler (1997) argued that parents use goals or personal rules to regulate how they interact with their child:

> Since all of the child's various behaviors and all of the parent's reactions must be detected, sorted, summarized, and compared over time, the task would seem impossible without a pattern or template outlining the recent matches between child and parent behavior. (p. 204)

There is growing empirical support for the link between parenting goals and parenting behaviors. Kuczynski (1984) found that mothers whose primary goal was their child's long-term socialization were more responsive and accepting than mothers who focused on short-term compliance. Hastings and Grusec (1998) also found that parenting goals influenced disciplinary choices: Parent-centered goals were associated with power assertion; child-centered goals with reasoning; and relationship-centered goals with warm, negotiating, and cooperative parenting.

How parents think about the job of parenting, therefore, is an important parameter for practitioners to consider. Patterson (1997) suggested that parents' implicit rules can persist despite being ineffective and can get in the way of treatment progress. Because RPT is based on a relationship model of children's socialization, parents who hold strongly to parent- or child-centered goals, regardless of the situation, may struggle in therapy. Conversely, parents who can shift their goals in more adaptive directions should benefit from therapy. For example, Hastings and Grusec (1998) found that parents who were asked to focus on relationship-centered goals displayed less negative emotions and greater sympathy for children.

An important link between parenting goals and disciplinary actions are parents' beliefs about what caused children to misbehave (Hastings & Grusec, 1998). Parents' attributions about their child's bad behavior can spur strong negative emotions that interfere with how parents think and act (Bugental, Blue, & Lewis, 1990; Bugental, Brown, & Reiss, 1996; Dix, 1991; Slep & O'Leary, 1998; Strassberg, 1997). Parents who feel they are to blame for their child's behavior will feel guilty or ashamed and may give in to unreasonable demands. Parents who see their children as defiant or malicious will feel angry or resentful and fail to recognize their part in the production of coercive exchanges. A particularly important target for parent therapists is the extent to which parents view their child's aversive behavior as voluntary or involuntary. Slep and O'Leary (1998) found that mothers who were told that children would misbehave voluntarily and do so with negative intent felt angrier and were rated as more overreactive in their discipline than mothers who were told that children were not to blame for misbehaving. The link between parents' goals and attributions suggests the need to clarify in therapy the degree to which children's dispositional traits and tendencies (i.e., *child effects*) can determine their behavior.

Understanding Parents' Current Goals

What is the best way to broach the topic of parenting goals? To my knowledge, this topic has not been addressed empirically. Clinically, it would seem prudent to begin by learning about parents' *current* goals. Below I describe two techniques that can assist in these efforts. Although any number of approaches is likely to enhance an earnest discussion of parents' current goals, these two provide a starting point for practitioners and perhaps an opportunity for interested researchers.

Letting Parents Tell Their Story

One of the more powerful ways to start is simply to listen as parents describe how their child's behavior has affected them and their relationship. As a supervisor, I frequently push students to learn more about parents' subjective experiences in dealing with their aggressive child. Most practitioners rarely practice outside of the clinic setting and thus may never fully appreciate what life is like in the homes of the families with whom they work. That is one reason why research using behavioral observations conducted in the home is such a valuable resource for practitioners. Practitioners who conduct home-based parent consultation can certainly attest to the insights gained from going "on location." Even then, however, our role as professionals may continue to shield us from important information about family functioning. A child psychologist once commented to me that in her role as a child's mentor—unburdened by the label *professional*—she was witness to many more insights than she had ever gained as a psychologist making home visits.

Because of the obstacles to understanding parents' everyday experiences, therapists should be especially attentive and sensitive as parents tell their story. As a clinician, I usually prompt the telling of this story by asking certain kinds of open-ended questions. These questions are uncommon enough that parents rarely have pat answers but not so odd and off-putting that parents consider these questions as irrelevant. Examples of such questions are, (a) "What is it like to be your child's parent?" (b) "What does it feel like being in your home, day-in and day-out?" and (c) "What is it like to have you as a parent?" There have been times when I have been amazed at parents' reactions to these questions. Parents have cast themselves as everything from "drill sergeants" to "pushovers" when asked what it is like to be parented by them. When comments like these are probed (e.g., "Tell me about being a drill sergeant") and parents are provided an atmosphere of understanding and support, practitioners can learn a great deal about the kinds of goals parents pursue when interacting with their aggressive child.

Exploring Parenting Myths

Another useful procedure is to share with parents a list of statements about parenting and ask them to discuss their views on each one (see Exhibit 4.1). These statements are myths about parenting in the sense that the veracity of each is unknown or would require strong qualification. Discussing the statements can create a lively and informative discussion about parents' perspectives on such issues as child effects, the role of discipline, and the importance of a caring parent–child relationship. Parents

Exhibit 4.1.   Statements to Promote the Discussion of Parenting Myths

Instructions: Please circle your answer.

1. Parenting is easy if you know what you're doing. *True   False   Maybe*

2. Children are always fair and reasonable if you are fair and reasonable.
   True   False   Maybe

3. Children should know not to ask for things that parents cannot give them.
   True   False   Maybe

4. Too much attention spoils a child. *True   False   Maybe*

5. The old ways of parenting are the best ways. *True   False   Maybe*

6. All children need is love. *True   False   Maybe*

7. A parent has to punish children for the little things so they will obey when it comes to big things. *True   False   Maybe*

8. Children should know when parents are in a bad mood, and they should be obedient. *True   False   Maybe*

9. Raising a child is a constant source of satisfaction and reward.
   True   False   Maybe

should be told there is not one way to view these statements but that it helps to know how they think about such ideas as "all that children need is love." This exercise fits well with a group format that allows parents to hear a range of differing opinions. Practitioners can revisit this list of statements midway through therapy and again at termination. Parents are usually surprised to learn how their views have shifted over the course of therapy.

Promoting the Goal of a Socializing Relationship

The macrolevel, relationship-based view inherent in RPT is at odds with models of socialization that place greater importance on parents' use of a particular type of discipline or on the extent to which parents effectively negotiate discrete disciplinary interactions. Of course, these more micro-level processes are the building blocks of a high-quality parent–child relationship, but too often relationship goals are overshadowed by other, more specific parenting goals. Narrower goals can distract parents from the importance of attending to the overall quality of the relationship with their child. For some parents, the goals of parenting reflect a misplaced emphasis on behaviors that are relatively unimportant to their child's long-term socialization and later adjustment (e.g., immediate, situational compliance). For other parents, the goals of parenting reflect a more serious problem, such as a strong feeling of hostility and rejection toward their child, a sense of powerlessness in the face of child coercion, or a faltering commitment to the job of parenting. The emphasis in RPT on socialization can be a novel and uncomfortable message for some parents. Especially reactive may be parents whose campaign for academic excellence, athletic prowess, religious piety, family togetherness, or some other admirable goal is valued without question. To ask parents to pull back from such campaigns may be akin to asking them to reject God, Country, and Mother. Parents who pursue other goals and accomplishments (e.g., athletic success, financial gain) to the neglect of their child's socialization may not appreciate the danger in this strategy or may fail to see that other goals usually emanate from a foundation in effective socialization.

Once practitioners understand how parents currently approach the task of parenting, the next step is to promote the goal of a socializing relationship. The task is not so much an eradication of parents' old goals as it is an attempt to reconcile important differences between current goals and the goals inherent in a socializing relationship. Typically, it is a process that requires more information than persuasion. General information about childhood aggression, specific information about their particular child, and clarification about the role of child effects versus parent effects in their troubled relationship are useful in this regard.

Educating Parents About Childhood Aggression

Parents of aggressive children often lack up-to-date information about the phenomena of childhood aggression. Without making statements about their child in particular, practitioners may want to highlight relevant pieces of normative information (e.g., causes, correlates, and consequences). Noting important differences that exist among aggressive children is also useful because parents will not be faced with the dilemma of having to accept or reject whether a singular view about childhood aggression applies to their child and their family. Practitioners can point out that aggressive children differ in etiology, in risk and protective factors, and in prognosis. Thus, rather than challenging or ignoring parents' goals, practitioners educate parents about the kinds of factors that are most critical to understanding and treating childhood aggression.

Reviewing Individual Assessment Results

Another useful way to build a consensus about what goals should be targeted is to review with parents the results of any assessments that have been conducted. The fact that parents typically complete the instruments used is helpful here. Reviewing assessment information can help orient parents to more adaptive goals (Blechman, 1996; Sanders & Lawton, 1993). Blechman (1996), for example, relied on 3 weeks of parent observation data obtained via daily telephone calls before meeting with families and establishing a shared set of goals. As a clinician, I have used the Child Behavior Checklist and the Teacher Report Form (Achenbach, 1991) as the basis for this kind of assessment review. When parents bring in the completed forms, I typically ask for their help in scoring the measures. I point out the various behavioral dimensions that will be scored and ask parents to predict on which dimensions (if any) they think their child will be elevated. Together, we then score the dimensions and go over what the data tell us. We examine whether parents were right about the scales that were elevated and we see if teachers held a similar view of the child. We then discuss any surprises and what they may mean. This approach helps to demystify clinicians' impressions and helps to build a collaborative partnership in which parents' views are strongly considered. This process can also serve as a vehicle for educating parents about the range and severity of problem behavior that their child is currently exhibiting. Pointing out the meaning of certain percentile scores and clinical elevations can reinforce parents' wisdom to seek help and practitioners' efforts to offer help.

Clarifying the Role of Child Effects Versus Parent Effects

A focus on the parent–child relationship and an emphasis on the role of child effects versus parent effects is uncommon among parent training programs (cf. Sheeber & Johnson, 1994). Instead, the message often conveyed to parents is that they are responsible for managing their child's behavior and that with sufficient training, they will be able to gain control over their child's actions. The assumption that difficult children are difficult because of parents' inept disciplinary practices is often explicit and is seldom qualified. The parent–child relationship is hierarchical in nature, but to ignore the characteristics and contributions of the younger, aggressive interactant is both naive and unfair to parents. Parents benefit when they fully appreciate the characteristics and tendencies of the other member of the parent–child dyad.

Some parents fail to recognize how their child's traits and tendencies contribute to a troubled parent–child relationship. Other parents fail to recognize their own contributions. Opening up for discussion the central question of what are child effects and what are parent effects lets parent trainers know what fundamental assumptions underlie parents' reactions to the goals and content of parent therapy, even though the question is not likely to be answered definitively. Is this parent able to appreciate the importance of fitting parenting goals to both child and parent effects? Is this parent willing to consider an approach to parenting that involves learning to accept and live with certain perturbing child effects? In what ways has this parent already adapted to the demands associated with their child's traits and tendencies? Helping parents see the value of pursuing a goal of establishing and maintaining a socializing parent–child relationship is greatly facilitated when child effects are addressed explicitly and early in the course of therapy. It is a necessary step in the process of determining what a socializing relationship would look like for a given parent and child.

Summary

Parents of aggressive children, although not a uniform population, are likely to share the common characteristics of feeling overwhelmed and defeated in their efforts to manage their child's behavior (Spitzer et al., 1991). Parents will interpret the causes and the consequences of this dilemma differently, however. Some recognize the seriousness of their child's antisocial demeanor and are working hard to regain parental control. Others are more fatalistic, feeling there is little they can do to alter their child's developmental trajectory. Many others will wax and wane between these two viewpoints. The task of the practitioner is to understand, support, and help these parents find a way to live more congenially and peaceably with their coercive child.

Under the best of circumstances, the task of improving the relationship between parents and aggressive, school-age children is a difficult one. Aggressive children need to be accepted and contained, but they are hard to like and they resist limits. And for many aggressive children, the circumstances in which they are raised are far from optimal. Significant and multiple stressors are common among these families. With these additional risk factors, a troubled relationship can become a troubling and possibly dangerous relationship that will affect more than just the lives of this one family. And yet, parents who seem most desperate and in need of help can often be the most resistant and punishing to practitioners. Unless practitioners can find a way to build and maintain a therapeutic relationship, they will be unlikely to benefit the parent–child relationship.

The task of forging and sustaining a therapeutic alliance is one that calls for expertise in teaching and training, understanding and supporting, and processing parents' thoughts and feelings. The effective use and integration of these skills takes the job of helping parents far beyond didactics. The clinical demands can be intense, and working with parents of aggressive children should never be confused with parent education. As a springboard for doing effective parenting work, practitioners are wise to focus initially on the gap between parents' current goals and the goals needed for a socializing relationship. Effectively working with parents requires a shared vision of parenting that is realistic in its assessment but hopeful in its promise. If parent therapists can accomplish this, they are well on their way to working effectively with parents of aggressive children.

5

Acceptance

The prior history of the relationship is surely something that matters a great deal in determining whether a child complies willingly with a given demand, and the relationship is not adequately described in terms of what the parents have reinforced or punished the child for. —Eleanor Maccoby (1980)

The phrase *positive parenting* is often used to describe those parenting skills that are distinct from discipline. There is little agreement, however, about how to define the concept of positive parenting. A laundry list of terms and techniques used to characterize this elusive concept adds to the confusion. Indeed, it would appear that positive parenting has been a kind of holy grail of parenting research (Cavell, 1999b). What is the most sensible way to define positive parenting? Is positive parenting best captured by the techniques of positive reinforcement (Forehand & McMahon, 1981) or is the core feature of positive parenting the display of warmth, affection, or positive involvement (Gardner, 1987; Patterson et al., 1992)? Or is it better to view positive parenting as sensitive caregiving that can foster a sense of felt security (Greenberg & Speltz, 1988)? My preference is to view positive parenting in terms of autonomy granting (Parpal & Maccoby, 1985), or what I generally call *parents' acceptance of children* (Cavell, 1999b).

This preference is based on the argument that the most important distinction to be made among various parenting behaviors is the distinction between accepting and controlling children's behavior. This is a crucial distinction that is not well articulated in the parent-training literature. Nearly 10 years ago, Jacobson (1992) leveled the same criticism at behavioral marital therapy. He argued that behavioral approaches to marital therapy emphasized changing partners' behavior—either through accommodation or compromise—to the neglect of accepting each other's behavior. He held that both are important for improving problematic relationships:

> A healthy marriage still involves the ability to compromise and accommodate, but it also involves the ability to accept the inherent unsolvability of some relationship problems, and better yet, the ability to turn those problems into sources of strength and intimacy. (p. 502)

In line with Jacobson (1992), I submit that behavioral approaches to parent training have neglected the role of acceptance when attempting to enhance troubled parent–child relationships (Cavell, 1999a, 1999b).

I should add, however, that the dichotomy between parental control and parental acceptance is in many ways false. My use of the term *acceptance* is not meant to imply that it is an inert activity on the part of parents. Indeed, without real benefits, it would be hard to imagine a significant role for this aspect of parenting. Acceptance is itself a change in how one construes the behavior of another, and acceptance can often lead to desired behavioral changes. Strategic therapists, for example, recognize that halting efforts to help resistant family members can often lead to changes made without that help.

A formal definition of *parental acceptance* is any behavior that fosters in children a sense of autonomy while not threatening their relationship security. The essence of acceptance is that parents are not trying to change their child's behavior. Children who are accepted by their parents feel comfortable acting on their own behalf: They neither fear nor expect retribution, intimidation, or intervention for the vast majority of behaviors, thoughts, and emotions they express. This sense of acceptance is qualified, of course, by the presence of certain behavioral limits. Without any limits, children will come to feel neglected or completely unrestrained in what they can do and say, neither of which is adaptive. However, in the phenomenology of the accepted child, behavioral limits are likely to operate more as background than foreground. Limits exist, but most behaviors are not going to be challenged by parents.

What does parental acceptance look like? What can parents do to promote in children a sense of autonomy that does not threaten their security? Parental acceptance is conveyed most compellingly when parents attend to their child's actions, communicate an understanding of those actions, and then refrain from efforts to change or stop those actions. The skills involved in child-directed play and reflective listening are quintessential examples of parental acceptance. These skills are valuable tools for parents who wish to convey to their child that he or she can act independently and safely as long as the child remains within the bounds of appropriate (i.e., nonaggressive) behavior.

Of course, parental acceptance does not always take on such grand forms as child-directed play or reflective listening. Parental acceptance can range widely from fairly subtle, indirect forms of acceptance to very explicit or direct forms of acceptance. Tacit acceptance may be little more than an unstated position of tolerance (see below). Active or explicitly stated acceptance, on the other hand, may be accompanied by positive emotion (e.g., warmth, fondness); physical affection; or statements of understanding, endorsement, and strong approval. The affective or evaluative valence with which parents regard their child's actions is not the critical parameter in parental acceptance. Instead, parents' ability to convey that a child's thoughts, feelings, or behaviors can be expressed freely and without undue risk to their relationship security are the key features of both tacit and active parental acceptance. The merits of distinguishing between tacit and active forms of acceptance are discussed later.

This definition of parental acceptance is intentionally broad and designed to encompass the vast majority of behaviors that parents use when interacting with their child. In a sense, acceptance should ideally serve as the default mode of parenting: Rather than assuming a child's actions will need frequent intervention, a posture of acceptance is characterized by the assumption that intervention will be the exception and not the rule. Of course, age, temperament, and a host of other factors (i.e., dispositional and contextual factors) will affect the particular mix of acceptance and control that parents use at any given time.

The Goals of Acceptance Skills Training

The reasons why parents should be accepting of their children are significant and varied (see Cavell, 1999b; Kuczynski & Hildebrandt, 1997; Maccoby & Martin, 1983). The reasons why parents of *aggressive* children should be accepting are perhaps more limited but no less important. If I were to capture these reasons in a single statement it would be that parental acceptance is critical if parents are going to matter to their aggressive children. The presumption here (discussed in chapter 3, this volume) is that for parents to have a socializing effect on their aggressive children, children must feel committed to and invested in the relationship. Stated differently, being accepted by one's parents reinforces a child's efforts to act, feel, and think as a full-fledged member of a prosocial system of commerce (Richters & Waters, 1991). Children who do not feel accepted by their parents will be less motivated to follow parents' examples and to internalize parents' lessons regarding behavioral conduct. If the lack of parental acceptance is severe, the values and behaviors espoused by parents may be rejected outright. It is critical that parents matter to their children, and parents who create and sustain in their children the proper blend of acceptance will matter most. All other goals associated with parental acceptance follow from this primary goal. Other, secondary goals of acceptance can be grouped into one of two overlapping categories: (a) sustaining a positive parent–child relationship and (b) promoting child compliance.

Sustaining a Positive Parent–Child Relationship

To keep a child invested over time in a family system assumes that a positive balance is maintained between those aspects of a parent-child relationship that are pleasant or rewarding and those aspects that are aversive or punishing. The primary medium in this system of exchange is emotion. Of all the ways to think about or measure the quality of a relationship, this parameter appears to be the most important. When the proportion of positive emotional experiences consistently exceeds the proportion of negative emotional experiences, relationships tend to be more stable and more satisfying (Dumas et al., 1995; Gottman, 1994). Dumas (1996) found that mothers of disruptive children expressed positive affect toward their children only 30% of the time, whereas mothers of average children expressed positive affect 80% of the time. Gottman (1994) reported a similar ratio of positive-to-negative emotions (5:1) among adult couples with stable marriages. For couples with unstable marriages, the ratio was closer to 1:1. Relationships with near-equal proportions of negative and positive emotions, whether between two spouses or between a parent and a child, can be filled with tension because the quality of that relationship is only as good as the last interaction. If parents and children repeatedly find that their relationship is emotionally dissatisfying, it not only loses its potential to be a vehicle for promoting greater prosocial behavior, but it can also become a vehicle for promoting antisocial behavior (Patterson et al., 1992; Wahler, 1994, 1997). Unlike marriages in which one or both partners can seek to dissolve the relationship, aversive parent–child relationships typically continue in their pernicious state unless the relationship improves or some cataclysmic event (e.g., child abuse, running away, residential placement) interrupts it. Therefore, it is imperative that parents of difficult, antisocial children find a system for sustaining a ratio of positive-to-negative experiences with which both they and their child can live. Without a workable system for maintaining positive social continuity (Wahler, 1994), aggressive children are likely to use coercive means to engage their parents. Many parents can appreciate the value of pursuing a more positive relationship with their difficult child, but few can easily reconcile that goal with the goal of reducing a child's misbehavior. The former has long-term implications and the latter is more of an immediate need. Therefore, practitioners may need to spend time processing with parents exactly what it means to establish and maintain an emotionally positive balance in the parent–child relationship.

What would such a workable system look like? What would it take to have a relationship that aggressive children would value and parents could sustain and survive, if not enjoy? Because of the coercive tendencies of aggressive children, perhaps the most critical issue in the relationship is the management of conflict. In the next chapter, I argue that aggressive children are better served if parental discipline is used to target specific acts of aggression and coercion, rather than noncompliance in general. In this way, parents reduce the amount of conflict with their children and decrease the frequency of negative emotional exchanges. Less conflict will not necessarily transform the parent–child relationship into a mutually satisfying enterprise, but it will certainly increase the odds that such an outcome can occur.

How parents should respond to all the other behaviors that children perform, some of which can lead to conflict, is an important issue relevant to acceptance skills training (the particulars of training parents to contain aggressive and coercive acts are covered in chapter 6, this volume). Parents of aggressive children struggle not only with permissiveness, but also with a tendency to use harsh, overly punitive forms of parenting. Patterson (1982) coined the term *nattering* to describe parents' tendency to use critical comments and idle threats when interacting with their children. Chronic nattering and other forms of harsh parenting can have an insidious effect on children's antisocial behavior and on the parent–child relationship. Parents of aggressive children often find it difficult to pull back from the constant effort to control children's behavior, despite the counterproductive nature of those efforts (Patterson, 1982). Whether it is the illusion of control or the perception that children's misdeeds and mishaps can be prevented, parents who natter and overreact find it a difficult habit to break.

In most parent training programs, positive parenting behaviors are offered as an alternative to parents' tendency to natter and overreact. However, some positive parenting behaviors convey messages of acceptance more so than others (Cavell, 1999b). Child-directed play and reflective listening skills, for example, are far less controlling than labeled praise, active ignoring, or imitative play, all of which are taught as part of the child's game (Forehand & McMahon, 1984). The assumption here is that significant reductions in nattering and emotionally harsh parenting are unlikely if parents simply trade one set of controlling behaviors (i.e., punishment) for another (i.e., reinforcement). To shift from harsh criticism and nattering, parents will need to adopt a posture of acceptance toward the child and toward their child's behavior.

A *posture of acceptance* refers to parents' cognitive and emotional capacity to tolerate and detach from those aspects of a child's behavior that are unpleasant and that invite unneeded intervention. A posture of acceptance can also be understood by relating it to the concept of personal or psychological *boundaries*. This more macrolevel construct is essentially that blend of thoughts, feelings, and actions that influence the extent to which one views another person as a separate being with distinct thoughts, feelings, and patterns of behaving (Minuchin, 1974). Helping parents to recognize and honor the psychological boundaries that separate them from their children is one approach to reducing harsh parenting and nattering. Although the construct of boundaries may be cumbersome psychometrically, parents are often open to the idea that they have personal boundaries that can be used to regulate the psychological space or emotional distance between themselves and their children. The relation between parental acceptance and psychological space or boundaries was evident in the process research conducted by Webster-Stratton and her colleagues (Spitzer et al., 1991; Webster-Stratton & Herbert, 1994). Their qualitative study of successful BMPT participation revealed that an important part of coping effectively as parents was "accepting and respecting the child" (Webster-Stratton & Herbert, 1994, p. 216). This point is well illustrated with comments made by parents who were feeling more efficacious by the 20th session. Included here are two such comments. In the first, the father argues for the importance of giving his child space—a message of acceptance that he learned not so much from the BMPT training curriculum as much as from the skilled trainer.

> *Father*: You know, something we haven't talked about specifically in this parenting class, although it is in everything you've talked about, is respecting children and their space in the world. You know they should be treated as human beings—it doesn't mean you don't set limits and all that stuff, but it means you know that they're human beings and as deserving of respect as you are. (Webster-Stratton & Herbert, 1994, pp. 216–217)

In the second comment, the mother also refers to the issue of giving her child space, but adds a point about looking into her child's eyes, a behavior that fits more with the goal of active acceptance:

> *Mother*: In the last three weeks I've noticed a synthesis of all the sessions we've had, and me basically changing the way I interact with Hannah in a dramatic way—spontaneously. Now when I interact with her I tend to look at her eyes and I realize I can't remember my parents ever doing that. I'm giving her more space and time—more room to make mistakes, screw up, and make messes. I'm trying to give her more independence, when she wants to do something let her do it, rather than saying you're going to spill the milk all over the floor. It's fine if she spills the milk, she'll learn what happens and we've actually been getting on really well. (Webster-Stratton & Herbert, 1994, p. 216)

The comments of these parents are impressive insights into the task of parenting and the importance of acceptance. They reveal the kind of overarching schema that can lead to wide-reaching and sustained changes in how to deal with children's misbehavior. And it is this kind of change that appears to be necessary to combat parents' tendencies to be emotionally reactive. The discussion of parents who participated in the RPT groups in chapter 2 revealed similar changes. As parents became more comfortable using the child-directed play skills and with a posture of acceptance, my colleagues and I would observe what appeared to be a fundamental shift in the dynamics of the parent–child relationship. It is almost as if parents had finally tuned their radio to a station that gave them just the right mix of music, only in this case they had discovered for the first time the proper ratio of acceptance and containment. As a result, they were able to alter the fundamental nature of the parent–child relationship.

Unless parents can find the right blend of acceptance and containment, the parent–child relationship is in danger of crumbling emotionally from the weight of recurring conflict. I am not proposing that parents of aggressive children should be conflict avoidant, but I am proposing that they be conflict selective. For aggressive children to sustain a commitment to and an investment in the parent–child relationship, it has to be a relationship in which the net effect of the interactions is a positive emotional experience for both parties. An analogy may help to explain the relations among acceptance, containment, and children's commitment to the relationship. In this analogy, which also has been used by Lykken (1995), I draw comparisons between parenting and the task of owning a pet dog.

Parents can readily accept the idea that dogs differ in their temperament, size, and need for room to exercise. I ask parents to imagine the problems that would come from trying to keep a large, spirited dog inside a small apartment. For some smaller dogs and perhaps older dogs, the setting might work, but for this kind of dog it would be a disaster. So what is the solution? Is it to focus on training the large, active dog to behave in those confined quarters, or is it to let the dog operate unchecked in the apartment despite the damage it would cause? The answer, of course, is neither. Instead, efforts should be made to find a setting that best fits the needs of this particular dog. So it is with parents and their aggressive children. The task of creating and sustaining a positive parent–child relationship may mean giving the child more "room to run" and recognizing that the degree of control parents have is not as important as whether the relationship is a satisfying one and whether the child's aggressive and coercive behaviors are contained. There are exceptions, of course. For extremely aggressive children who are frequently violent, the effort needed to contain them may override any efforts used to accept them. In families with such children, parents' socialization efforts may not be productive unless other interventions (e.g., medication, residential treatment, foster care) are used first to reduce the amount of violent behavior. Aside from such extreme cases, it should be possible for parents to create a system in which the proportion of positive emotional exchanges would generally exceed the proportion of negative exchanges. For pet owners and their dogs, that system may be one in which the interactions between them are limited to daily feedings and brief romps in the field: The dog is not allowed indoors, and the owner seldom ventures outdoors. Similarly for parents of aggressive children, the only viable system for maintaining good relations may be one in which parents and children limit their interactions to those situations that ultimately sum to a net positive experience for both parties. Situations and topics that invite conflict (e.g., trips to visit grandparents, choice of music, neatness of a bedroom) may need to be avoided, and situations and topics that lead to greater harmony and understanding (e.g., shared hobbies, television shows) should be pursued regularly.

Practitioners should be aware that the system of relating proposed here is such a radical departure from parenting as usual because parenting an aggressive child is often an unusual task. Although most parents can expect and insist on a wide array of behaviors from their children, parents of aggressive children do not have that luxury. Perhaps they did when their child was much younger, but by school age, this issue is typically moot.

Many aggressive children will make the costs of enforcing rules and following through with chores so aversive that the effort can be both punishing and unsustainable. Therefore, parents have to choose wisely which behaviors warrant their intervention (see also chapter 6, this volume). For example, one young boy with whom I worked was very sneaky with his antisocial acts such as secretly vandalizing cars at times when he was angry. He also lied often, which aggravated his mother greatly. She often began our sessions with the latest reports of his misdeeds, laying out a perfectly reasonable and logical argument why he should have done this or should not have done that. In one session, she reported that he had on several occasions failed to perform his morning chores. The chores were not unreasonable, although they did benefit his mother more than him. However, because their relationship was feeling the strain of this mother's constant criticism and negativity, I felt it necessary for her to choose, in effect, between her son and these chores. I let her know that I could help her devise a plan to increase the performance of his chores or I could help her and her son achieve a more positive and rewarding relationship, but that doing both was not likely given their traits, tendencies, and circumstances. The meaning of this mother's decision to relieve him of these chores—at least temporarily—was at issue here. Was this a mistake, an example of reinforcing a child for bad behavior? Was she being taken advantage of, and was he likely to become even less responsible? The answer to both questions would be "yes" if the quality of their relationship did not improve to the point where his mother actually saw the benefit of pulling back from his assigned chores. However, this mother had been fairly persistent in her previous efforts and in her expectations about his chores. So for her to intensify these efforts seemed potentially damaging to a relationship that was already strained. Interestingly, the boy's immediate response to his mother's concession was to assist her voluntarily with the chores, a feat that gave his mother ample reason to be positive and loving toward him.

Promoting Children's Compliance

There is evidence to suggest that parents who convey greater acceptance will enjoy increased compliance from their children. Correlational studies document a positive association between maternal compliance and children's compliance and between a mutually cooperative parent–child relationship and committed compliance in temperamentally fearless children (e.g., Kochanska, Aksan, & Koenig, 1995; Parpal & Maccoby, 1985). There have also been experimental studies showing that parents' efforts to be more compliant and to grant more autonomy could lead to greater child compliance (e.g., Wahler & Bellamy, 1997). However, whether these findings replicate and whether they apply to parents of aggressive children are still unresolved issues. As a practitioner, I am wary of predicting that aggressive children will become more compliant if parents began engaging in child-directed, reflective listening or some other acceptance-based interaction. The state of research knowledge in this area does not yet support such a prediction, and some children may never demonstrate significant gains in immediate compliance following parents' enhanced use of acceptance. Moreover, if greater compliance did result, it may be preceded by an initial period of intense noncompliant behavior. The idea that child-centered, nondisciplinary techniques such as child-directed play and reflective listening can promote greater compliance is also a hard sell clinically. It seems much easier for parents to believe that acceptance is essential if their examples for behaving and lessons for living are to be internalized by their child. Therefore, I may mention to parents the *possibility* of greater compliance if they were to use their newfound acceptance skills, but I then downplay the developmental significance of short-term changes in compliance. Instead, I emphasize the long-term goal of sustaining a child's participation in a prosocial family system and the child's internalization of the values espoused by that system. This decoupling of immediate compliance and enhanced socialization may seem odd, but it reflects recent advances by developmental researchers in understanding of compliance, internalization, conscience, and socialization (e.g., Kochanska, 1995; Kuczynski & Hildebrandt, 1997).

That is not to say that increased acceptance will have no effect on the goal of increasing children's compliance. Several recent studies document the phenomenon, and it is certainly one I have witnessed clinically. However, researchers in this area know too little about this process to say when or why it works. Is it because children are left in a more positive mood by a parent's accepting actions (Lay, Waters, & Park, 1989), or because children tend to reciprocate when a parent complies with their requests (Parpal & Maccoby, 1985)? Is it because children who feel accepted are likely to emulate the prosocial behavior of their parent, or because children learn to regulate their emotions when parents routinely validate their comments and feelings? All of these are possibilities (Cavell, 1999b), but more research is needed before one can speak confidently with parents about this reason for their being more accepting.

Acceptance Skills Training

As stated previously, the skills involved in child-directed play and reflective listening are quintessential examples of parental acceptance. To the extent parents can acquire and use these skills, they enhance their capacity to convey messages of acceptance to their children. In discussing the process of acceptance skills training, it is helpful to refer to a typology of these various skills. This typology segments the skills into meaningful subgroups to simplify the tasks of teaching and learning acceptance. It is not an empirically derived typology, but one that reflects extensive clinical experience teaching these skills to parents of aggressive children.

A Typology of Parental Acceptance Skills

One way to categorize acceptance skills is based on the saliency or explicitness of parents' acceptance. Are parents tacitly accepting a behavior, or is there an effort to actively endorse the behavior? A second distinction that can be made is between the simpler versions of acceptance and those versions that are subtle and complex. That is not to say that simple acceptance skills are easy to train and easy to use. In fact, even the simplest forms of acceptance can seem like a distant goal to some parents with aggressive children. Nevertheless, it does help to begin acceptance skills training with a focus on the rudimentary skills before moving on to the more complex ones.

Simple Tacit Acceptance

By definition, all forms of parental acceptance involve refraining from efforts to control or change a child's behavior. In the case of *tacit acceptance*, the parent does little else vis-à-vis the child. Topographically, tacit acceptance can take many forms, and the most basic is simply doing nothing. J. J. Snyder and Patterson showed (1995), however, that the simplicity of doing nothing belies its potential benefits. In their study, it was parents of nonaggressive children who often made no response when their child tried to influence them in maladaptive ways. Were these parents caught off guard and simply too stunned to respond? J. J. Snyder and Patterson (1995) did not address this possibility, but I suspect that for most parents the act of doing nothing is a much more complex phenomenon than simply being caught off guard. For some parents, the act of doing nothing—of not intervening—is incredibly foreign and difficult to learn. Making no response, especially in the light of behaviors that are inappropriate or annoying, can feel awkward and unnatural. Some parents may feel it is their duty to be helpful and corrective whenever the opportunity arises. Other parents simply know of no other way to respond.

In the context of child-directed play, tacit acceptance is evinced when parents passively attend to their child's play. Of course, the opportunity to play under parents' watchful eyes will seem like active endorsement to some children, particularly children whose parents rarely play with them. In the context of reflective listening, tacit acceptance essentially means do not interrupt and let the child speak. But most parents are not simply inert and passive, at least not for very long, so most of the skills of child-centered play and reflective listening are techniques of active acceptance (see below). It is also true, however, that both parents and children have lives filled with an array of activities and pursuits that preclude the use of intense, uninterrupted play and listening sessions. And it is during these other activities—the primary fabric of families' lives—that the skills of tacit acceptance are most useful.

Because the only goal of tacit acceptance is to leave children free to act on their own accord (while leaving intact their sense of relationship security), the specific skills parents use are less important than the degree to which parents maintain a posture of acceptance. Framed in this way, the "skills" of tacit acceptance encompass virtually any behavior other than unnecessary parental intervention. So to keep from intervening and micromanaging their child's behavior, parents have to find a way to manage their own behavior. Paradoxically, the most effective way that parents can maintain a posture of acceptance is to attend less to their child's concerns and more to their own concerns. Stated differently, parents who understand and practice the concept of having a life separate from that of their children should have little difficulty with tacit acceptance. For parents who struggle to appreciate this point, I often use metaphors and visual imagery to illustrate what it looks and feels like when parents adopt a posture of tacit acceptance. In one metaphor, I invoke the image of a soccer field. I begin by stating that the lines around the soccer field are to keep parents out. I then suggest that a child's soccer game is a microcosm for a child's life. If children are misbehaving during a soccer game, teammates, opponents, coaches, and referees will intervene well before there is a need for parents to do so. If children are seriously hurt or hurting others, then parents can leave their chairs, venture onto the field, and intervene as needed. However, the main job for parents is to stay in their seats.

In another exercise, I ask parents to imagine leaning over their child, hovering and waiting for the first sign that corrective action is needed. I then ask them to imagine standing straight up, slowly turning around, and walking away to resume their own life with their back to their child. I suggest that rather than turning toward their children and pressing them to perform this or that behavior, it is better for parents to turn away and lead the healthiest life they can as an example for their children. This metaphor also serves as a springboard for discussion about what parents can do with their life, especially if the goal is to make it healthier and a better example for their children. In other words, the behavioral void that is created when parents begin to "do nothing" is best filled by parents' enhanced self-care (see chapter 9, this volume). Of all the skills parents can use to avoid unwanted control of their children, the best are those irrelevant to children but central to parents. To the degree parents can separate psychologically, emotionally, and behaviorally from their children, they will find it easier to be accepting of them.

Complex Tacit Acceptance

Aside from making no response at all, or pursuing their own self-care agenda, what else can parents do to exercise tacit acceptance? A more advanced approach to tacit acceptance is to use verbal *mirroring* skills. I am referring here to the practice of parroting a child's comments or describing a child's actions in a simple, straightforward manner without added commentary or judgment. In essence, parents can function as verbal mirrors that offer children an opportunity to learn what others hear and see when children speak and act as they do (Faber & Mazlish, 1980; Ginott, 1976; Gottman, Katz, & Hooven, 1997). For example, imagine a mother whose 9-year-old son is angry and says to her, "I hate you! I wish you were dead!" Rather than being pulled into an unwarranted disciplinary conflict, the mother could parrot her son's anger-filled words: "You hate me and you wish I were dead." Parroting a child's angry or inappropriate comments may seem like an odd tactic given the common recommendation to ignore minor misbehaviors, but ignoring is meant to extinguish misbehavior, and therein lies a potential problem. Children who use angry or inappropriate words that fail to get the desired effect will abandon the use of hurtful words, but they may escalate to using hurtful actions. The former can certainly unnerve parents, but the latter are unacceptable and portend serious maladjustment. But what of the danger of reinforcing a child's use of angry, hurtful words? If parents had a choice between bad words and good words, they would surely choose good words; however, parents of aggressive children often have to choose between bad words and bad deeds, and bad words are clearly preferred. Words are a safer way to influence others and a more appropriate way to express feelings and desires. Words are also less likely to cause damage that cannot be undone or hurt that cannot be recanted. As long as parents of aggressive children effectively contain hurtful behavior, listening to hurtful words may actually benefit children.

Now imagine this same mother adding a descriptive comment about her child's emotional state: "You look pretty mad." With this reflective comment, the child is given even more feedback about his current behavior and his efforts to manage it. By reflecting for children what they seem to be experiencing, parents can promote the development of their child's emotional regulatory skills. In this example, the mother scaffolds for her son the words he can use to express his own emotions (Gottman, Katz, & Hooven, 1996). She is not condoning or endorsing her son's angry sentiments, but she is also not insisting that he not be angry. If she was concerned that he might interpret her mirroring comments as endorsements, she could also add a comment such as the following: "I get really mad, too, sometimes, and I think about hurting the person I'm mad at. But I don't hurt them. I just tell them how mad I am." As a final descriptive comment, she could note that he has only spoken about his feelings and has not acted on them.

Parents' use of tacit acceptance to convey tolerance for but not approval of their child's behavior is perhaps most valuable as a tactic for terminating potentially conflicted interactions (Snyder & Patterson, 1995). Consider the following example of a father who is unhappy about his daughter's use of the word *stupid* to describe her younger brother. Note that he is neither endorsing nor containing his daughter's ugly comments:

> *Father*: I really don't like it when you call your brother stupid.
> *Daughter*: But he acts so stupid!
> *Father*: Maybe. But it bothers me when you call him that.

In this example, the father is clearly stating his views about his daughter's name-calling, but he is not insisting that she cease. His disapproval is stated as opinion or information and not as a directive. Of course, his daughter is free to dismiss this information if she chooses. If the father says these words calmly or at least without rancor, is he still operating from a position of acceptance? The answer, it seems, is both yes and no. Critical to conveying a sense of acceptance is that parents defer to children when deciding which behaviors are to be performed. In this example, the father may clearly prefer that his daughter stop calling her brother *stupid*, but—for the moment—he is leaving that decision to her.

On the other hand, the father left little doubt that he did not approve of the name-calling.

What if the girl stopped calling her brother stupid after hearing her father's comment? Would the father's comment then be an externally imposed punisher? Perhaps, but it would seem that something more important is operating: The father's comment is unlikely to reduce his daughter's name-calling unless she values her father's beliefs and then acts more or less autonomously to bring her behavior in line with his. Moreover, her tendency to act on his comments and to internalize his standards will likely depend on the quality of their relationship, in particular the extent to which she has been allowed to act autonomously and securely in the past (Grusec & Goodnow, 1994; Kuczynski & Hildebrandt, 1997). In a sense, one could argue that punishment in this instance would be self-imposed and would not be delivered by the girl's father. If the father did punish his daughter, perhaps by sending her to time-out, then name-calling should also decrease. However, under this scenario, a reduction in name-calling could operate independently of whether the girl internalized her father's values and with the possibility of a negative effect on the father–daughter relationship.

In a sense, tacit acceptance combined with parents' expressed disdain for a given behavior functions as a valuable third option for parents who feel caught between standing firm or giving in. Parents of aggressive children often appear torn between these two strategies, switching inconsistently from one to the other (Dumas et al., 1995; Patterson et al., 1992). By recognizing children's autonomy and by respecting the choices they make, parents can pursue a third strategy that is not otherwise apparent: Accept the child's choice of behavior, but make it clear that you do not endorse it. If parents have been clear and consistent in the past about what is strictly prohibited, then tacitly accepting a given behavior should not be mistaken as a signal that parents agree with every decision a child makes. And if parents have a history of typically granting autonomy to their child, then disapproving of that behavior should not be taken as insistence to stop. I am not aware of empirical research on this topic, but it appears that this third option represents a useful alternative for dealing with child behaviors that can lead to greater conflict. It would seem that a strategy of nonintervention coupled with open disapproval (or verbal mirroring) is an approach that goes beyond the technique of ignoring offered in most BMPT curricula. Ignoring can be useful at times, but simple ignoring lacks any sort of guidance about how children can better manage emotions and resolve conflict. Chapter 7 further discusses this third option and suggests that it can be used as a way to endorse parents' prosocial beliefs and values.

J. J. Snyder and Patterson (1995) found that parents of nonaggressive children also used humor to diffuse their child's inappropriate influence attempts. This is an intriguing finding, but I am not aware of any empirical research on parents' use of humor as a socialization or conflict-management tool. I commonly use humor when demonstrating certain acceptance skills, but I have not explicitly trained parents to use humor.

Because the use of humor often requires spontaneous reactions that may be state dependent (e.g., relaxed, confident), it seems a particularly complex skill to teach. However, there may be value in helping parents adopt one or two behavioral scripts that involve the use of humor. For example, parents may be able to develop a nickname for their child that captures, in a humorous but noncritical way, those times when the child's behavior is bothersome to parents. Oppositional, defiant children can be "Mr./Miss Opposite" or "my opposite child," overly excited and rambunctious children can be "Mr./Miss Excitement," and bossy children can be "my assistant-junior-parent-who-I-didn't-hire." To the extent such terms of endearment are used sparingly and humorously to convey the impact that a child's behavior is having on family members, everyone benefits. However, if overused or if used in a mean-spirited way, such nicknames can be hurtful and not helpful. Practitioners should be judicious in recommending this method of infusing humor into parent–child interactions. There are other humor-related scripts that parents can use when faced with minor misbehaviors. These include funny facial expressions, silly or made-up words to describe the behavior of concern (e.g., "tough guy talk"), or patently hollow and whimsical ways to deal with children who misbehave ("I will put you on the moon!"). Many of these can take the form of pretend fighting or verbal sparring that has a game-like feel to it. Very often children will begin such games, but their parents fail to see the opportunity to respond with feigned sternness and bluster rather than with power-assertive parenting.

Simple Active Acceptance

Unlike tacit acceptance skills, *active acceptance* skills are designed to communicate that parents actually value the behaviors in which the children are engaged. Moreover, active acceptance skills can be used to enhance or repair the parent–child relationship by increasing its positive emotional tone and by drawing attention to the many ways in which parents understand and hold dear their child's sense of self. Parents who display active acceptance convey more than a simple message of nonintervention; they demonstrate that they are caring and curious witnesses to their child's life.

When teaching parents skills that convey a sense of interest and esteem, it is useful to remind them about also refraining from intervening unnecessarily. When the goal is active acceptance, parents can be intrusive in rather subtle ways. For example, parents may praise, teach, or help children when it is not needed. These behaviors are not inherently wrong or inappropriate, for clearly there are times when children need parents' assistance. However, for parents of aggressive children, the first order of business is to establish a relationship that is characterized more by prosocial harmony than by coercive exchanges. When parents zealously push other goals for their children (e.g., academics, chores, athletics, music), the proper blend of acceptance and containment can be jeopardized. A child who is a talented pianist or a gifted athlete may be less likely to be aggressive, but these talents do not preclude a child from becoming antisocial. Therefore, parents should be careful about parenting goals that can spoil or taint an effective socializing relationship (see chapter 4, this volume).

Resisting the temptation to correct their child's mistakes, solve their child's problems, answer their child's questions, and boost their child's morale will be particularly difficult for some parents. Like feeding, clothing, and sheltering children, helping them through their dilemmas is an obvious way for parents to prove their worth. I worked with one mother who had a 9-year-old son with a history of defiant and aggressive behavior. Previous treatment had centered on BMPT for the mother, and thus she was familiar with the concept of special playtime. However, when the family presented, mother and son had a strained relationship, and his behavior continued to be disruptive at home and at school. After spending considerable time and effort on the parents' role in the socializing relationship, I then began child-directed play skills training. When the mother practiced using these skills, I was initially quite impressed and thought that she needed little if any coaching or constructive feedback. Gradually, however, I began to notice a pattern to her play that had a subtly controlling feel to it. For example, she would make suggestions as he pieced together a puzzle, ask questions about his play, and tease him in ways that were funny and related to his play. These behaviors began slowly and then increased in frequency, possibly because she felt more relaxed playing in my presence. It was soon apparent that these minor intrusions began to come at such a pace that her son had virtually lost all control of the play. In processing with this mother later, she admitted to having trouble curtailing her strong mothering tendencies—tendencies she believed she had learned from her own mother.

There are many reasons why parents might assert undue control as their child plays or speaks. They may be bored by the slowness of play, frustrated by the child's inability to execute a simple task or state a point, or discomfited by the child's heightened activity or intensity of emotions. Such factors can cause parents to exercise more control than is needed, and sometimes the controlling actions are task related and difficult to detect by parents and parent trainers. For this reason, I often suggest to parents that the goal of child-directed play is to be with children *as they play* and not necessarily to *play with* children. This can be helpful not only to parents who are too playful (and thus too controlling), but also to parents who would prefer not to play.

If the goal of child-directed play is one of active acceptance, the void created by no longer asserting control is best filled by something other than ambiguous silence and stillness. Attending closely to the child's play, making eye contact, positioning one's self close enough to the play but not so close as to impede the play, and making facial expressions or vocalizations (e.g., "Ooh," "Wow") that match the emotional tone of the play are all examples of simple active acceptance skills. Once again, however, the simplicity of these skills belies their potency when used effectively. Other examples of relatively simple active acceptance skills are parroting and paraphrasing the child's comments and describing a child's actions. These play skills are essential features of reflective listening, so it is critical that parents gain some facility with these aspects of child-directed play. For most parents, repeating a child's words is easier than describing the specifics of play. When a child speaks, it functions as a prompt for parents to speak in return. The child's play activity is not punctuated by such prompts, and parents can occasionally lapse into long silences if their child plays quietly. Another relatively easy skill for parents to master is joining in the child's play if invited to do so. Despite the recommendation to "be with" rather than "play with," parents should not refuse their child's invitation to play.

Simple active acceptance skills communicate in compelling ways parents' willingness and capacity to be curious about and caring of their children. Fortunately, these rudimentary skills do not require a great deal of psychological sophistication on the part of parents. Most parents should be well equipped to conduct this level of child-directed play and reflective listening after only 3 to 6 training sessions.

Complex Active Acceptance

There are some skills related to play and listening that do not come so easily for parents. The effective use of these acceptance skills generally requires greater psychological-mindedness and more time and opportunity for rehearsal and skill integration. These more complex skills require parents to distance themselves emotionally, understand their child's point of view, and infer accurately their child's emotions.

One such skill involves stepping out of role after having been invited to play by the child. By stepping out of role, parents can check in with children about how they are to act in their invited role. For instance, a father who is invited by his son to play with plastic army figures could begin by asking, "What should I do?" His son may want him to be on his side, or he may want him to be "the enemy." By not assuming either position and by not choosing, this father not only provides his son with greater autonomy, he also learns something about his son and his son's play that he would have not known otherwise. As the play proceeds, this father can continue to step out of role and inquire—perhaps in a whispered, "conspiratorial" aside—about what his next move is to be. In this way, the child has the joy of playing with his father but without losing control of the play session. The ability to step out of role and to focus more on their child than the play itself is not an easy skill for some parents. It requires that they reverse what has been familiar figure and ground. To attend to their child may mean deviating from the precise rules of a game. It may mean not attending to who is winning a game or even what the score is. It may mean watching closely and intently a child's facial expressions, but glancing only occasionally at the object of the child's attention. In short, to step out of a play role means preserving the child-directed nature of the play session. Even parents who enjoy enacting the play role to their own liking can benefit from at least minimal training in this area. If they temporarily can suspend their ideas or rules about how to play and spend more time simply being with their child, these parents can learn a great deal about their child.

A second, advanced active acceptance skill is the practice of *summarizing* what a child has done or said. For example, a mother may comment that her daughter has played a certain game each time they had a play session. Another mother may summarize her son's play by saying, "You have certainly been active today. I believe you played with every toy we have." The skill of summarizing a child's behavior is not limited to play, of course. In fact, summary statements are a valuable listening tool, providing for children (and parents) a look at the bigger picture that is often overlooked. For example, a mother listening to her son's comments about school may offer the following summary, "You know, whenever I ask about your day at school, you almost always talk about lunch and gym class. Those must be your two favorite school activities."

A third advanced acceptance skill is the *reflection* of children's feelings. The ability to reflect a child's feeling can be difficult because parents may not be sure what their child is feeling. Some children openly state that they are angry, scared, or mad, but using language to express emotion is less common among aggressive children (see chapter 1, this volume). Facial expressions can offer clues as to the child's emotional state, but aggressive children may respond to emotionally charged situations by suppressing emotional expression or by denying negative or vulnerable states (Lochman & Dodge, 1994). As a result, the task of identifying and reflecting an aggressive child's feelings should be done tentatively in case the feelings were misidentified or denied. For example, rather than assuming that a child is mad because he lost a game, it is better to begin with a tentative description of the child's overt reaction to the event: "When you lost the game, you were upset but I couldn't tell if you were mad or sad." For some aggressive children, describing their emotional reactions can be a rather novel thing to hear from parents. Parents' harsh demands to end quickly the display of strong emotion may be more familiar. For many aggressive children, emotional arousal can be a confusing state, and reflective comments provide emotional labels that help children understand and cope more effectively with their emotional states (Gottman et al., 1997). Accurately labeling a child's feelings may also serve to soothe the child. Once children realize that a parent understands and accepts that they are experiencing strong emotions, they will feel less threatened by their emotions and may eventually learn to self-soothe. In describing the value of reflecting children's feelings, I sometimes remind parents that when children were very young, we held, rocked, or suckled them in an effort to sooth them emotionally. As children grow older and more verbal, parents' words take on more of that soothing role. Strong emotions can also accompany a range of behaviors, so parents have myriad opportunities to reflect a child's feelings. Of course, parents welcome some of these behaviors, only tolerate other behaviors, and probably contain the rest. In fact, the next chapter on containment revisits the issue of reflecting a child's feelings and discusses its use when the goal is to not accept children's behavior.

Many parents fail to recognize the soothing value of their words or have had poor models for how to use words in this way. Some parents may feel that children do not need or deserve their soothing words. Children may also complicate matters by expressing their emotional needs in ways that are frustrating and confusing to parents. For example, feelings of fear or sadness may be covered all too quickly by acts of anger or defiance that fail to elicit any sympathy from parents. When children are using emotional displays in a purely instrumental and coercive manner, parents may need to combine acceptance with containment (see chapter 6, this volume). Despite the many factors that conspire to disrupt parents' use of soothing comments, those who use these skills routinely will find that they can "hold" their children with their words just as they once held their infants with their arms. Children who sense that their parents accurately appreciate and openly accept their feelings are, of course, apt to convey more of their inner selves. The net effect of this increased understanding, disclosure, and acceptance is an enhanced parent–child relationship, the foundation of more effective socialization. Thus, parents' use of reflective comments to acknowledge and accept their child's feelings is an extremely useful skill to acquire. Some parents will lack the capacity for reflecting feelings, however, and parent trainers will need to adjust their goals accordingly. At minimum, parents may be able to learn new scripts for responding when their child's strong emotions cause them discomfort or tension. Without an alternative script (one that can become more automatic with practice), parents may continue to treat their child's emotional displays as "bad behavior" worthy of eradication.

The last advanced, active acceptance skill is *personalizing*. *Personalizing* means that parents acknowledge more clearly a child's particular desires and goals as expressed during the interaction. Play or conversation that is personalized keeps the focus on the child despite shifts in the object of play or in the topic of conversation. For example, a father whose son is knocking toy figures off an imaginary building might describe the play by saying, "Those guys are crashing to the ground." But if he were to personalize the play interaction, the father might say, "You're knocking those guys off the building, and they're crashing to the ground." When parents personalize an interaction, their child's desires and sentiments are clearly identified rather than implied or understood. Imagine a mother whose daughter remarks that her science teacher is a "real witch." Paraphrasing this comment without personalizing it might sound like this: "She's pretty mean, huh." Personalizing the conversation would produce a paraphrase more like the following: "You really don't like her." The difference between these two statements may seem trivial, but parents who are able to personalize their interactions bring an added intensity to their acceptance efforts. They are better able to convey a willingness to attend to their child's perspective and to discern their child's unique perspective. This point is perhaps best illustrated with an extended example:

Daughter: My science teacher is a real witch!

Mother: You really don't like her. [vs. "She's pretty mean, huh."]

Daughter: She picks on me, and she treats those other kids as her favorites.

Mother: You think other kids are treated better than you. [vs. "She's not very fair."]

Daughter: Monica doesn't like her either. She talks back to her—tells her she has dumb rules.

Mother: You know other kids who feel the same way you do, although they talk back to the teacher. [vs. "Monica gets so mad that she talks back to your teacher."]

Daughter: I'm glad somebody tells her something. I hate her!

Mother: You want this teacher to know how you feel. [vs. "So it's good that Monica talks back to her?"]

Daughter: At least my English teacher, Mrs. Levitt, is nice. She treats everybody fair.

Mother: You don't think your science teacher is being fair, but you like your English teacher. [vs. "Mrs. Levitt is fair."]

The skill of personalizing is a subtle one, but it is an effective way to keep children as the focus of parents' attention. It also provides children with important feedback about how their comments and actions are viewed by others. In this last example, the daughter's feelings and wishes remain a prominent part of the conversation. If her mother had not personalized her comments, the focus of the conversation would have shifted from the science teacher, to Monica, to Mrs. Levitt, thereby relegating her daughter's perspective to a kind of secondary role.

Summary

The typology of acceptance skills presented here is meant to serve as a heuristic for practitioners and perhaps an agenda for interested investigators. The categorization is neither definitive nor exhaustive, and more research is needed to understand fully what parents do when they elect not to intervene in their child's behavior. The following focuses more directly on the task of training parents to be more accepting.

Promoting Parents' Use of Acceptance Skills

The assumptions underlying the use of parental acceptance must be clear and convincing if parents of aggressive children are to engage in and benefit from acceptance skills training. Even parents who see the value of acceptance may feel uneasy or awkward if these skills are unfamiliar, and others may lack the social–cognitive abilities to use more complex forms of acceptance. Below are a number of suggestions that can help practitioners in their effort to promote greater parental acceptance.

Train Slowly, Support Often, Process Regularly

There are two points to be made here. First, practitioners are reminded of the importance of establishing and sustaining a strong therapeutic alliance, particularly as more demands are made of parents (see chapter 4, this volume). Second, acceptance skills training should not be underestimated, either in its potential to affect the parent–child relationship or in the degree to which it represents a formidable obstacle for parents of aggressive children. Because the task of being accepting may present a significant challenge for parents with aggressive children, practitioners must train slowly, support often, and process regularly. Instructions and examples should be presented in an organized fashion at a pace that is in line with parents' capabilities. Role-play exercises that involve modeling and rehearsal opportunities should not be hurried along. Parents' efforts and accomplishments during the training should be acknowledged, along with those occasions when parents feel tentative or discouraged. And because of the difficulty of distinguishing between parents' need for more support or more training, practitioners will need to process with parents so that their unstated reactions to the training are not overlooked. Perhaps the best way to summarize this particular point is to suggest that there is considerable risk to the success of acceptance skills training when practitioners move too quickly and assume too much. Practitioners who are used to following a BMPT curriculum should be particularly cautious. Most BMPT programs devote only 2 to 3 sessions to the topic of parent–child play (see chapter 2, this volume), focusing primarily on the skill of following a child's lead during play and not on the broader goal of parental acceptance. When one considers the challenge of trying to forge and sustain a harmonious relationship with a troubling child, it is vital that efforts to train parents correspond to the scope and significance of the skills involved. By moving slowly and in constant collaboration with parents, practitioners will increase the chances that training will have the desired effect.

I recently worked with a divorced mother whose two children were exhibiting a mix of both externalizing and internalizing symptoms. Although she was emotionally damaged by an abusive childhood, this mother had no difficulty displaying personal power, particularly when threatened by others. Unfortunately, her tendency to see threat and provocation was rather acute, and her children often experienced harsh treatment when she was upset. I found it necessary and helpful to spend a great deal of time accepting this mother before mentioning the goal of accepting her children. I was initially encouraged because she seemed to recognize the need to be more accepting, but she had no clue about how to do it. She faltered in her first attempt, in large part because I had assumed that her intelligence and my demonstrations were sufficient preparation for a first rehearsal. She then missed the next session (reportedly because her daughter was ill) and in the session following she arrived extremely angry and in near crisis about all that was happening to her. Although I had hoped to resume skills training (and correct my earlier error), it was clear that she needed me to listen to her. As she described in great detail the negative incidents of the past few days, I began to realize that listening to this mother was providing her with an opportunity to experience fully what it meant to be accepted. I must confess that I had quite a strong urge to stop her complaining. I had suspected, however, that until I listened to her story, she would not settle emotionally and she would not hear anything I had to say. In the next session, we were able to process her reaction to that first rehearsal, and she agreed to do two more practice sessions. This time, she was not only open and responsive to my feedback, she also demonstrated incredible improvement in her ability to be accepting of her children.

Build a Shared Perspective of Parental Acceptance

Acceptance skills training is enhanced when parents and practitioners have a common understanding of what parental acceptance is and why it is important. This point is particularly important for acceptance skills training that involves parent–child play. Unless practitioners proceed cautiously, parents may confuse acceptance—as reflected in parent–child play—with any number of activities that fail to leave a child with a sense of acceptance. For example, granting a child's request for special prizes or privileges, rewarding or praising a child for good behavior, or going to a special event (e.g., the circus) can all be misconstrued as accepting. There also exist activities that fit well with a goal of parental acceptance but that may not be recognized as such by parents. Saturday morning errands, family chores or projects, long car or bus rides, meal times, and trips to the doctor's office that involve long waits can all be occasions for promoting a child's sense of acceptance, if used well.

As discussed in chapter 4, parents can differ widely in their understanding of acceptance and the value of a positive parent–child relationship. I try to create a shared understanding of acceptance by using a succinct and memorable phrase often borrowed from the words used by parents themselves. I then use this phrase frequently during training to keep at the fore the reasons why we—parents and I—are doing this collaborative work on parental acceptance. I have used such phrases as (a) "so your values and beliefs will matter to your child," (b) "so your child will feel more a part of this family and have a reason to behave," and (c) "so you and your child will have the kind of relationship that is best for both of you." Such phrases help motivate parents to begin the work of acceptance skills training, but their cognitive and emotional reactions to training should be continually processed. Of course, parents' success with skills acquisition and implementation can also improve their understanding of acceptance. But if parents struggle to learn these skills, then any positive views about acceptance may be quickly eroded. As discussed in chapter 4, practitioners who face this dilemma may need to suspend training temporarily, support parents in their struggle, and process with them their reactions to training.

Set Realistic Training Goals

The need to set training goals that are not beyond parents' reach is related to building a common perspective of acceptance. Although I described earlier a number of skills that can be used to convey acceptance, training should not be driven by a need to cover every skill possible. Rather, practitioners should regard these skills more like paints on a palette that can be chosen and mixed in a variety of ways. The job of the practitioner is to identify that set of acceptance skills that works best for parents. For some parents, that may mean a great deal of active acceptance, mixing both simple and complex techniques. For others, it may mean adhering primarily to simple, tacit acceptance skills, in particular the strategy of pursuing their own self-care in order to avoid unneeded and counterproductive interactions with their child. Parent–child dyads will differ in which combination of acceptance skills will give them the optimal, maintainable relationship.

Practitioners should ask themselves the following question: Under what conditions could a relationship between this parent and this child be positive and sustainable? By focusing on the answer to this question, and by regularly processing with parents the reasonableness and accuracy of their answer, practitioners are more likely to set realistic training goals. Practitioners who focus on this question may also avoid the mistake of casting every parent–child dyad as one that can enjoy a close, affectionate bond. Socializing relationships between aggressive children and their parents, by definition, are not based on coercive exchanges, but these relationships may well lack for closeness and affection. To strive for such desirable extras may be unrealistic and hazardous for parent–child dyads that struggle with negotiating intimacy, interdependence, and power. Recognizing the influence of both child and parent effects is critical to successfully articulating the parameters of a sustainable socializing relationship. As Gottman (1994) discovered in his research on couples in stable marriages, therapeutic notions about effective relationships do not always match with what occurs naturally.

Avoid Training Stops and Starts

To the extent it is possible, practitioners should avoid frequent shifts away from acceptance skills training to other seemingly relevant but distracting issues. Opportunities to lose focus on acceptance are common as stressful events throw parents into crisis and other training goals are put forth as more relevant. For example, it would not be uncommon for questions about containment to arise during acceptance skills training. As discussed in chapter 3, there appears to be little empirical support for placing acceptance skills training before containment skills training, and vice versa. As such, parents who raise containment issues early and often may be better served by reversing what has come to be the conventional sequence. However, shifting between these two dyadic skills would not seem advisable.

The conceptual and practical linkages between the two are complex and often subtle, and to move back and forth between them may only confuse parents and dilute the training for each type of skill. In the case earlier of the mother who arrived angry and in crisis, I was not sure that my decision to listen to her story would allow me to return the following week to a training agenda. If that had not been possible—if she returned with yet another crisis to handle—I would have been faced with the difficult decision of going forward or postponing acceptance skills training. Before making such a decision, practitioners need to consider whether any time is likely to be less stressful for the family than any other. If the answer is "no," then the benefits of parents mastering a set of important skills must be weighed against the hope of quieting the recurring stress that families face. Practitioners should also recognize that parents who are resistant to change and to learning new skills are more prone to experiencing and reporting obstacles to skills training (Patterson & Forgatch, 1985).

Maintaining a persistent focus on acceptance skills training in the face of parents' other concerns is frequently a daunting task. Knowing how to respond to crises-ridden or training-resistant parents is not always clear. At a minimum, however, efforts to support and process with parents should include an accurate and sincere acknowledgment of their concerns. Once acknowledged, practitioners and parents can then work collaboratively to decide what to do about these concerns during this phase of training. Options include deferring training until the concern is settled, tabling the concern until later in training, scheduling a time apart from training to meet and discuss the issue, or dedicating the last few minutes of a training session to the concern. Another strategy is to begin each training session with an opportunity for parents to update the trainer with any new issues or events that are noteworthy. The benefits of this approach are that practitioners can learn from the start of a session if a parent's mind is preoccupied by concerns that are unrelated to acceptance skills training. My own preference is to begin with this type of check-in procedure, but only after I have reminded parents of the agenda for that session. In this way parents are not surprised if I ask, "How should we deal with this issue and not lose focus on the skills training?" Many times, however, the issues raised are not so urgent or complex as to require a great deal of in-session time. Skilled practitioners will often find ways to reframe parents' concerns as further justification for continuing with the present training agenda or for waiting until more time and attention can be devoted to dealing more effectively with what may be a very significant concern or question. The down side to opening each session with this check-in opportunity is that practitioners may not be able to return parents to the training agenda without feeling unduly controlling or rude. Also, when working with a group of parents, the time required for the check-in can be prohibitive. On the other hand, the structure of a group format should also function to keep the focus of training on the stated agenda. Again, if practitioners can train slowly, support often, and process regularly, they will be more likely to avoid unneeded stops and starts.

Start Simply

As suggested by the typology presented earlier, some acceptance skills are easier to comprehend and simpler to use than others. Parents seem to find summarizing, personalizing, and reflecting more difficult to learn than parroting and describing. Because basic skills are easier to learn, practitioners should begin there and add more complex skills to the mix as parents demonstrate facility and confidence with previously learned skills. In the RPT groups described in chapter 2, child-directed-play skills training began with the first seven skills shown in Table 5.1. Most of the materials used to support child-directed-play skills training were adapted from those used in CREFT (Guerney, 1983). Short labels have been assigned to each of the play skills so that parents and parent trainers can

Table 5.1.   Child-Directed Play Skills

Number	Action	Skill
	Try to . . .	
1.	Wait for your child to lead the play.	Holding back
2.	Repeat your child's words.	Parroting
3.	Paraphrase or re-paraphrase your child's words.	Paraphrasing
4.	Describe out loud and in detail your child's play.	Play-by-play announcing
5.	Get close enough so you can watch carefully as your child plays. (Try sitting on the floor!)	
6.	Make facial expressions, gestures, and sound effects (e.g., "Boom!" "Oh no!") that match your child's play.	
7.	Join in your child's play if invited to do so.	
8.	If invited to play, continue to check in with your child about what and how you should play.	Stepping out of role
9.	Let your child have "wrong" ideas, facts, and notions.	
10.	Summarize your child's play now and then.	Summarizing
11.	Look for and describe your child's feelings (e.g., "You look really mad!").	Identifying feelings
12.	Connect your children's goals to his or her behaviors and comments (e.g., "You wanted those cars to crash together").	Personalizing
	Try not to . . .	
1.	Change the way your child plays.	
2.	Evaluate the play using praise or criticism.	
3.	Teach or correct your child's mistakes.	
4.	Ask a lot of questions.	
5.	Answer questions that your child can answer.	
6.	Solve problems that your child can solve.	
7.	Tell your child what to feel.	

refer to them quickly. Parents who can reliably perform the first seven skills will have a good grounding in the strategy of parental acceptance. The skills of holding back, parroting or paraphrasing, and describing are particularly important. In fact, these three can be thought of as a kind of triad of core acceptance skills. Child-directed play sessions are greatly enhanced when this triad of skills comes readily and easily to parents. As noted previously, describing tends to be the most difficult of the three because parents are not prompted to speak when children play silently.

Some parents, of course, will be able to move beyond the simpler skills to those that require greater interpersonal sophistication. These are listed in Table 5.1 as numbers 8 to 12. Of these four skills, stepping out of role is perhaps the easiest for parents to learn, especially if it becomes an automatic response to children's play instructions. The other three skills are less likely to be used in an automatic fashion. However, these three advanced skills are particularly useful when the parent–child interaction is conversational and not play based. Because conversations are likely to occur more frequently than play interactions, parents who can tap into these skills are better able to convey an overall posture of acceptance to their children.

Build New Habits Before Critiquing Old Habits

Table 5.1 presents not only skills that parents should try to use but also skills to avoid. Parents participating in the RPT groups were given this list of prohibitions toward the end of the acceptance skills training phase. Our experience in pilot training groups was that if these unwanted behaviors were presented too early, parents were less likely to focus on the new skills. Instead, their attention and their energies were centered on behaviors to avoid. In some cases, parents would hesitate, seemingly paralyzed by the fear of performing a proscribed behavior. Parents also may not be able to appreciate the reasons for avoiding these behaviors until after they have experienced the benefits of using child-directed play skills. Asking parents not to praise, ask or answer questions, and correct their child's mistaken ideas and facts is a rather bold request. For parents who see themselves as competent mothers and fathers, these actions are fairly salient ways to demonstrate one's care and concern.

The admonition against correcting the child's mistaken ideas and beliefs is especially trying for some parents. During play, a child's misinformation can be manifested in a number of ways. Misinformation can reflect a lack of knowledge or experience, a slight misunderstanding of what is accurate, or a firm belief in a wrong piece of information. For example, a child may believe that professional basketball player Michael Jordan has never lost a game. At other times, the misinformation may be instrumental in that it supports a child's argument or actions in some way. For example, a boy losing a game of checkers may suddenly "remember" a rule that benefits him but not his father. Some parents fear that allowing a child to

make up new rules will be teaching them that it is permissible to change
the rules whenever one is losing. If this were true, then parents may well
be concerned. On the other hand, if parents intervene they miss those
occasions when parental acceptance is followed by children self-correcting
their reliance on new rules. Practitioners can also point out that siblings
and peers are unlikely to allow such rules and that it may be better for
the corrections to come from these sources. The classic example of this
phenomenon, of course, is a child's belief about such mythical figures as
Santa Claus and the Tooth Fairy. Parents can go a lifetime without challenging their child's beliefs about these figures and not fear that these
myths will persist into adulthood.

Another example of misinformation that pulls for parent intervention
is when children offer dubious facts about a deviant friend in order to
justify continued contact. Parents may challenge the child's misinformation as a way to justify a decision to prohibit continued contact or because
they fear their child is being overly naive about this friend. Both reasons
may be shortsighted and unnecessary, however. Children may be naive
about their friends and the hazards of their friendship, but there may be
little to gain from parents' challenging that perspective. For one thing,
children are likely to learn from other peers and from their own experiences the kind of information that parents fear is overlooked. Challenging
children's beliefs about deviant peers may inoculate them against the very
arguments parents are making and lead children to present parents only
with information that contradicts parents' perceptions. Little is gained
when parents try to convince their child that a friend is deviant; the emphasis should be on parents' prohibition against continued contact. In fact,
when working with parents of older children and adolescents, I often suggest that parents concede that their perspective (e.g., whether a child's
friend is deviant) and their decisions are often flawed, but that as parents,
they are committed to the decisions they do make.

A final reason to wait before presenting the list of behaviors to avoid
is that such recommendations often require discussion and clarification.
Such discussion is usually better left until after parents have become more
familiar with the concept and skills of parental acceptance. This is especially important for parents who would experience a vast behavioral void
if they suddenly ceased using the seven behaviors to be avoided during
child-directed play (e.g., correcting; praising). By equipping parents with
ready substitutes for more controlling actions, practitioners ease the way
for successfully presenting these prohibitions.

Foster a Relaxed Training Atmosphere

Because parents often feel anxious about learning new parenting skills,
training can be made smoother by an atmosphere that is not only safe and
supportive, but also relaxed and at times fun. Simply acknowledging the
"weirdness" of having to practice these skills in front of someone else can
be extremely helpful. It can also be helpful to ask parents to describe their

personal views about play or their experiences playing as a child. Recounting their favorite childhood toys and games can also set the kind of relaxed, playful tone that may put parents at ease and allow them to learn more. Practitioners should recognize, however, that not all parents speak fondly or positively about play or their play experiences. I have had parents announce, "I do not play" or "I am not a player." Statements like these should be taken seriously and not trivialized. For this kind of parent, a playful atmosphere may not be relaxing. Instead, speaking in a tone that reflects parents' concerns may work better at promoting skills acquisition.

Recognize the Importance of Assigning, Planning, and Reviewing
Acceptance Skills Homework

Acceptance skills only benefit the parent–child relationship when used at home, either in or outside of play. Before parents can transfer newly acquired acceptance skills to the home, however, they will need to do homework that specifically promotes skills transfer. For parents who are able and willing to hold play sessions at home, I make the standard CREFT recommendation of once a week for 30 minutes (see chapter 2, this volume). To prepare for home play sessions, parents are given instructions and training on such issues as how to begin and end play, how to set limits during play, when and where to hold play sessions, and the types of toys and games suitable for child-directed play. Tables 5.2 and 5.3 and Exhibits 5.1 and 5.2 present examples of the handouts used in this preparation. Note that many of these handouts are modifications of those used in CREFT.

Instruction and training on how to begin and end play, as well as on how to set limits during play, are especially important for parents whose aggressive children are likely to find it difficult initially to remain within the temporal and behavioral boundaries of parent–child play. Although issues involving limits on play behavior relate more directly to the concept of containment, parents should be made aware of these simple techniques for improving the experience of parent–child play. The handout devoted to special considerations for home play lists a number of issues that parents should consider prior to beginning. There are few definitive answers to the questions raised by this handout because each home, each dyad, and each family is likely to have its own set of circumstances that bear on these issues. Also, for some families there may be no good answers to the questions raised, in which case practitioners will certainly need to attend to issues involving family structure (see chapter 8, this volume).

Practitioners should also recognize that parents are usually quite eager to discuss a successful home play session and equally eager to avoid discussing an unsuccessful attempt at home play. Either way, parents are likely to have strong feelings about the use of home play, especially when starting out. Therefore, practitioners should plan to spend sufficient time

Table 5.2.   Suggestions for Beginning and Ending Play

Suggestion	Example
Beginning play	
When ready to begin, give an introductory message.	"Okay, let's begin our special play time. You get to choose what we play and how we play. If there is something you can't do, I'll let you know."
Ending play	
Give 2 time warnings before ending the play session.	
Give the first warning 5 minutes before the end of play, and the second warning 1 minute before the end of play.	"Joey, we only have 5 more minutes to play."
End play firmly but calmly.	"Our play time is up now. We have to quit."
If the child is reluctant to stop playing, reflect his or her feelings and restate that play has ended.	Use your body and voice to stress this point.
Begin putting away the play materials.	
Reflect the child's desire to continue playing, but insist on ending the play.	"I know you want to keep playing, but we're finished playing for the day."
Toy pick-up	
Do not insist that children pick up toys by themselves.	Parents pick up toys and children often follow along.

processing parents' experiences and reactions. Practitioners should make few assumptions about how well the play went at home lest parents censor their accounts to match these expectations. Broadly worded statements, such as "I'd like to hear about the home play session," may work best when beginning the review of play skills homework. Practitioners can then use reflective listening skills to support parents and to learn what the experience meant to them. In fact, it may be necessary and beneficial to devote the major part of a therapy session to processing parents' home play sessions. Understanding what transpired at home may require briefly interviewing the child, an additional in-session practice session, or a role-play exercise in which the parent is in the role of either the parent or the child, depending on what was needed. Because home play sessions can produce strong emotional responses in some parents, going over the particulars can help parents reach a sense of closure and understanding that promotes another attempt (if parents felt unsuccessful) or continued use (if parents felt successful).

Table 5.3. Special Considerations for Home Play Sessions

Type of Consideration	Considerations
Physical–structural	1. What should your child do when beginning the play sessions at home?
	2. What is the best place to have a play session?
	3. Will water be allowed?
	4. What furniture would you worry about? What could you do about it?
	5. What can you do to make the room more "playable"?
Time	1. Considering the needs of your children and you, what would be the best day and time to have play sessions?
	2. Is the room you have selected for play sessions scheduled for some other activity when you planned to use it? (For example, you have chosen the kitchen, but the time you chose interferes with preparing dinner or doing the dishes.)
	3. How will you set up play sessions for two or more children?
	4. How will you accommodate other children who are too old or too young for the play session?
	5. What if it is absolutely necessary for you to cancel a play session?
	6. With what other interests might the play session be competing?
Possible interruptions	1. What will you do if the telephone rings? Would you leave it off the hook? Ignore it? Have someone else answer it?
	2. What if someone should come to the door? Would you leave a note on the door? Ignore it? Have someone else answer it?
	3. What if one of the other children interrupts a play session?

Emphasize the "Portability" of Reflective Listening Skills

As a clinician, I have witnessed often the power of child-directed play to convey to children that they are accepted and valued. Indeed, I have often felt there is no better gift that parents can give their children than time spent in child-directed play. However, as a vehicle for directly conveying parental acceptance and for promoting a more positive parent–child relationship, child-directed play is not very practical. Even when used only once a week for 30 minutes, regular home play sessions are often not feasible given the demands some parents face. Single parents with multiple children often have the hardest time with this task. If the single parent works outside the home, the children are very young, or the home is only one or two rooms, then home play becomes even more impractical. If home play is not a viable option, parents can still convey a posture of active acceptance through other kinds of parent–child interactions, in particular those that allow for the use of reflective listening skills.

Exhibit 5.1.   Limit Setting During Play

<hr>

What Is a Limit?

A *limit* is a guideline for behavior that is enforced by imposing consequences. During child-directed play, few limits are ever needed. However, sometimes children play in ways that are dangerous or destructive. Following the steps below should help if such behaviors occur.

Steps in Setting Limits

First occasion:	Determine if the behavior should be stopped. That is, ask yourself if a limit is needed (Is the behavior dangerous or destructive?).
	State the limit to the child (e.g., "Joey, one thing you can't do when we play is hit me with the ball.").
	Give the child an alternative (e.g., "But you can hit this doll or the Bop Bag if you want to.").
Second occasion:	Set the limit again, and warn the child that the play will end if the behavior is repeated (e.g., "Remember: You can't hit me with the ball. If you do it again, we'll have to stop playing.").
Third occasion:	State the limit again, and end the play (e.g., "We're going to stop now because you hit me with the ball.").

<hr>

Because reflective listening is embedded in child-directed play, the transition from play to non-play acceptance is often an easy one for parents to make. Indeed, parents comfortable with their play skills often report using the skills in non-play situations without any prompting from therapists. For other parents, the transition from play-based to conversation-based acceptance is not so smooth or natural. These parents may benefit from practitioners making explicit the relation between play and listening skills and from casting the latter as portable enough to go anywhere and to be used anytime. For parents who struggle to maintain a regular play time, the portability of listening skills is usually an attractive option.

That is not to say that parents who can arrange regular home play sessions should not be encouraged to extend their message of active acceptance beyond the play setting. Reflective listening applied to everyday, non-play situations may be even more beneficial to children because everyday situations are both more real and more frequent than play situations. Of course the portability of reflective skills does not mean that some parents will not struggle to understand and use these skills effectively. Listening skills that convey parental acceptance can be every bit as difficult to learn as child-directed-play skills. Parents may need a great deal of in-session modeling and rehearsal before they can use these skills adequately. One useful way to model the effective use of reflective listening skills is to role-play recent parent–child interactions that parents felt were handled poorly. These exercises can be helpful because parents have an opportunity to use on the parent therapist the kind of comments their child uses on them. By modeling reflective listening skills, parents can

Exhibit 5.2

Toys and Games for Home Play Sessions

Some toys and games are better than others for the type of play we're doing. Toys and games to avoid are those that can be played in only one way, do not allow for general conversation, or are not so engaging. The best toys and games are those that children enjoy playing with someone else and that allow for creative and imaginative play. Below are toys and games that would be appropriate for this type of play. We encourage you and your child to think of others.

crayons or markers	construction paper	tea set
sand (or pea gravel)	Velcro darts	masks
baby bottle	toy food and kitchen	playing cards
watering can and bucket	doll house with furniture	watercolor paints
PlayDough	family dolls, puppets, little people	bop bag
Mr. Potato Head	building blocks (Lego, tinker toys)	ring toss
toy knife or gun	army men/other miniature figures	blowing bubbles

learn new ways to respond to their child. Parents should be encouraged to listen for lines that they can use and to recognize that a few well-chosen phrases can apply to a host of situations. Moreover, by relying on the three most basic skills of child-directed play and listening—holding back, parroting and paraphrasing, and describing—parents do not have to be clever to respond effectively to their child; they only need to look and listen with a posture of acceptance.

Summary

Teaching parents to be more accepting is often a challenging enterprise. When faced with the day-to-day struggles of parenting an aggressive child, learning skills that promote acceptance may seem odd or even detrimental. Therefore, it is important that parents understand the purpose of acceptance. Acceptance skills training that is poorly understood and that is taken out of the larger context of socialization may indeed be detrimental. On the other hand, parent therapy that ignores the quality and the sustainability of the parent–child relationship may also be detrimental to parents and their aggressive children. The capacity to let children make decisions on their own, to watch and listen as children express their thoughts and feelings, and to see the value of "doing nothing" as children engage in minor misbehaviors is best taught in the context of child-directed play and reflective listening. Whether the goal is to convey explicitly their sense of acceptance or simply to refrain from unnecessary intervention, parents can use acceptance skills to create and maintain the kind of relationship that children will see as worthy of investment and that parents will see as workable and perhaps rewarding.

6 _____

Containment

Every child has the right to be loved, but that right may be denied if parents lack the requisite skills to first teach children to be reasonably compliant and noncoercive. —Gerald Patterson (1986)

The preceding chapter described a number of skills by which parents can convey to their child a sense of being accepted. In this chapter, the focus is on those skills that leave children feeling constrained in their freedom to act. Before outlining the particulars of containment skills training, I first present a conceptual overview of containment and its fundamental goals and then describe the characteristics of adaptive containment scripts. I then offer a four-step model of containment, review a number of optional containment skills, and cover ways that practitioners can custom fit parents' limit-setting scripts. I end by discussing two important issues related to the topic of containment: responding to sibling conflict and parental supervision.

A Conceptual Overview of Parental Containment

I define *parental containment* as any behavior that fosters in children a sense of restraint while not threatening their relationship security. Children who are contained by their parents feel restricted from acting on their own behalf but do not feel personally or relationally threatened by this restriction. Parental containment skills convey to children that their behaviors are limited in reliable and specific ways. As outlined in chapter 3, parental containment is only one part of a larger strategy that parents can use to socialize aggressive children. The socialization of aggressive children does not succeed or fail solely on the basis of whether parents gain control over their children's performance of antisocial behavior. Instead, children are socialized when they participate in a sustained relationship with a prosocial adult and the relationship entails both containment and acceptance.

To create and sustain a positive, accepting relationship with aggressive children, parents must be selective in how they use containing actions. Because conflict and the potential for conflict occur more often in the homes of aggressive children, the challenge of forming and maintaining an emotionally positive relationship can be met only if parents limit their use of containment (Cavell, 1999a). Effective parent therapy helps parents and their aggressive children settle into a pattern of interacting that, over time, blends containment with acceptance in a way that has a net positive effect on the parent–child relationship and on the family's emotional climate. That is not to say that parents should avoid all disciplinary conflict with their aggressive children or that parent–child interactions can be free of negative affect. However, if emotionally negative situations and ugly exchanges are offset by a predominant theme of acceptance and mutual respect, then the parent–child relationship will promote children's socialization.

The term *containment* is used to emphasize that parents of aggressive children should reserve their disciplinary efforts for when children are acting in violent, antisocial, or coercive ways. Aggressive children, generally speaking, tend to defy and resist parents' efforts to control them. They seldom comply—willingly or unwillingly—to parents' *don't* commands and they can find any number of ways to circumvent parents' *do* commands. Many aggressive children are so adept in their ability to defy parental authority that they establish themselves as the most powerful person in the family (Patterson et al., 1992). Compared to nonaggressive children, aggressive children are more likely to engage in extended coercive exchanges with parents and are more likely to prevail in those exchanges (Dumas et al., 1995; Patterson et al., 1992). When aggressive children wield excessive power in the home, the risk for developing antisocial tendencies increases tremendously. Such children not only participate in the basic training of coercion (Patterson, 1982), they also live in a family system that distorts the meaning of such concepts as boundaries, power, and hierarchy (Dumas et al., 1995; Minuchin, 1974). Therefore, effectively containing aggressive children not only limits their use of coercion but also promotes a family hierarchy in which parents are the dominant figures.

When one considers the developing self-system of aggressive children, the goals of containment take on even greater significance. Because the most aggressive children are often those who have inflated self-views (Edens et al., 1999; Hughes et al., 1997), parents can ill afford to abdicate their position of authority. Paradoxically, it is the child's self-system that offers parents a means by which they can limit their efforts to contain aggressive children. If the goal of discipline is to leave children with a sense that they do not have ultimate authority in the family, then parents need not win every disciplinary encounter. Instead, parents need only to prevail in those exchanges that are necessary to maintain their position of authority as perceived by the child. For temperamentally inhibited children, this may mean little more than a stern look delivered now and then. For very strong-willed children, the process of learning the limits of their own power is likely to be slower and more effortful, at least on the part of parents. Schneider, Cavell, Hughes, and Oxford (1999) studied the degree to which aggressive children doubted their parents' ability to contain them. Aggressive children's self-rated sense of containment interacted with parenting practices to predict composite ratings of externalizing behavior problems. Externalizing scores for those aggressive children with a sense of containment were directly related to the level of harsh and inconsistent parenting that was used. For those children with a lower sense of containment, poor parenting was unrelated to externalizing problems. These findings suggest that improved disciplinary practices may lead to minimal gains if aggressive children doubt a parent's willingness or ability to contain them.

To develop a sense of containment, the learning trials that children undergo must be handled in clear and consistent ways. Ideally, children should be able to discriminate rather easily between behaviors that are allowed and behaviors that are not allowed. The consequences that follow the former should be distinctly and consistently different from the consequences that follow the latter (Wahler & Dumas, 1986). Most often the task of containing aggressive children involves the consistent application of strict limits on their use of aggression and coercion. Performing this task is fraught with potential problems. If the number of prohibited behaviors is excessive, then parents will find it much harder to be consistent. The costs mentally, physically, and emotionally of excessive containment can slowly erode parents' ability to sustain a long list of prohibitions. Children will fail to get clear and consistent messages about limits and about the ability of parents to contain them. If parents happen to gain the upper hand on aggressive children by working hard to sustain external control, it may come at the cost of children no longer feeling accepted and possibly rejecting (or failing to internalize) the values and norms of their prosocial parents.

Parents of aggressive children are better served when they focus their disciplinary energies on those behaviors that are most important to their child's later development and to the family's health and well-being. As such, aggressive and extremely coercive acts are the most appropriate disciplinary targets. Allowing these behaviors to continue creates negative consequences for the child, for parents, and for other family members. Successfully containing these antisocial behaviors is the most effective way that parents can (a) maintain a position of authority, (b) put an end to the use of coercion, and (c) let children know they live in a system in which there are real constraints on their behavior.

The Primary Goals of Containment

Based on the RPT model of parental containment, there are three fundamental goals to keep in mind when helping parents become more effective in their use of discipline. These three goals are essentially the criteria by which therapists can evaluate parents' use of various containment skills.

Stop Victimization by the Child

Parents should not be chronic, unwitting victims of their child's antisocial behavior. Parents may not always be capable of halting such victimization, but they certainly do not deserve it. This is essentially the minimum criterion for evaluating how effectively parents are containing their aggressive children. All other goals must follow this one. If parents and other family members are not safe in their home, then it is nearly impossible to pursue other tasks, including the socialization of the aggressive child. A strong message to parents that they need not be their child's victims is one that becomes increasingly important as aggressive children expand the severity, frequency, and breadth of their antisocial behavior. No one benefits when parents place the positive, accepting aspects of parenting ahead of putting an end to being hit, robbed, or vandalized.

When parents "circle the wagons" to protect themselves and other family members from a victimizing child, they are asserting the norms for conduct in their family system. They also present their child with the minimum conditions for participation as a family member. In the final analysis, parents must come to value their safety and the safety of other family members more than they value the hope or desire to change their aggressive child. Unfortunately, some aggressive children ignore or defy prohibitions against victimization and thereby risk further distancing from the family when they are placed out of the home. Some parents find this possibility so unpleasant that they remain in debilitating relationships with children who continue to victimize them. These parents will need a great deal of support for their efforts to end the victimization in the home. They are also likely to need to process thoughts and feelings that can disrupt efforts to take a stand against victimization. They may feel extremely guilty, see themselves as failures, or fear others will see them in a negative light. Parents who cannot appreciate how they are being victimized by their children are often asked to read the book *Before It's Too Late* by Stanton Samenow (1989). Samenow presents parents with a sobering account of the developing criminal mind. Parents who are victims of their children's aggression may also benefit from participation in Al-Anon, the support group for loved ones of alcoholics. The tenets of Al-Anon emphasize (a) the limits of control one has over the alcoholic and (b) the importance of taking care of one's self. Now that I have issued such a strident argument against allowing children to victimize parents and other family members, let me qualify it. The goal of ending victimization by aggressive children is a kind of last resort for parents and parent therapists. When parents are faced with an aggressive child who has resisted all previous socialization efforts, then a strategy of not being a victim may be all that remains.

Consider the case of Reggie. Reggie was a 10-year-old boy adopted by his parents when he was roughly 7 years old. He had been neglected as a very young child (and probably abused physically), and had lived for 1 to 2 years with a foster family before being adopted. His behavior at the time I met him was marked by antisocial tendencies both overt and covert. His adoptive parents had successfully raised three children of their own, but they found the going quite tough with Reggie. In one of our earliest sessions, his adoptive mother appeared spent and frustrated, and she expressed a feeling of being at the end of her rope. She used parenting strategies that involved a number of contingency management techniques—token systems, behavioral contracts, and the like—that contributed to her fatigue and frustration. She and her husband felt that Reggie needed a great deal of structure because he was ADHD as well as aggressive. However, previously unsuccessful efforts to control their son's behavior left them entertaining thoughts of ending their role as Reggie's adoptive parents. Because they were so desperate, I discussed with them the idea of changing their strategy for dealing with and living with Reggie.

I suggested that their energies as Reggie's parents would be better served by a strategy in which they reduced their own victimization and promoted their own health and well-being. I reasoned that if they no longer waged a campaign to change Reggie, then they might find a way to live with him. At a minimum, they had to be ready to put a halt to victimization. But to pursue even this limited agenda would be difficult, so any attempts they made to refuel and support each other would also help their cause. I also suspected that Reggie's behavior would not improve appreciably over time (given his developmental history), but that this new strategy would be the easiest one for them to sustain. Moreover, if Reggie became more amenable to their socialization efforts, it would likely be due to their willingness and ability to maintain an emotionally positive relationship with him over time. In essence, this new strategy of resisting victimization and engaging in better self-care represented a win–win scenario. They could stop being his victims and perhaps find a way to keep him in the fold and thus more likely to benefit from their prosocial lessons and examples.

This strategy is also useful for parents whose older children and adolescents are involved in deviant behaviors maintained by forces beyond parents' control. In working with such parents, I summarize the strategy by reminding them, "Don't be victimized. Live the healthiest life you can, and then pray that your child follows your example." I refer to this strategy as *life-line therapy*: Parents provide a life line for their children, should they want one, but the costs of extending that life line should not involve their being victimized. The image that comes to mind is one in which parents stay safely "on the bank" rather than jumping in to save their child, lest they risk their own "drowning." The reader may also note similarities between these recommendations and those advocated by the support group Tough Love (i.e., a support group for parents that pushes parents to regain control over wayward teens). Similarities aside, it should be clear that I am not endorsing radical, desperate acts by parents as a means of regaining control over their children. Such brinkmanship should never be used as a tool for gaining compliance from children or as a strategy of forced submission. Threatening to call the police or to place a child out of the home (e.g., with a relative, in a foster home) or some other last-ditch measure should only be used if it is needed to preserve the safety and well-being of parents and other family members. These are actions that should convey to children, "I may not be able to control your behavior, but I can control mine. And I will act to keep from being your victim." Saying "no" to victimization also may well benefit the aggressive child, but that is not its purpose. It is intended to benefit those who are being victimized. It is a defensive posture, not an offensive weapon. Children should not be pushed out of the family as a threat to see if they will come around. Rather, they should be invited to join the family but under conditions that promote each member's safety.

Enhance Children's Sense of Containment

If parents are not concerned with the problem of recurring victimization by their child, then the opportunity exists for devoting more time, attention, and effort to their child's socialization. In essence, children who do not chronically victimize parents retain the right to be socialized, or at least the right to expect that parents will attempt to socialize them. As stated earlier, the key to promoting a sense of containment in children is to respond to prohibited behaviors in a way that removes any ambiguity about whether these behaviors are allowed or even up for negotiation. Containment, in essence, is discrimination training for children and parents (Dumas & Wahler, 1985; Wahler & Dumas, 1989). Children must be taught that certain behaviors are simply not permitted. Also, when containment occurs in the context of an accepting parent–child relationship, the distinction between parents' response to prohibited versus permitted behaviors should be clear. However, if the relationship history and context is one of negativity and nattering, then it becomes harder for children to make the necessary distinctions between prohibited and permitted behaviors.

Parents who engage in unremitting criticism and correction of behavior make it hard for children to determine which restrictions are fundamentally important for prosocial commerce. In the face of ambiguity about which behaviors are the most important to suppress, children are unlikely to make important moral discriminations. One would then predict, based on the application of the matching law hypothesis (J. J. Snyder & Patterson, 1995), that children's use of coercive behaviors will vary as a function of the relative level of reinforcement that exists for such behaviors. That is, to the extent there are payoffs for acting aggressively and coercively, children whose parents provide a poor context for discrimination learning will use such behaviors commensurate with these payoffs, even if they are told not to do so. Positive reinforcement (e.g., praise, rewards) for good behavior can sometimes help children distinguish good from bad behavior, but most child behaviors lack the moral valence and saliency needed to make parents' use of positive reinforcement an efficient form of discrimination training. *Desirable* and *undesirable* are more inclusive terms for the things children generally do, but these categories can be redefined too quickly and too easily for either parents or children to keep up with which is which. Instead of being tied to predetermined criteria for what is best for children's socialization, the parameters for undesirable behaviors wax and wane as a function of parents' mood and children's efforts at persuasion. Contributing to this dance of negativity is a desire for predictability by children who are unclear of what is currently desirable and undesirable (Dumas & Wahler, 1985; Wahler & Dumas, 1989).

If parents' efforts at containment are characterized by lax or even indulgent parenting, then children will have a different discrimination problem. The difficulty will not be which *Stop that!* to take seriously; rather, the problem will be knowing that a pained expression or a plaintive sigh is really meant as a message to desist. Under these conditions the consequences for performing prohibited behaviors are not clearly and consistently distinguished from consequences for permissible behaviors. Many parents who struggle with this kind of parenting problem can benefit from skills training designed to increase the clarity and specificity of their commands. In fact, Roberts and Powers' (1988) compliance test is designed to distinguish between those children who comply when given clear instructions and those children who remain oppositional despite being given clear commands. Unfortunately, the likelihood that children can be contained simply by issuing clear commands appears to decrease the longer they have resisted containment and the more coercive and aggressive their behavior has become.

In sum, the goal of increasing a child's sense of containment can be promoted by parents who create and maintain the proper conditions under which children can learn to discriminate behaviors that are acceptable from behaviors that are prohibited by parents and are antagonistic to the family's functioning. The challenge, of course, is to identify those conditions that accomplish this task in a way that is realistic and can be sustained over time. This issue is covered later, but for now, the emphasis is that a sense of containment is the goal to be pursued. And as overwhelming as this task may seem, it is far more reasonable and practical than a goal of making aggressive, school-age children comply with parents' every request. Some parents will have trouble letting go of the goal of having children who are quick to comply, who seldom challenge their parents' authority, and who are ready to defer to parents whenever parents raise their voices or their eyebrows. Most aggressive children will not experience the kind of anxiety that promotes this kind of internalization process (Kochanska, 1995). Their parents are often puzzled and shocked that their children are not bothered by prohibitions and punishments. These parents expect children to react emotionally and behaviorally as they reacted to their own parents. They fail to recognize the likelihood of important differences between themselves and their children in how they respond to punishment. These parents will need help accepting the goal of reducing aggression and coercion while letting go of the goal of quick, reliable compliance (Cavell, 1999a). Other parents will have difficulty fulfilling their responsibility to follow through with behavioral prohibitions. Their impediments can be many and varied. They may be overwhelmed by a whole panoply of stressors or they may simply find it too aversive to engage their child in conflict. They may lack skills and scripts or they may fail to appreciate the insidious nature of their child's developing antisocial nature. As is true with acceptance skills training, a shared vision of what it means to contain an aggressive child is needed if parents and practitioners are to work effectively on the acquisition of containment skills.

Limit the Exchange of Negative Emotions

Effectively containing an aggressive child will not eliminate the exchange of negative emotions. Indeed, it would not be surprising if a shift to more effective containment leads to a temporary increase in the display of negative feelings in some homes. However, for those parents whose past disciplinary efforts were marked by harsh, critical, and perhaps explosive discipline, improved containment skills should eventually produce an overall reduction in negative affect. Their children will benefit, not only because of firmer limits on their coercive acts, but also because the relationship as a whole is made more enjoyable and mutually satisfying. The ability to manage one's emotions when disciplining a defiant, misbehaving child is likely to range widely among parents. Of course, parents of aggressive children are likely to find it very difficult to alter their emotional reactions to children's misdeeds. Their harsh ways of responding have been acquired, in part, through hundreds of learning trials with their children. Harsh reactions that have become standard features of parental discipline are negatively reinforced by the cessation of children's coercive or annoying behavior. Because of the strength of this kind of escape conditioning, the tendency to react harshly is not easily vanquished. The knowledge that one is being too harsh or wishes to keep calm will not suffice in the face of strongly conditioned cues to react as one has done many times before.

For this reason, comprehensive containment skills training should include the goal of reducing parents' use of overly harsh discipline. More importantly, training should focus on how parents can deal effectively with those occasions when disciplinary conflict does escalate into negative emotional exchanges. Rather than assuming that skills training will lead to the complete eradication of overly harsh parenting, it is more realistic to prepare parents for when it does happen. That is not to say that parents cannot acquire new disciplinary skills that are less affectively charged. Many can and do, and parents' use of new, effective containment scripts can be trapped by the reinforcing contingencies that exist naturally in the environment (e.g., increased prosocial child behavior, more rewarding parent–child interactions). Still, if parent trainers hope to reduce the level of negativity in the parent–child relationship, then they must also recognize the limits of parental change. The goal of containing children with a minimum of negative affect becomes more reasonable when parents are taught how to discipline firmly and how to limit the emotional fallout that often accompanies disciplinary conflict.

Guidelines for Containment Skills Training

In this section, I strive once again to strike a balance between the need for a detailed prescription of skills training and the importance of providing basic training principles from which practitioners can deviate when necessary. I discuss the characteristics of effective containment scripts, the four basic steps of containment, optional skills parents can use to enhance containment, and guidelines for custom-fitting parents' containment scripts. I also include in this section a discussion of parents' response to sibling conflict and the importance of parental supervision. I begin, however, with a brief commentary on preparing parents for training in the area of child containment.

Preparing Parents for Training in Containment

For parents of aggressive children, discussions about how to discipline should be treated with reverence. The fact that such discussions are even needed can be an unpleasant reminder of the many defeats parents have suffered at the hands of their coercive children. As a practitioner, I often struggle with the desire to rush in and rid parents of their "mistaken" notions ("If only they would allow me to enlighten them with my clinical insights and brilliant recommendations!"). However, if I fail to recognize and inhibit my overeagerness, I run the risk of pushing parents away from this important opportunity to improve their skills. Earlier I discussed the task of building a collaborative alliance of parents through the use of supporting, processing, and training efforts. I also emphasized the value of letting parents tell their story. I repeat that emphasis here and add the following recommendation: Before asking parents to hear your perspective on discipline, hear theirs.

Characteristics of Adaptive Containment Scripts

A critical assumption made here is that disciplinary encounters with an aggressive child can often undermine parents' use of adaptive strategies because containment can be a stressful, emotionally charged event. Given this assumption, it follows that parents are likely to develop behavioral scripts for containment. *Scripts* are overlearned action patterns that are invoked and discharged in a rather automatic, nonreflective manner. In the language of computers, a behavioral script is rather like a *macro*—a sequence of small steps that are consolidated and implemented as a unit. An important task for practitioners is to help parents establish more adaptive scripts to use when containing their difficult child. What would such a script look like? I suggest that six features characterize adaptive scripts used to contain aggressive children: Scripts are seldom invoked, are consistently applied, are fully discharged, raise the cost of aggressive acts, are feasibly sustained, or are nonviolent.

Seldom Invoked

The seldom-invoked script places heavy emphasis on the socializing power of positive parent–child relationships. As such, any containment script used so frequently as to preclude the possibility of a positive parent–child relationship is not adaptive, at least for the child in need of socialization. One of the greatest challenges for practitioners is to help parents of aggressive children reduce their harsh, nattering behaviors. I argue the best strategy for doing this is for parents to concentrate their containment efforts on children's use of physical aggression and other forms of antisocial behavior (Cavell, 1999a). Childhood aggression is a reliable predictor of later maladjustment, and to target it, alone, creates inherent limits on the frequency with which parents engage in containment efforts. Another potential governor over parents' use of containment is to use it primarily to enforce *don't* commands. Because of studies suggesting that *do* commands are harder for parents to enforce and harder for children to internalize (e.g., Kochanska, 1995), parents who limit their containment scripts to the enforcement of *don't* commands should enjoy less conflicted and more positive relationships with their children.

The *five-or-less rule*, a mnemonic device I often use with parents, states that parents' short list of target behaviors should always number five or fewer specific behaviors. (I sometimes joke that this "handy" rule allows for one target behavior per finger.) The choice of five or less is rather arbitrary but designed to prevent parents' overuse of containment while not being too restrictive in the eyes of parents. The task of deciding which and how many behaviors go on the short list is done by parents with assistance from the practitioner. Of course, I strongly encourage parents to include among their target behaviors acts of aggression and other forms of antisocial conduct. Depending on the family, I have also recommended targeting either antisocial acts only or adding one or two *do* commands to the list. I recommend the former when parents are struggling to contain a very defiant child who is engaging in frequent acts of aggression. For families whose children are not too old or too big for time-out but whose parents have yet to establish time-out as an effective sanction, restricting the list of targeted behaviors to specific acts of aggression (e.g., hitting, kicking, biting, pushing, grabbing) can be especially critical. In fact, establishing time-out when there has been no history of its effective use can represent such a demanding task for parents that little else can reasonably fit on a list of target behaviors. However, if children are infrequently acting in an aggressive fashion, parents may have the luxury of adding to their short list one or two *do* commands. When this opportunity arises, I often advise parents to consider *do* commands that have potentially widespread, systemic benefits. For example, children's adherence to bed-time curfews and to rules about where to eat or where to play can help the whole family. As children become less difficult to manage (i.e., less coercive), parents can also add age-appropriate chores to their list of target behaviors. Note that parents should not wait till children are reasonably compliant before expecting their children to perform age-appropriate chores; rather, I am recommending that parents simply not impose strong sanctions for failure to complete chores until children's level of coercion subsides enough to where parental sanctions are not occurring at an excessive rate. (In the next chapter, I elaborate on the value of maintaining parental expectations even if children are presently not meeting these expectations.)

For some parents, firmly and consistently containing five or fewer target behaviors will mean an increase in how controlling they are. For other parents, containing only the behaviors on their short list will mean a reduction in how aversive and controlling they are. The goal for both types of parents is the right mix of behavioral resistance and behavioral tolerance that promotes in children a sense of containment but does not preclude a sense of acceptance. For parents who are extremely harsh and overcontrolling, sticking to the behaviors on the short list is particularly important. For parents who struggle with being firm, containing the nonnegotiable behaviors on their short list is their disciplinary bottom line.

But how should parents respond when children perform one of the many undesirable behaviors that are considered negotiable by virtue of the fact they are not on the short list? Patterson (1982) described a process in nonreferred families whereby parents tend to overlook or deflect child behaviors that are not considered important enough to confront: "Mothers of normal children tend to issue one or two commands and then ignore the outcome if the issue is not important" (p. 46). This chapter later discusses how parents can use natural consequences as a way to respond to undesirable child behaviors.

Consistently Applied

Containment scripts, by definition, are consistently applied. Hard-to-manage children who get away with antisocial acts are unlikely to develop a sense that they are contained by parents and restricted in their behavior. Therefore, it is incumbent on parents to shift into their containing mode whenever they witness misdeeds that are on their short list of target behaviors. To emphasize this point to parents, I often suggest to them that containment of target behaviors should ideally take place 100% of the time. This slight exaggeration also helps to reinforce the notion that parents' list of target behaviors should be very short and well thought out.

As children begin to spend less time under the supervision of parents and other caring adults, the task of consistently containing their antisocial behavior becomes increasingly difficult. Instead of discriminating between acceptable and unacceptable behaviors, older aggressive children may learn to discriminate between conditions under which they can and cannot perform antisocial acts. Even younger, well-supervised children with antisocial tendencies may be drawn to this deleterious form of discrimination training. Indeed, children who are successful and well practiced in the art of covert antisocial behavior (e.g., lying, stealing) can be difficult to contain because so many of their misdeeds go undetected. Patterson (1982) reported that some parents of covertly antisocial children are quick to contain overt aggression directed at them by their children but seem unconcerned about antisocial acts committed by their children outside the home. How common a pattern this is among the parents of covertly antisocial children is unclear, but there is evidence that children can follow an exclusively covert path on their way to later delinquency (Loeber et al., 1993). The main point, however, is that children's sense of containment is threatened when they can perform antisocial acts with impunity. Although consistently containing all target behaviors does not guarantee a sense of containment in the covertly antisocial child, it remains the right thing to do.

Fully Discharged

Patterson (1982) uses the term *confrontation* to describe parents' successful efforts to halt a child's coercive actions and reduce the likelihood of their recurrence. He observed that parents of aggressive children often threaten and nag but fail to confront their children. Following through with threats of punishment is the key in a fully discharged containment script. Parents and their aggressive children tend to engage in extended chains of coercion that typically end with parents as losers. Thus it becomes important for parents of aggressive children to be able to persist in their containment efforts, once started. Adaptive scripts will equip parents with the tools they need to bring their disciplinary efforts to a successful resolution. The idea of a fully discharged containment script brings to mind that feature of instinctual behavior that entails completion of an entire script once it is released. Similarly, containment scripts that enable parents to doggedly and more or less automatically pursue an effective halt to children's coercion are useful when parents are confronted with the spirited defiance and vigor of an aggressive child. Keep in mind, however, that with automaticity comes a loss in flexibility. Once invoked, automatic containment scripts are hard to modify, particularly if such scripts are enacted during states of high emotional arousal. Those parents who can shift easily from following through when needed to ignoring or deflecting when containment is not needed are fortunate. Because most parents of aggressive children cannot be expected to make such moment-to-moment shifts, containment scripts should be used with both caution and commitment.

Effectively Raising the Costs of Performing Antisocial Acts

For containment to be adaptive, it must lower the rewards for acting in antisocial ways. Given that children's rate of aggressive behavior tends to match the likelihood that such behavior will be reinforced (J. J. Snyder & Patterson, 1995), parents of these children must find ways to make such behavior more costly. However, it is the relative reinforcement value of a behavior that is associated with its rate of occurrence. In the context of an accepting parent–child relationship, the task of lowering the relative value of antisocial behavior is made easier because many other behaviors lead to desired payoffs. In a reinforcement-lean, nonaccepting parent–child relationship, this same task can be nearly impossible because a floor effect makes further reductions in the value of coercive behavior unlikely. The importance of an accepting context aside, parents' success at raising the costs of antisocial behavior is itself an important feature of containment.

Gauging the costs or benefits of children performing antisocial behaviors is not always easy. The most useful barometer is whether the child continues to use the offending behavior. Far less useful is the child's immediate response to containment. Most practitioners have heard parents complain that a given approach to discipline does not work. Although such complaints are often a by-product of parents' failure to follow through or be consistent, there may be other reasons why punishment seems to fail. Children with conduct problems who show high levels of callous and unemotional traits may be impervious to the disciplinary efforts of their parents (Wooten et al., 1997). Another possibility is that despite raising the costs of committing antisocial acts, parents will not see significant changes until their aggressive children have had sufficient time to appreciate the impact of containment on the parent–child relationship. Some children will require a greater number of learning trials before they change their perceptions and use of antisocial behavior. Practically speaking, this means that parents will have to persist in their use of containment even when it seems to be doing no good. As noted earlier, containing aggression and other forms of coercion serves to protect parents from being victimized and promotes their children's socialization. Even if raising the costs of antisocial behavior never leads to a significant reduction in such behavior, parents should not abandon their efforts.

Rather than focusing on the immediate impact of punishment to gauge the relative cost of aggressive behavior, parents would do better to focus on the degree to which containment restricts their child's choice of behaviors. Time-out and withdrawal of privileges are two disciplinary techniques designed to do just that. The reasoning behind this recommendation is that children, left to their own devices, will behave in ways that optimize their payoffs. Therefore, restricting their choice of behaviors is likely to result in a drop in the payoffs for antisocial behavior. Sometimes parents are concerned that their aggressive children do not protest or seem bothered when punished. Restricting a child's choice of behaviors may not elicit complaints, but parents should recognize that the costs of antisocial behavior are affected when there is a reduction in children's autonomy.

Feasibly Sustained

Socializing an aggressive child can be a lengthy, arduous process. Parents need to be equipped for the long haul. Containment scripts that carry a lot of punch but cannot be sustained over time are not adaptive. The most useful containment scripts can be enacted repeatedly and with minimal cost to parents. Only in these instances will parents be able to sustain the kind of containment that is needed to meet the conditions of a socializing relationship. Of course, differences in parents' abilities and motivation will greatly influence the durability of a given containment script. Individual differences aside, however, there are ways that parents can modify their scripts to reduce the costs of containment and render them more sustainable. In fact, the primary reason parents should consider using a set script is to manage the costs of containment. Later, I review the components of containment and discuss specific ways that parents can make their scripts less costly and more sustainable.

Nonviolent

This last characteristic of adaptive containment should be obvious, but the prohibition against violent forms of discipline bears repeating. For one thing, parents who currently use violent forms of discipline often do so in a scripted manner. Violent parents generally act out during conditions of high stress and overarousal, and their reactions to children can become rather automatic (Wekrerle & Wolfe, 1996). Violent disciplinary scripts can possess many other features of adaptive containment (e.g., consistently applied, seldom invoked). However, increasingly intense physical punishment is abusive and leads to more, not less, antisocial behavior. This seems to be true regardless of how normative physical punishment might be in the family subculture (Deater-Deckard & Dodge, 1997).

A Four-Step Model of Containment

I offer here a fairly simple, step-by-step procedure for understanding and implementing child containment. The first three steps—*instruct, warn,* and *sanction*—are common foci of disciplinary skills training. Via these three steps, children learn about limits on specific behaviors, are warned of the consequences that will follow if limits are not heeded, and are then sanctioned for crossing these limits. Most readers should be familiar with these three steps, although the terms *command* and *punish* are often used in place of *instruct* and *sanction*, respectively. Practitioners who have not seen these skills performed effectively should either view a set of commercially available videotapes (e.g., Webster-Stratton, 1987) or ask their supervisor or an experienced colleague to model these skills. These steps also parallel the three-step procedure used in CREFT (L. F. Guerney, 1983) to set limits on children's behavior during play. I make this point so readers are aware of this link between acceptance skills training and containment skills training. Parents who have mastered the procedure for setting limits during play are thus well positioned to benefit from containment skills training. The fourth step in this procedure—*reconnecting*—is probably less familiar to most. I use the term *reconnecting* to describe a specific kind of parent–child interaction in which parents reaffirm their reasons for imposing a sanction but remind children of their place in the family. Table 6.1 summarizes and gives examples of this four-step procedure.

Table 6.1.   The Four-Step Approach to Containment and Other Related Skills

Approach	Explanation (example)
Four steps to containment	
1. Instruct	State the limit in a clear, firm, and direct manner. Change your facial expression, posture, and voice so that your child knows you are serious about containment. (e.g., "Sally, we can't drive off until you put your seat belt on.")
2. Warn	If your child fails to follow the instruction, state the limit again, and inform you child of the ensuing sanctions. (e.g., "Sally, if you don't buckle your seat belt, I'll have to leave you here with Grandma.")
3. Sanction	If your child fails to heed the warning, impose the sanction as indicated. (e.g., "Sally, you're going to stay here with Grandma.")
4. Reconnect	When suitable, calmly emphasize these three main points: your child is accepted; your child will be contained; and the misdeed is incongruent with the family's values. (e.g., "Sally, you are a valued member of this family, and I love you dearly. However, I can't let you ride in the car without a seat belt. That is not what we do. It's too dangerous.")

Skill	*Optional skills* Suggestion (example)
Reflect	Reflect your child's comments, feelings, and desires. (e.g., "Sally, I know you don't like seat belts, but you have to wear one.")
Redirect	Redirect your child to more appropriate behavior. (e.g., "Sally, I don't mind your complaining about the seat belt, but I can't let you ride unbuckled.")
Reason	Give your child a reason for the limit. (e.g., "Sally, it's just too risky to ride without a seat belt.")

Instructions

Instruction is the task of conveying simply and clearly that a given behavior is not allowed. Of course, instructions can also be used to request a specific behavior of children. However, given the emphasis here on enforcing *don't* commands, I restrict my discussion to parental prohibitions. The manner in which parents deliver their instructions can be a major determinant of their child's compliance (Roberts, McMahon, Forehand, & Humphreys, 1978; Roberts & Powers, 1988). This is particularly true for parents who perceive themselves as lacking in power. Children tend to tune out less powerful parents who are more likely to use ambiguous instructions (Bugental, Lyon, Lin, McGrath, & Bimbela, 1999). The most effective are instructions that address in plainly understood language a single behavior at a time. For example, imagine a mother whose neighbor asks her to watch her 4-year-old son (Cedric) for an hour even though this mother is cooking dinner and supervising her own 8-year-old son (Tony) and 9-year-old daughter (Joyce). Now imagine that Cedric stands absentmindedly between Tony and the television. The mother looks in just as Tony pushes Cedric out of his line of vision. A simple instruction that could be used in this instance is "Tony, don't push Cedric." Less specific and presumably less effective instructions include "I saw that!" "What are you doing?" "Do I need to go in there and deal with you?" or "Don't make me come in there!" The value of the first instruction is in its simplicity and clarity. Also, the use of Tony's name can help gain his attention so he actually hears the instruction given by his mother. Of course, starting an instruction with a child's name is no guarantee that the child will hear it. Also helpful in gaining a child's attention are the nonverbal cues parents use to package their instruction. Included here are such factors as parents' proximity to the child; whether they are standing or sitting; the use of gestures; the degree of contact made; and the volume, tone, and firmness of a parent's voice. Parents can use these cues to convey in a more convincing way that they have temporarily altered their posture of acceptance and have now shifted into a potentially containing mode. The use of nonverbal cues may be especially helpful to parents whose manner of speaking is less imposing than that of others.

Orgel (1980), borrowing from Ginott (1976), suggested a slightly different twist in instruction giving that would seem particularly helpful when the instructions involve *don't* commands. Orgel recommends that parents shy away from such direct commands as "Tony, don't push Cedric!" He argues that a better, more relationship-sensitive technique is to place emphasis on the "offending" action or object and not on the child himself or herself. In the example above, Orgel's twist might yield the following instruction, "Tony, Cedric is not for pushing." Orgel suggests this approach is less damning of the child's feelings (e.g., anger) and desires (to watch television) but retains a clear focus on the limits of behavior. I know of no empirical study that has examined the value of this approach. My clinical experience suggests it has some merit but it is fairly awkward to use. I believe there is value in giving instructions that do not sound overly critical, but parents cannot be expected to learn to speak in such odd ways. My own variant of Orgel's recommendation also emphasizes the offending action but carries with it the implication that parents are allies in children's prosocial development. The key to this variant is the use of *I* and *we* language. Staying with the example above, Tony's mother could say "Tony, we don't push people in this house" or "Tony, I'm not going to let you push Cedric like that." This type of instruction is more than a simple prohibition against pushing; it is a direct reminder of parents' prosocial beliefs and their commitment to enforce those beliefs for the sake of all family members. It is also a lot easier to use. Of course, as with Orgel's approach, this manner of instruction giving has not been examined empirically.

Warnings

Parental warnings are statements made to children that typically convey two points. The first is a reminder of a previously given instruction and the second is notice of the consequence that will follow any recurrence of the misbehavior. For example, in the above situation involving Tony, a warning from his mother might be "Tony, I've told you that we don't push. If you push again, I'll have to put you in time-out." Warnings can serve a number of important functions, most of which relate to the potential to avoid the use of sanctions. If parents can contain aggression and other antisocial acts without using sanctions, the parent–child relationship benefits from not having to endure the emotional costs of a disciplinary conflict. Given that sustaining an emotionally positive parent–child relationship is fundamental to the socialization of aggressive children, warnings and other parenting techniques that lower the frequency of parent–child conflict are valuable training targets. Warnings can also be helpful to parents whose children are highly impulsive or cognitively immature. Such children may find themselves frequently ensnared in parents' sanctions unless they are given a warning. Warnings can also serve as a reminder to children of a standing rule. For example, instead of responding to Tony's pushing with an instruction to cease, his mother could have responded with a warning if the family already had a rule about not pushing others (see chapter 8, this volume, for a discussion of household rules).

There are times when a warning is not appropriate. Consider, for example, if Tony had not simply pushed Cedric out of his line of vision but had kicked him roughly in the back. Both actions are aggressive, but one is more violent than the other. If such a violent act as kicking Cedric in the back occurs infrequently, Tony's mother would be remiss if she only warned him. Rather than learning that aggression is not allowed, Tony may learn that aggression is okay if used in certain situations or in certain ways (e.g., only one). Given the importance of containing aggression and other severe forms of coercion, I generally advise parents to eschew warnings when children act aggressively. Frankly, many parents cannot and should not have to decide whether a certain act of aggression is violent enough to bypass a warning. Therefore, warnings can serve helpful functions in parents' efforts to contain their children, but like most parenting skills, warnings must be used judiciously.

Sanctions

Effective use of instructions and warnings can reduce but not eliminate the need for parental sanctions. Parents of aggressive children also need to use effective sanctions. Practitioners should recognize that it is the advice on the use of sanctions that parents of aggressive children most want to hear. Because parents are often reluctant or unable to let go of current methods of discipline, even if these are not working, I try to avoid pushing a particular type of sanction. Instead, I present parents with a number of options and then discuss with them the pros and cons of each type of sanction. Figure 6.1 is an attempt to categorize different sanctions based on two important parameters. The first parameter is whether the sanction involves the imposition or removal of a stimulus. The second parameter is whether the sanction can be imposed by parents alone or whether it requires the cooperation of the child. From this two-by-two typology come four distinct ways to impose sanctions.

The first sanction, *response cost*, involves parents removing from or not presenting to the child a previously attractive object or activity. The term reflects the fact that a child's response has resulted in a cost. This kind of sanction is often referred to as a *loss* or a *withdrawal of privileges*. Older children usually experience this sanction as grounding. The primary advantage to the response–cost method is that it is perhaps the easiest to use. Taking away a valued game, toy, activity, or privilege can typically be done without the child's cooperation. Of course, aggressive children often challenge and circumvent parents' use of response costs, so in that sense parents do need their children's cooperation. But compared to other sanctions, response–cost methods are primarily parent driven.

There are ways that parents can minimize the chance that children sabotage response–cost efforts. These essentially involve having strict control over the child's access to the desired object or activity. For example, taking away the privilege of playing a video game is less easily circumvented if the games are placed in a locked and secure place (e.g., the trunk of a car). Also, withdrawing a privilege is made easier if it can only happen with parents' cooperation. The best example of this involves occasions when children need to be driven to a desired event or activity. Even the most timid of parents can use this sanction successfully by simply refusing to drive the car. In this example, parents not only act alone (i.e., without the child) but also remain passive (e.g., do not act at all) to impose the sanction. Parents who have the luxury of providing their children with an allowance, however meager, can also use this "passive" response–cost approach when they refuse to give the full allowance to children who act aggressively.

Another commonly used form of passive response cost is the practice of letting children suffer the *natural consequences* of their actions. For most aggressive children, there exist myriad punishing consequences that naturally follow their undesirable actions, even if parents never lifted a finger to contain them. At school, children may be criticized or ostracized by peers for acting rudely, and they may miss the opportunity for extracurricular activities if their classroom behavior is poor or their academic work is unsatisfactory. At home, aggressive children have to endure the costs of breaking their own toys or failing to complete their homework in time for a favorite television show. Of course, some parents may actually interfere with the occurrence of natural consequences because they are uncomfortable witnessing their children struggle or complain about any ensuing hardship.

The primary disadvantages to the response–cost method—aside from the possibility that children will work around the imposed sanction—is that it may have minimal effect on the relative cost of acting antisocially. Children with little adult supervision, abundant material possessions, or a laundry list of daily or weekly activities may be nonplussed by the loss of a single possession or activity. However, if parents keep in mind the goal of raising the relative cost of antisocial behavior, they may be able to make response–cost an effective sanction. For example, among teenagers who drive, little else costs them as dearly as taking away their access to a vehicle. There are also disadvantages to using natural consequences when the goal of containment is children's use of aggressive and antisocial acts. Allowing siblings and peers to counterattack when a child hits them may be a reliable and natural consequence of childhood aggression, but it is unlikely to benefit anyone involved. Also, relying solely on natural consequences as a way to sanction increasingly irresponsible and antisocial behavior is unlikely to increase a child's sense of containment. The costs are often too far removed from the misconduct and the sanctions are generally not imposed by a prosocial adult who also accepts them.

Another caveat regarding the use of response cost relates to its reusability. Parents who raise the costs of a response too high or do so too quickly may find that they have prematurely exhausted their ability to impose sanctions. Recall the scenario involving Tony and Cedric. If his mother takes away a privilege (e.g., television viewing) for the next several days, she cannot use this same sanction the next day. In other words, children may be little affected by losing what is already lost, even if the period of loss is extended. Practitioners may need to help parents adjust the duration of a response–cost period to fit the frequency with which their children act aggressively. A once-a-week infraction rate would allow for a multiple-day response–cost period. However, a once-per-day infraction rate would require a briefer response–cost period. This task is made difficult, of course, by the aforementioned possibility that a brief response–cost period may have little effect on the relative value of acting aggressively. In balancing these competing demands, I typically advise parents to err in the direction of greater reusability rather than in the direction of increased cost. I base this recommendation on two points: (a) the recognition that socializing an aggressive child is a process that takes place over several years and (b) the possibility that heavy-handed use of response costs can leave some aggressive children feeling bankrupted and believing there is nothing left to lose. Such sentiments are the seeds of disaffection and can lead too often to a sense of alienation. Therefore, I see serious risks to using sanctions that drive children in this dangerous direction.

Physical discipline is a second type of sanction available to parents. Physical discipline can involve holding a child or spanking a child. For most school-age children, physical restraint or holding is no longer a reasonable option, although it can be a useful tool when establishing time-out (see below). Physical discipline differs from response cost in that it involves the presentation of a presumably aversive stimulus. It is similar to response cost in that it does not depend on the cooperation of the child to any great degree.

An important caveat regarding parents' use of physical discipline is, of course, its potential to lead to physically abusive parenting. Spanking, more so than holding, also represents a relatively violent form of sanction even at nonabusive levels. This fact can be particularly problematic if parents are hoping to promote a general family rule of "no hitting" or "no hurting." There is also evidence that even mild or infrequent spanking is associated with children's greater use of peer aggression (Strassberg, Dodge, Pettit, & Bates, 1994). On the other hand, surveys of parents in this country typically find that 80 to 90% report having spanked their child (Strauss & Gelles, 1990). If the base rate for psychopathology during and after childhood is less than 80 to 90%, then one would have to conclude that many spanked children are not maladjusted. In a review of 166 empirical studies on the topic of spanking, Larzelere (1996) found only 35 that were adequately designed. Of these, 26% found mainly beneficial effects of spanking, 34% found predominantly detrimental outcomes, and 40% found neutral outcomes. Recent work has also shown that both the level and the context of spanking are important parameters in determining whether a child's functioning is helped, hurt, or unaffected by physical discipline. For example, Deater-Deckard and Dodge (1997) found that physical discipline by African American parents was not related to children's level of externalizing behavior except when it reached abusive levels. However, nonabusive physical discipline was significantly related to externalizing behaviors when the relationship between African American parents and their children was relatively cold. Deater-Deckard and Dodge (1997) also found preliminary evidence that African American parents view spanking as compatible with a generally positive approach to parenting (unlike European American parents). Therefore, practitioners should be cautious about assuming that spanking, especially by African American parents, is either causing children's aggression or is indicative of a poor parent–child relationship. Unknown at this point is whether the use of physical discipline differs in cold versus warm parent–child relationships. If it does, then practitioners will need to attend to the emotional tenor of the parent–child relationship when deciding if physical discipline is perhaps damaging to a child. As suggested by the work of Deater-Deckard and Dodge (1997), assessing parents' beliefs about physical discipline may be a convenient way to determine the emotional context of future spankings.

Importantly, studies of spanking and other forms of nonabusive physical discipline do not support the use of physical discipline as an effective way to reduce children's level of aggression. Such a finding may be difficult to detect, however, given the many other differences that exist between spanking and nonspanking parents. Experimental studies that examine the effects of varying levels of spanking within emotionally positive parent–child relationships are needed, although it seems that such studies would be nearly impossible to conduct. An alternative approach would be to assess the effects of improving the emotional quality of the parent–child relationship in families that currently rely on spanking as a disciplinary technique. The results of such a study would be particularly helpful to practitioners who, wisely enough, are reluctant to criticize parents unwilling to halt their use of spanking. In fact, the most reasonable strategy regarding physical discipline as a type of sanction is to educate and assist parents who do use it, but to not recommend it to parents who have not used it. This strategy is at odds with parent training programs that train parents to spank children who are escaping from time-out (e.g., Forehand & McMahon, 1981; Hembree-Kigin & McNeil, 1995). If parents are not currently using spanking, then one would suspect that these parents view spanking as an overly harsh form of discipline. For practitioners to recommend it may seem odd and perhaps misinterpreted as permission to act more harshly. For parents who do use spanking, educating them on ways they can reduce its harmful effects makes considerable sense. Such work will need to be informed by an assessment of (a) the quality of the parent–child relationship, (b) parents' beliefs about physical discipline, and (c) the particulars of how and when parents presently use physical discipline. This approach is likely to be much more productive when working with parents who have settled, more or less, on nonabusive physical discipline as their sanction of choice.

One of the most widely recommended sanctions is *time-out*. As Figure 6.1 shows, time-out is similar to response cost in that a previously attractive stimulus is removed. However, it differs from both response cost and physical discipline in that its successful implementation does require some level of cooperation on the part of the child. Unless a child remains in the time-out spot, time-out does not exist. Some parents may lock a child in a room, thereby obviating the need for their cooperation, but I typically advise parents against this practice. I question both its safety and its usefulness, especially if children are free to be destructive or self-injurious when behind locked doors. Therefore, I see time-out as distinct from those sanctions that can be imposed without children's cooperation. The term *time-out* is actually shorthand for "time-out from reinforcement" and it refers to the fact that placing a child in an isolated area prevents access to normally available reinforcers. This is an important point to cover with parents who restrict children to a bedroom equipped with an array of modern conveniences (e.g., television, CD player, video games) that allow continued access to reinforcing stimuli. Conducting time-out in a reinforcement-lean environment is not the only feature to address, how-

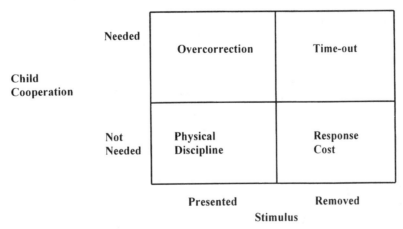

Figure 6.1. Sanctions parents can use to raise the cost of misbehavior.

ever. There are other aspects of time-out that one should also consider. Some view time-out as an opportunity for out-of-control children to calm down. When viewed this way, adults may instruct children to take voluntary time-outs when feeling upset or angry. There certainly is value in using time-out in this way, although I would question the applicability of this approach for aggressive, school-age children. Those who possess both the ability and the motivation to take a voluntary time-out are unlikely to be severely aggressive.

A more meaningful perspective is to recognize that a child remaining in time-out—without benefit of a locked door or parents' physical restraint —is exercising self-control. Admittedly, the duration and level of self-control that some aggressive children display in time-out is extremely limited. Nevertheless, I have often marveled at the potential socializing power inherent in a child's decision to remain in an assigned area when they could easily walk away. Although some severely antisocial children (e.g., those who engage in primarily covert acts) may go willingly to time-out, most are likely to resist or escape. Therefore, a decision to remain in time-out when told to do so by parents can represent an important interaction in the history of the parent–child relationship. Unlike response cost and physical discipline, children who remain in time-out are deferring (at least temporarily) to parental authority. In short, time-out is a kind of two-for-one sanction: Not only does it raise the relative cost of committing antisocial acts, it is also more conducive to the larger goal of instilling in children a sense of containment.

The added features of time-out come at a cost, however. Because some degree of child cooperation is required, time-out is a more difficult sanction to use. More accurately stated, time-out is a much harder sanction to start. Effectively establishing time-out is critical to its success. In my experience, parents who label time-out as a technique that "didn't work" almost never established time-out in the first place. Establishing time-out means that parents have used it at least once successfully, and they are able to reuse it as a sanction whenever necessary. Recall that reusability is an important aspect of containment scripts that are feasibly sustained by parents. For time-out to be feasibly reused, children must remain in time-out with minimal insistence on the part of parents. Once children no longer try to escape from time-out, it becomes a convenient and effective parental sanction. Therefore, it is not time-out that "didn't work" for many aggressive children; what didn't work was parents' attempt to establish time-out. The point is not merely a semantic one. Once children learn that time-out is an inevitable consequence of their misbehavior, they are much less likely to resist its reuse. However, it is true that establishing time-out can be a trying task for parents of aggressive children. Indeed, asking parents to establish time-out with an aggressive child can be one of the most demanding tasks given to them. Many will refuse to do so on the grounds that their child cannot be made to stay in time-out.

Sometimes parents are correct in asserting that time-out is an inappropriate sanction for them to use with their child. Other adults may be successful in getting their child to remain in time-out, and other children may stay in time-out when told to do so by these parents. But for certain parent–child dyads, time-out is not a viable option. Child factors to consider here include the child's age, size, and history of defiance and violence. Parent factors to consider include parents' size and health, their level of perceived power within the family, and their history of violence. These are important factors because attempts to establish time-out often depend on parents' ability to impose a different sanction if the child attempts to escape; typically that sanction is physical discipline. Rather than advising parents to spank to enforce time-out, I generally recommend physical restraint or holding (McNeil, Clemens-Mowrer, Gurwitch, & Funderburk, 1994). Thus, if children resist staying in time-out, parents may have to physically restrain them until they agree to stay on their own. Given this possibility, practitioners should be cautious about asking parents to establish time-out if their use of physical discipline is likely to be unsuccessful or violent (Lutzker, 1994). The child and parent factors listed above are important considerations when making these judgments, but definitive criteria for these variables do not exist.

Parents who are unable or unwilling to impose physical discipline can use an alternative set of tactics for establishing time-out. The most obvious is to place the child in a room and lock the door. Again, there are significant risks associated with this tactic, but some parents report using it successfully. Roberts (1988) trained mothers of defiant preschoolers to use it effectively. A less obvious tactic is to use a more severe response–cost sanction as a way to enforce time-out. The advantage of this approach is that it avoids the use of physical force and allows parents to use a potentially powerful (but less reusable) sanction to establish a different, potentially powerful (but reusable) sanction. I am unaware of empirical studies that have evaluated the benefits of using this combination with aggressive children, but it appears to be a reasonable hypothesis.

A third tactic, oddly enough, is sheer persistence. This is an even more speculative notion than the others, but it is based on my experience with parents (usually mothers) who were not successful in their attempts to establish time-out. Children who experienced mothers persisting but failing in their initial attempts to establish time-out sometimes decided that resistance was not worth the effort. I suspect that these persistent parents made the value of remaining in time-out more attractive than the value of resisting. Children whose parents are willing to be persistent are fortunate indeed, and I often remind parents that persistence is itself a message to children about what is and is not acceptable behavior.

A final tactic to consider is one in which children are apprised beforehand of parents' intentions to begin using time-out. What little research has been conducted on this tactic is not wholly supportive, however (e.g., Roberts, 1984). The lack of positive findings may mean that children prone to aggressive and oppositional behavior are unlikely to lower their resistance to time-out simply because parents tell them about it ahead of time. As a practitioner, I routinely recommend this tactic, but I downplay the likelihood that it will lower a child's resistance to time-out. I still recommend it because children should know if there is to be a major shift in their parents' choice of sanctions. Little purpose is served when parents surprise children with their decision to use time-out. I also modify the tactic of forewarning children by framing time-out as a way for parents to help children learn to be less aggressive. Therefore, I ask children to help their parents select the particulars of how time-out is to be used in their home. Of course, it is much easier to sell this to younger children than to older children, who are more likely to be suspicious of parents' help. And there are some parameters of time-out that are not negotiable. One is when (i.e., for which misdeeds) time-out is to be used, and the other is whether children will have to remain by themselves. Still, it can be empowering to children when they help make decisions about where time-out will take place, how long it will last, whether they will stand or sit, whether they must be quiet or not, and which clock parents will use to gauge the length of time-out. These are merely suggested areas in which parents have some latitude; parents may want to bend on some and not others. Asking children to coconstruct the details of their sanctions can be used with any of the sanctions discussed in this chapter. Although it remains to be seen whether this tactic can reduce children's resistance to sanctions, it does afford parents an opportunity to build a "partnership" with their aggressive children on a topic that can be emotionally charged. Parents' efforts to form such partnerships—even when it does not lead to less resistance—can help keep children invested in the family and its values.

The time-out parameters that I see as negotiable may surprise readers who are used to viewing time-out in more definitive ways. Most parent training programs specify precisely where and how time-out is to be administered (e.g., Forehand & McMahon, 1981). Most programs recommend that time-out should last about 1 minute for each year of the child's age, that children sit and remain seated, and that children be quiet during or prior to release from time-out. I view all three of these recommendations as expendable because they are not so essential to the successful use of time-out that parents can implement time-out only with these features in place. Recall my earlier points regarding both the importance and the challenge of establishing time-out with an aggressive child. I see little reason to make the task of establishing time-out more challenging by adding requirements that are not fundamental (Roberts, 1982; Roberts & Powers, 1990). If time-out (a) is used primarily as a sanction for acts of aggression (and other behaviors on the five-or-less list) and (b) is conducted in a relatively nonreinforcing setting, and (c) children remain there without door locks or physical restraint, then the critical features are achieved. This perspective implies that children might stand up, complain loudly, and remain in time-out for far less than 1 minute per each year of their age. If parents insist on children's adherence to these nonessential features, they may be fighting the wrong battles. Whenever I discuss these more expendable features of time-out, I am reminded of the joke about a group of "thugs" who do all sorts of unspeakable acts to someone as the victim's friend looks on and laughs. The friend had been told by the thugs to stay behind a line drawn in the dirt and was laughing because he had been able to step over the line several times during the assault. Whatever humor lies in this joke is due to the fact that the amused friend seems clueless about the thugs' abuse of power and what is really important. Similarly, I would prefer that parents focus on the most essential elements of time-out rather than its nonessential elements. In sum, I want them to appreciate the value of successfully insisting that their child remain in an area when absolutely no one was holding them. Whether their child is standing, yelling, or demonstrating only brief moments of self-restraint is less important. This last point is a key one. Some aggressive children may stay in time-out for only a few seconds initially. To call such a brief stay *time-out* may seem preposterous, but a few seconds is often a reasonable start when the goal is to establish time-out as a reusable sanction.

It is hard to overemphasize how important it is to successfully plan parents' efforts to establish time-out. This is because a lot is at stake if parents fail, but more importantly, a lot can be gained if parents succeed. In fact, I would hypothesize that the regular use of time-out is associated with relatively less improvement in aggressive children's behavior than that realized when time-out is first established. This rather provocative hypothesis should underscore what I see as most important to know and to teach about time-out. Besides making sure that parents understand and can execute the skills needed to place a child in time-out, I prepare them for the challenge ahead by making three additional recommendations. First, I discourage them from attempting to establish time-out unless they have the time to devote to it. For some parents and children, this could mean 30 minutes and for others this could mean several hours over multiple days! Second, I encourage parents to be fully rested before forging ahead. Finally, I strongly advise those parents with partners to schedule their initial attempts at time-out during a time when partners are there to lend emotional support. I do not recommend that partners assist physically because to do so would dilute the first parent's efforts to build a relationship with the child that sends a clear message of containment. In addition to making these recommendations, I also try to inoculate parents against the sheer "messiness" that can occur when an earnest attempt at time-out is made. I describe for them the possibility that they will be worn physically and spent emotionally by the time they are done. I also let parents know, however, that once they get beyond the messiness of children's frantic, initial escape efforts, subsequent efforts to use time-out are often much easier.

The last type of sanction listed in Figure 6.1 is *overcorrection*. Like time-out, overcorrection requires the cooperation of the child; unlike time-out, which strives to remove children from readily available reinforcing stimuli, overcorrection involves presenting children with unattractive, punishing stimuli. Typically, these punishing stimuli involve some kind of chore or work. In fact, the phrase *correcting work* may be a more accurate description of what is involved. The *over* part of *overcorrection* refers to the practice of having children do more than is needed to repair whatever damage they have done. For example, a child who punches a hole in a wall may be given the work of repairing the hole and then painting all the walls in the room. When a child damages another person physically or emotionally, parents will have to be more creative in their use of overcorrection. For example, the aggressive child may be asked to provide the injured party with a combination of completed chores, special favors, and sincere apologies.

The primary advantage to using overcorrection is that children not only endure the costs of acting antisocially, but they are also required to act prosocially. Therefore, overcorrection might help to promote both a sense of containment and a sense of prosocial efficacy. Overcorrection can even be used to promote a child's sense of acceptance. This is possible when parents join with children in completing the correcting chore. Such joint efforts can lead to temporary partnerships between parent and child that produce an outcome for which they can both be proud.

Because of the potential benefits associated with overcorrection, it is an important sanction for parents to consider. There are also disadvantages to its use, however. The most obvious disadvantage is that aggressive children may not comply with parents' request to do the correcting work. Parents may be able to use physical prompts to get younger children to comply, but this approach is unlikely to work with older children. Parents can use time-out or response cost to enforce compliance with overcorrection, and some of the techniques designed to reduce children's resistance to time-out may be helpful (see above), particularly having children coconstruct the overcorrection plan. One problem with this last approach, and a second disadvantage of overcorrection, is that parents and children may create a plan that has a negligible impact on the relative costs of acting antisocially. For example, if the only sanction for an aggressive act is a curt "Sorry," then children are unlikely to feel contained. Parents and children may enjoy the short-term drop in conflict, but they are likely to suffer from a long-term increase in acts of aggression.

The four types of sanction described above offer a variety of advantages and disadvantages. Sanctions that are easier to use tend to be less effective than sanctions that require the child's participation. Therefore, an important role for practitioners is to guide parents as they select and learn to use the type of sanction that works best for them and their child.

Reconnecting

It is imperative that parents place strict limits on their children's use of aggressive actions. And yet, that goal may yield little in the way of increased socialization if children withdraw emotionally and relationally from the family system. Connell (1990) has described *disaffected children* as those whose sense of self is organized around beliefs, perceptions, and feelings that one is not tied relationally to others in their home, school, or peer environments. Although we do not typically think of children as disaffected or alienated, these attributes are often characteristic of aggressive children whose parents find it difficult to balance strong containment with consistent acceptance. Parents often sense the growing distance between the target child and the rest of the family, but they may not be able to articulate or stop it. To make the phenomenon of relational distancing or disaffection more concrete, I have given young clients a sheet of paper and asked them to draw a circle representing their family. I then ask them to place an *X* on the spot that depicts their position vis-à-vis the family. Disaffected children typically make marks on, near, or beyond the perimeter. Their marks are sometimes accompanied by statements that everybody hates them, that they are the bad child, or that no one cares about or understands them. To help parents appreciate their child's sense of disaffection, I have occasionally assigned the task of reading "Baa Baa Black-sheep," a short story by Rudyard Kipling (1982). This story, told in the first person, is about a boy whose parents are living abroad and who feels misunderstood and rejected by his temporary caregiver. The boy's ensuing misbehavior is closely tied to his feelings of disaffection. Not all parents are capable of benefitting from this exercise, but for those who can this story effectively illustrates how a child's sense of alienation can lead to even more coercive behavior.

The notion that parental discipline can influence children's sense of commitment to the family has received little attention from researchers who develop and evaluate parent training programs. Consider, for example, the parenting practice usually recommended for a child who has just been punished via time-out. Most training programs advise parents to reinforce children for any subsequent acts of desirable behavior (e.g., complying with a command). If parents' goal was to maintain their child's investment in the family system, it is unclear that contingently reinforcing a child for preferred behavior after a time-out punishment is the most effective plan. In fact, there may be an unrecognized down side to this strategy. Harter and colleagues (Harter, Marold, Whitesell, & Cobbs, 1996) found that highly contingent parenting was associated with adolescents' tendency to engage in *false self behavior*, a pattern of behavior characterized by a lack of commitment and a heightened risk for psychopathology. Thus, parents who want to keep children invested in the family's value system may need to use a different strategy when limiting children's use of aggression.

Rather than viewing the postpunishment period simply as a time to look for and reward good behavior, families may benefit if it is viewed as a chance to debrief and *reconnect* emotionally with difficult children. Framed in this way, the postpunishment phase becomes an opportunity to clarify the message behind parents' discipline and to correct any possible misinterpretations children may have. More importantly, postpunishment encounters can serve to repair any emotional damage incurred by the parent–child relationship as a result of needed containment. I often describe this approach as one of bringing children back into the fold after they have been disciplined and after the bad behavior has been halted. This strategy also reflects a shift from parents' role as adversary to that of collaborative partner interested in resolving the issues that led originally to the disciplinary conflict.

Importantly, parents should not pursue a reconnecting exchange before a sanction is imposed. However, there appears to be little danger in reconnecting if it occurs after children have completed their sanction. For example, if a sanction is used to enforce compliance with a *do* command (e.g., take out the garbage), then complying with that request should be a prerequisite to parents' efforts to reaffirm their child's place in the family. If parents reconnect without first insisting on compliance, children are essentially reinforced for actions that allowed them to escape parental demands. Because I have argued that containing aggressive children should emphasize prohibitions against aggressive and coercive acts (i.e, *don't* commands) and not the enforcement of *do* commands, the likelihood of this kind of mistake occurring should be minimal. One exception to waiting until the postpunishment period before reconnecting is when parental sanctions take several hours or days to implement. For example, response–cost sanctions (e.g., withdrawing privileges) often take longer to implement than an 8- to 10-minute time-out. If a boy loses a Saturday morning privilege because he committed a transgression on Tuesday, should his parents wait till Saturday afternoon to pursue the goal of keeping their son in the fold? Aggressive children are certainly not likely to wait till Saturday afternoon before expressing their discontent over the sanction. Notwithstanding the issue of a consequence being too far removed from the transgression, I see parents' efforts to keep children connected to the family as beneficial even as children continue to endure the burden of imposed sanctions. As long as parents do not give in to children's complaints or protests, the parent–child relationship is likely to profit when parents remain supportive while children experience and learn from the unyielding nature of parents' limits.

Presumably, the manner by which parents reconnect with their children after an imposed sanction can vary greatly. Unfortunately, parents' behavior during the postpunishment period has not been systematically studied. The following example offers suggestions for teaching parents about reconnecting, but the lack of empirical research makes it difficult to recommend one technique above the others. Recall Tony, the boy who had pushed Cedric. Imagine that Tony's mother feels it necessary to put Tony in time-out for his aggressive actions. Once time-out is over, his mother can look for a chance to visit with him briefly. If he returns immediately to watching television or is so angry that any interaction will lead to an escalation of conflict, then his mother is wise to wait until later. I would recommend—when she and Tony are both ready for a brief interaction—that the mother reconnect with Tony by emphasizing three main points: First and foremost is that Tony remains a valued member of the family despite the earlier disciplinary conflict. Second, his mother is committed to containing his aggressive behavior through the use of needed sanctions. Finally, his aggressive acts are not in keeping with the values and beliefs of their family. An example of how all this might be phrased is as follows:

> Tony, I know you didn't like being put in time-out. I didn't like it either because I love you and you are important to me and important to this

family. However, I'm not going to let you hurt other children. Each time you push or hit, I will put you back in time-out. In our family, we don't hurt others.

The three goals of reconnecting—all reflected in this brief encounter—represent the three conditions necessary for parent–child relationships to have a socializing influence on aggressive children. In this one interaction, Tony's mother touches on acceptance, containment, and prosocial values. The fact that all three socializing components are involved in the post-punishment reconnection may explain why the process of struggling and working through conflict is such a pivotal aspect of positive, transforming relationships (e.g., Stoolmiller et al., 1993). The effective use of containment that includes regular reconnecting is also a useful way to integrate differing views about discipline from the developmental and the clinical literatures (Larzelere, Sather, Schneider, Larson, & Pike, 1998). Larzelere and his colleagues noted that developmental studies with nonselect samples of children tend to support the value of parents' use of reasoning or induction. Clinical models of effective discipline place emphasis on strict limits and decry the overuse of verbal interchanges. With a procedure like reconnecting, parents can impose strict limits without unwittingly reinforcing escape behavior, and they can address the reasons for the limits in a more inductive manner.

Summary

The four-step approach to containment offered here is meant to form the foundation for parents' containment scripts. Parents who can successfully apply these four steps have a greater chance of not being victimized, of promoting their child's sense of containment, and of limiting the exchange of negative emotion with their children. Parents of aggressive children may possess the ability to perform some of these steps, but perhaps not all. More importantly, they may need help in recognizing the importance of being an effective and consistent container of their child's antisocial behavior. Therefore, a critical task for practitioners is helping parents of aggressive children build a containment script that is effective and likely to be used. Parents' choice of sanctions is a key feature of that script. Parents and practitioners will need to keep in mind both the advantages and the disadvantages of each type of sanction. Practitioners will also have to teach parents the value of and skills for punctuating their containment scripts with a reconnecting encounter. By reconnecting with aggressive children, parents move closer to providing the full complement of their socializing influence.

Optional Containment Skills

The four-step approach to containment is generally all that parents of aggressive children will need. However, other skills and techniques that may further improve the quality of parental containment exist. These skills are not included in the four-step model, and practitioners should view them as options that parents may or may not build into their limit-setting scripts. These optional skills can also be used to enhance the likelihood that aggressive children will comply with requests for behaviors that are not on parents' short list. Because most of the behaviors requested of aggressive children are not behaviors that parents must strictly and consistently enforce, parents may want to use these optional skills to promote their child's cooperation. Table 6.1 summarizes and gives examples of these optional skills. I organize my discussion of these skills around the functions they can serve.

Skills to Improve Children's Immediate Response to Containment

What can parents do to increase the odds that discipline will go smoothly and that children will be less likely to resist their containment efforts? For parents of aggressive children, perhaps not much. However, it still may be useful to consider skills that can potentially facilitate a child's response to parental discipline. Aggressive children are not uniform in their opposition to discipline, and techniques supported by research with nonaggressive samples may prove beneficial to some parents with aggressive children. I am referring to techniques that can soften or enhance parents' use of emotionally charged, power-assertive discipline. Although intense parental emotion can occasionally lead quickly and quietly to a child's compliance, it can also disrupt and undermine parents' socialization goals.

To soften containment scripts that rely too heavily on intense power-assertive tactics, parents have three options: redirecting, reflecting, and reasoning. *Redirecting* refers to the technique of coupling an instruction with a description of what is permitted. For example, a child who violates a family rule by bringing toys into the kitchen can be reminded that it is okay to play with the toys in the bedroom or living room, but not the kitchen. *Reflecting* refers to statements made by parents that convey an understanding and an acceptance of a child's feelings. In the short run, reflective comments may help by soothing the child and reducing the need to defy parents. For example, a boy who is told that the television must be turned off may benefit if his parents reflect his ensuing feelings of anger and disappointment (e.g., "I know you hate it when you don't get to watch the whole show"). *Reasoning* refers to efforts by parents to provide children with a rationale for an instruction. Giving children reasons—especially if they are unaware of the reasons—can at times enhance cooperation. For example, a girl who is told "Don't throw rocks" may be more willing to comply if the potential dangers of this behavior were made clear to her (e.g., "Thrown rocks can accidentally hurt other kids").

Having noted the potential of these techniques for increasing the short-term success of containment, I again caution practitioners about overselling them to parents of aggressive children. As stated earlier, aggressive children may be less moved by redirects, reflective comments, and reasons for limits than is the case for nonaggressive children. Also, these potentially helpful add-ons may not be as meaningful to parents whose children are repeatedly and chronically violating rules. Parents of aggressive children may find that redirecting, reflecting, and giving reasons are hard to do when they feel under siege and forced to act in expedient ways. Practitioners should avoid overstating the benefits of these skills as well as their expectations for parents using them.

Skills to Improve Children's Long-Term Response to Containment

The same skills designed to increase the short-term success of containment can also be used to promote long-term gains. How critical are these skills to the socialization of aggressive children? The RPT model posits that parents' observable reactions to children's misbehavior are less important to socialization than children's participation in a relationship in which they feel accepted and contained by a prosocial adult. Although children are more apt to feel contained when parents prevail in a disciplinary encounter, it is not simply prevailing per se that promotes a child's socialization. Of course, efforts to socialize aggressive children do not simply depend on parents' use of reflective comments or moral messages. This caveat aside, parents of aggressive children should be aware that subtle modifications in their disciplinary practices and containment scripts may lead to important gains in their child's later functioning. If parents can persevere in the use of redirects, reflections, and reasons despite a lack of immediate change in their child's behavior, they are likely to reap benefits later.

One strategy involves parents' recurring efforts to combine prohibitions against and sanctions for aggressive behavior with prosocial redirecting. For example, parents can redirect their aggressive child by saying "You can use your words if you're mad, but I can't let you hit others." If this is done routinely, children will have opportunities to learn about prosocial behavior during their disciplinary conflicts with parents. Reflecting back to children an awareness of the feelings they are experiencing during a disciplinary encounter can also have this kind of beneficial sleeper effect. Parents who couple a firm posture of containment with an accurate reflection of feelings can help children in ways that are not immediately apparent. The practice of restricting behaviors while accepting feelings can be foreign to some parents. The oddness of this recommendation is due to parents' tendency to perceive a child's "bad feeling" as all part of the same package of bad behavior. Reflecting a child's feelings while standing firm on a behavioral limit uncouples feelings from behavior for both parents and children. Reflective comments also (a) help children recognize when they are in a state of overarousal, (b) provide children with words they can use to label these states, and (c) convey to children the idea that negative emotions do not have to result in coercive actions.

When parents reflect children's negative feelings, disciplinary encounters become opportunities to learn important emotional regulatory skills. Consider, for example, occasions when children feel hurt, disappointed, or cheated but express only anger. Comments such as "It hurt your feelings when I punished you" or "You're disappointed because I said no" are the kind of responses that enhance children's ability to manage their own emotions (Gottman et al., 1997). Parents of aggressive children may not see immediate payoffs for their efforts to be "emotion coaches," so the practice of reflecting feelings will have to be incorporated into an overlearned containment script if it is to be sustained. Similarly, children who are given reasons for the limits that parents impose may not immediately lower their resistance to these limits, but they can develop a clearer understanding of the necessity for these limits ("In our family we don't hurt people to get what we want"). Combining moral lessons with firm limits may seem a futile effort, but parents should be reminded that aggressive children's knowledge about the rules of conduct is not always apparent from their adherence to these rules. If parents are comfortable knowing that clear reasons for imposed limits may not affect children's immediate behavior, then they might consider the potential long-term gains that can come from this strategy.

Skills to Help Parents Manage the Costs of Containment

Effectively countering a child's antisocial behavior can take its toll on parents. Sometimes the costs are physical in that parents may be fatigued by the effort needed to prevail. Sometimes the costs can be social in that effective containment in certain settings (e.g., a school fair) may require an immediate departure for the entire family. At other times, the costs can be of an economic nature. Parents who choose to prioritize the containment of their child may be late for work or miss work entirely, may have damaged walls or torn clothing, and may be spending money on ways to cope with the added stress of parenting (e.g., substitute child care, prescription medicine). For the most part, however, the costs of containing an aggressive child will be cognitive and emotional in nature. Feelings of anger, resentment, guilt, and hopelessness are all likely when parents engage aggressive children in disciplinary conflicts. Parents may also begin to see themselves as mean, unloving, or incompetent, even when they are containing effectively. Parents' negative thoughts and feelings may extend to their children. Children may be seen as ungrateful, vindictive, or malicious. Regardless of the nature of these costs, if the price of containing an aggressive child is too high (or too high for too long), then parents might give up the goal of containment. The rewards of improved child behavior can counter the punishing costs of containment, but too often these rewards are delayed and may be no match for the potent reinforcement of immediately escaping a child's aversive demeanor.

Experienced practitioners recognize these potential costs and train parents in containment skills that invite a minimum of costs. However, published parent training programs rarely target the emotional fallout that accompanies parents' efforts to set firm limits. Parents may be warned that extinction bursts (i.e., increases in the frequency and intensity of previously rewarded behavior) can occur when children are first confronted with attempts to ignore or punish misbehavior. And most BMPT curricula emphasize that parents' use of commands, warnings, and time-outs should be delivered in a standard fashion without the kind of intense emotion that detracts from the disciplinary message. However, there is little else to guide practitioners who want to prepare parents for the costs of being firm. In CREFT, leaders process parents' cognitive and emotional reactions to setting limits on their child's behavior. Processing can help parents to recognize the kinds of obstacles that get in the way of their taking charge in an effective and nonviolent manner. Less clearly articulated, however, is how CREFT leaders can help parents learn to counter interfering thoughts or corrosive feelings. Helping parents manage the costs of containment is likely to require aspects of both the BMPT and the CREFT models. By processing parents' thoughts and feelings about the costs of containment, practitioners can help generate adaptive containment scripts that are rehearsed and refined.

Helping Parents Develop New Containment Scripts

A commonly used technique in assertiveness training is called the *broken record*. As its name implies, the technique involves repeating as often as needed a simple, assertive message (e.g., "I can't help you right now. . . . I can't help you right now"). The idea behind this technique is that locking in a set response obviates the need to think quickly and cleverly in the face of strong persuasion. Most people find it hard to think clearly when the normal way of viewing things is openly challenged by another person. We get flustered and fail to respond, or we react in awkward, less competent ways. Eventually, with repeated challenges, we can develop a pat response that we deliver in a rather mechanistic fashion whenever we encounter a similar challenge. With the broken-record technique, our limited ability to think on our feet is bypassed in favor of a prepackaged, overlearned response. To the degree this automatic response has use across situations, we are now capable of acting more assertively.

Parents of aggressive children also need pat responses that allow them to react promptly and competently when faced with disciplinary challenges. I have referred to this kind of response as a *containment script*. Containment scripts are basically a set of overlearned behaviors and cognitions that parents use to enforce a limit on their child's behavior. Parents may already have a scripted response to disciplinary conflict, but old scripts often contain features that mitigate successful containment. For example, old scripts may include memories, images, and self-statements insinuating that their child is attacking them personally, that attempts to socialize their child are futile, or that it is not worth the time and effort to contain their child right now. A practitioner's task is to learn about these preexisting scripts and to build new ones that contain empowering images, corrective self-talk, and effective actions.

Ideally, actions that convey verbally and nonverbally that parents are serious about setting a limit should be supported by mental images of being a strong but caring parent whose wisdom and persistence will allow both parents and children to weather each disciplinary conflict. A favorite image I often relate to parents is that of a huge bear—one that is soft to the touch but very big and slow to move. Parents can also benefit when scripts include features that help them lower or cope with their own emotional arousal. For example, parents may want to use a standard posture that creates proprioceptive cues associated with less arousal (e.g., sitting down, hands in pockets). A standard verbal script can also help parents manage their arousal. In fact, the same skills designed to enhance children's response to containment (see above) can also benefit parents—even if children are unaffected. Parents can use redirects, reflective comments, and reasoning as a way to counter their own negative thoughts and feelings about setting a limit. Parents who fear they are being mean when they set a limit or who tend to react harshly can benefit when they hear themselves using limit-setting scripts that incorporate these softer, inductive features. Imagine how much harder it would be for parents to act harshly or to see themselves as mean if they made the following comments when containing a child who in this example was aggressive towards a sibling: "I know you were mad, and I know that you think I'm mean and hateful. But I care about you and your brother, and I am not going to let you hurt him." By carefully analyzing old scripts and by building effective new scripts, parents can develop a pattern of responding to their child's antisocial actions that will not only be more effective, but also less costly. Below I discuss three approaches to script building that practitioners can use to help parents generate the scripts that suit them and their family best. Helping parents to develop more adaptive scripts assumes, of course, that practitioners are aware of the critical features and range of skills that make for good scripts (see the earlier discussion). Drawing on that knowledge, practitioners can help parents personalize, internalize, and mechanize more effective ways to contain their aggressive children.

Personalizing Scripts

There does not appear to be a one-size-fits-all containment script. Rather, practitioners and parents will need to custom build a pattern of responding that fits the strengths, weaknesses, and circumstance of the individual parent. In fact, effective containment scripts are probably dyad specific because what a parent does with one child may not work with that child's sibling. One of the more important goals of personalization is deciding which type of sanction parents are to use. For example, if time-out is being considered, then practitioners need to assess whether it can be implemented by a particular parent with that parent's child. But other factors also shape a script, such as, how authoritative parents look and sound when giving instructions. How simple must the words and actions be for parents and for children? What are the weak links in parents' containment chain? Are they too sarcastic? Are they too wimpish? Does the parent fear behavioral reprisal or emotional rejection? What are the distorted beliefs and strong emotions that interfere with the parent's goal?

Although practitioners may find it daunting to sift through such an array of issues, one should consider that for parents the focus is entirely on them—what they can and cannot do and what will and will not work for them and their child. Parent training programs that take a uniform approach to teaching discipline can leave parents feeling misunderstood and wanting. In fact, one way to begin the process of developing a more adaptive script is to ask parents about their current patterns of responding when children act coercively. When does it work and when does it fail? Which parts of the script appeal to parents, and which parts bother them? Have they considered any other approaches? Do they know parents of hard-to-manage children who use a different, perhaps better, approach? Is it possible for them to imitate these parents? Questions like these speak directly to issues that concern and confuse parents the most. The discussion generated by these questions lets practitioners know which aspects of parents' current scripts are sound and which need improvement. More importantly, this kind of discussion can guide practitioners and parents as they make specific choices when forming new containment scripts. "Off-the-rack" containment scripts are easier to incorporate into a parent training curriculum, but a "custom-fitted" script will take time and effort as practitioners get to know the parents and the challenges they face.

Internalizing Scripts

As discussed in chapter 4, skills training can be augmented through open discussion of parents' cognitive and emotional reactions to new skills. Parents' perception of the similarities and differences between new skills and current modes of behaving should also be a part of this discussion. Constantin and Cavell (1999b) found that processing enhanced mothers' skills implementation in the home. They hypothesized that processing allowed mothers to understand and internalize newfound skills. Processing may have also helped to reduce the likelihood that new skills were viewed as odd appendages with little real-world utility. Because parents of aggressive children are often sensitive to criticism about their disciplinary skills, script building may appear to progress more smoothly than is actually the case. Parents may nod in agreement when suggestions are made about the use of a particular type of sanction or when asked about their confidence in following through with a particular script. Unless practitioners engage parents in candid discussions about their internal reactions to new scripts, parents may hide the fact that proposed changes are not for them. When probing parents' reactions to potential scripts (see Table 4.1), therapists should focus on parents' cognitions (e.g., "What thoughts ran through your mind as you _____") and emotions (e.g., "You seemed _____. Were you?"), as well as the relation between new and old behaviors (e.g., "How different was it to use this approach?" "Can you imagine using this approach on a regular basis?").

Mechanizing Scripts

Mechanizing a script simply means making it more mechanical or automatic. Although inflexibility is not always a positive attribute when the goal is disciplining children, there does appear to be value in making at least some aspects of discipline rather mechanical (see the earlier discussion). Shifting performance of a behavior from a conscious, deliberate effort to a more reflexive, automatic response requires that the new behavior be overlearned. *Overlearning* requires expanding the length, breadth, and depth of training. Practitioners can promote overlearning by creating opportunities wherein parents participate in frequent and intensive skills rehearsal. Also helpful are scripts that are simply constructed and that do not feel too uncomfortable or awkward to use. It is also helpful to break scripts into smaller subunits that can be addressed sequentially. Practitioners can then ensure that a particular skill is fully acquired and readily accessible to parents before moving on to the next skill. In sum, mechanizing a containment script means following through with the best available practices of behavioral skills training.

Sibling Aggression and Parental Monitoring

Thus far this chapter has focused on the goals, the skills, and the scripts of effective containment. In the final two sections of this chapter, I discuss two more issues that are related to parents' efforts to counter their child's antisocial behavior. I first narrow the discussion by focusing on a specific kind of aggression and then widen it to focus on an issue that goes beyond containment: The first issue is sibling aggression and the second issue is parental monitoring.

Responding Effectively to Sibling Aggression

Aggressive children tend to fight with their brothers and sisters (Patterson, 1982; Patterson et al., 1992). In fact, it is not uncommon for parents of aggressive children to identify sibling aggression as the most troublesome behavior exhibited by their child. In some cases, aggressive children victimize their younger, weaker, and less aggressive siblings. If the victimization is extreme, parents' failure to intervene can constitute neglect. Even if sibling aggression does not involve victimization, recurring bouts of sibling aggression operate to extend the basic training of aggression beyond parent–child conflict (Patterson et al., 1992). Sibling interactions also function as practice opportunities for later peer interactions. A recent study by MacKinnon-Lewis, Starnes, Volling, and Johnson (1997) found that sibling aggression was predictive of peer-rated aggression and that sibling conflict partly mediated the relation between maternal rejection and peer aggression. It appears, therefore, that children who learn to use aggression to resolve sibling disputes are likely to use aggression to resolve conflicts with peers.

Implicit in the findings of MacKinnon-Lewis et al. (1997) is that children who learn to resolve sibling conflicts peacefully without resorting to acts of aggression should be more likely to experience successful and prosocial peer relationships. Therefore, parents may lower their child's risk of acting aggressively toward peers to the degree that they can respond effectively to sibling conflict. I frame the issue in this way because parents' goal in the face of sibling conflict is not simply to stop it. A better goal is to use sibling conflict as an opportunity for children to learn important prosocial skills that will transfer to other relationships (Perlman & Ross, 1997).

Practitioners should be particularly concerned about parents who respond to sibling conflict in one of two extreme ways. One is a *laissez-faire* approach to sibling conflict that can inadvertently give children license to act in whatever manner they wish—aggressive or otherwise—as long as children work it out themselves. The dangers of adopting this strategy should be obvious, especially for families with aggressive children. Even when this strategy is used by parents of nonreferred children, the outcome is likely to be an increase in sibling aggression (Vickerman, Reed, & Roberts, 1997). The lone advantage to this approach is that uninterrupted sibling conflict could lead to a more stable dominance hierarchy and less aggressive behavior among siblings (Felson & Russo, 1997). At the other extreme of the *laissez-faire* approach are parents who tend to intervene at the first sign of any sibling dispute. The advantage to this approach is that sibling aggression is thwarted as long as parents are there to observe it and intercede (Vickerman et al., 1997). The down side is that parental intervention can interfere with the establishment of a stable dominance hierarchy among siblings (Brody, Stoneman, McCoy, & Forehand, 1992). Also, opportunities for siblings to practice and benefit from successful conflict resolution are greatly reduced when parents intervene too early (Dunn, 1995).

Instead of these two extreme positions, I recommend that parents adopt a more intermediate position when responding to sibling conflict (Dunn, 1995). A key aspect of this position is to intervene when sibling conflict involves the use of aggression by one or both children. According to Dunn (1995), intervening only when conflict is overly intense helps parents to avoid perceived favoritism and gives children a chance to resolve conflicts on their own. Another goal of this intermediate position is to assist children who are struggling to resolve sibling disputes nonviolently. In much the same way that Gottman et al. (1997) spoke of emotion coaches, parents can also serve as "conflict coaches" assisting their children through conflict rather than insisting on the suppression of conflict. As with emotion coaching, children can benefit from conflict coaching when their ability to manage conflict is exceeded by the demands of the situation (Perlman & Ross, 1997). Exhibit 6.1 summarizes the principles and procedures that parents can use when coaching their children through sibling conflict.

The first two points remind parents to be selective when intervening in sibling conflict. Parents should not allow children to use aggression as

Exhibit 6.1.   Suggestions for Coaching Children Through Sibling Conflict

---

What to Do When Siblings Argue

If your children ask for help during an argument, coach them. But when siblings argue, your main goal is not to referee the argument. Try to follow these guidelines.

Staying out of the conflict. If a situation is not extreme (i.e., not violent; no "teaming up") and if children do not ask for help or "tattle," then stay out of the conflict. Of course, this can be hard because children may try to settle things in noisy and angry, emotionally immature, or unequal or unfair ways.

Responding to tattling. When a child tattles, you should coach that child through the conflict.

Coaching. Help your children with the words and the behaviors they can use to settle their conflicts. (e.g., "Billy, tell Michael you don't like to be hit. Tell him you want him to stop it." "Jane, I bet that hurt your feelings when Robert took your toy. But I can't let you hit him. We can't do that. If you're mad, use your words. Say to him, 'Robert, it makes me mad when you take my toy. I want it back.'")

Stepping in. You should step in and stop a conflict only if there is either (a) physical violence or (b) *teaming up* (two or more kids against one).

Violence. There should be a time-out or a loss of privilege for all children who were violent. However, don't punish simply on the word of another child.

Teaming up. If there is teaming up, simply announce to all children that there is to be no teaming up.

---

a way to deal with conflict, but sibling disputes should be ignored if they are proceeding in a nonviolent manner. One exception to intervening only when conflict becomes violent is when two or more children are teaming up against a single child. By not allowing children to form teams or alliances against a lone child, parents convey that to do so is unfair—a message echoed by the recently popularized schoolyard dictum "You can't say, you can't play." Prohibiting children from teaming up also teaches that each child should speak for himself or herself and not side with others who speak for them. Intervening when children are teaming up can also prevent the lone child from feeling pushed out and alienated from the rest of the family. A line I offer to parents is "There's no teaming up in this family. The only teams are the kid team and the parent team." This message reminds children that the family structure does not allow for unhealthy alliances either within or across generations.

Parents are also cautioned that sibling conflict can proceed in ways that make parents uncomfortable. Children's way of resolving conflict is not always calm, reasoned, or even logical. Instead, children can be noisy, their arguments can be emotionally messy, and their solutions may be unequal or impractical. Still, if children navigate their way through a dispute without resorting to aggression, then they benefit regardless of the solution. If all parties feel good about the outcome and positive interactions resume, then children will have learned important lessons about making relationships work over time. Parents who intervene prematurely in sibling conflict may rob children of the chance to learn these lessons. For those occasions when sibling conflict is simply too loud or too disruptive (but not violent), parents can benefit by insisting that children settle their arguments outside or in another room. If this is not possible, parents can either seek their own solitude (e.g., go to another room, leave the house, put on headphones) or request that children settle their disputes more quietly. This latter recommendation may lead, however, to parents being pulled into the conflict (e.g., "He's the one who is being so loud").

Parents can shift to a more active coaching mode when one child complains about or tattles on the other or when parents have to intervene because of aggression or teaming up. The goal of coaching is to teach children the skills they can use to resolve conflict optimally and nonviolently. My preference for how to teach these skills is to give children detailed scripts they can use. For example, a boy who complains that his older sister is cheating at a game may be coached to return to his sister and say "I don't like it when you cheat. It's not fair. I want you to stop." This example illustrates a number of points. First, the child was not asked to deliver a message for the parent, which can seem like an intrusion by the parent and a crossgenerational teaming up against the other child. Second, the child is given examples of helpful *I* statements and not criticizing *you* statements. Third, the form of the script is one that has been used successfully to coach aggressive children to act more prosocially (Prinz et al., 1994). The form is one in which the child describes the offending behavior, reports how it makes him or her feel, and then states a request for a behavior change (e.g., "I don't like it when you _____. It makes me feel _____. I would like you to _____."). If parents reliably coach children to use this adaptive form of problem-solving communication whenever children tattle, they essentially create a learning laboratory for healthy conflict resolution skills. Eventually, as children's skills increase, they will need less detail and fewer scripts; however, parents may still need to remind children to use their words (and not act aggressively) and to take their words directly to their siblings.

Monitoring: A Multidimensional Construct

Parents' failure to monitor or supervise their children has been shown to be a reliable predictor of later delinquency (Loeber et al., 1991; Patterson, 1982; Patterson et al., 1992). The predictive value associated with parental monitoring also appears to increase as children begin engaging in more peer-related activities (Loeber et al., 1991). The functional relation between parental monitoring and children's subsequent antisocial behavior has found support in the intervention findings reported by Forgatch (1991). In fact, Forgatch (1991) found that improvement in parental monitoring was more predictive of children's outcome than improvement in discipline. However, only 16% of the parents treated were able to reach the criterion for improved monitoring (30% gains over baseline). What is it about this aspect of parenting that makes it such a reliable predictor of children's externalizing behavior but also such a difficult variable to affect? I submit that the answer lies in its multidimensional nature.

Past attempts to measure the construct of monitoring reveal its multidimensional nature (Patterson, 1982; Patterson et al., 1992). Attempts to assess parents' awareness of children's whereabouts, their involvement in deviant behavior, and their associations with deviant peers are reflected in these indices. The extent to which children *inform* parents of their whereabouts, their activities, and their friends is also assessed. Assessment of monitoring has also included parents' insistence on and children's compliance with bedtimes, curfews, and other aspects of a family's routine. Patterson (1982) has even considered mealtime conversations about the day's events as a critical part of parental supervision:

> The child's report elicited both sustained interest and a discussion with the parents. I suspect that these periods of shared information are a powerful mechanism for shaping the child's values and interests. Given that this was a frequent occurrence, one would expect that the members of normal families would be more homogeneous than distressed families in values, interests, and recreational activities. (p. 227)

At a minimum, one can question whether indices of monitoring assess only parents' skill or whether significant aspects of children's behavior are also being assessed. One reason that monitoring may have less predictive value for children under 10 years of age is that younger children have yet to exhibit the kinds of behavior problems that are typically embedded in a measure of monitoring (e.g., associating with deviant peers, breaking curfew). This reason seems more plausible than arguing that parents' monitoring skills are relatively intact when their child is young but somehow become less reliable as their children grow older. It seems more parsimonious to explain this age-related shift in terms of child effects and not parent effects.

It would also seem that monitoring taps into a wide range of parenting factors. For example, Patterson's (1982) description of the daily conversations held by parents and their nondeviant children would suggest features of parental acceptance, parents' promotion of prosocial norms, and family structure. One could also argue that parents who lack the energy or motivation to adequately supervise their children are most in need of assistance with self-care skills. Indeed, the converse of a capable, committed monitor would appear to be a parent who is defeated and withdrawn or distressed and overwhelmed. Either way, simple skills-training approaches are unlikely to be sufficient to offset the emotional inertia such parents experience. Of course, successfully limiting children's involvement with deviant peers and their access to delinquent activities are also important containment skills.

What does it mean, therapeutically, if parental monitoring is in fact a multidimensional construct? Should practitioners eschew intervention approaches that take a strictly parent-effects stance? Given both the empirical relation and the conceptual link between monitoring and discipline, it seems reasonable to address this issue primarily in the context of containment skills training. Parents should be advised that as children become more independent in their daily tasks and activities, monitoring takes on increased importance in their containment efforts. As mentioned earlier, some children respond to parents' containment efforts by learning to discriminate between settings in which they are likely or unlikely to be punished and not between which behaviors are or are not allowed. To the extent parents adequately supervise children and keep abreast of their activities across multiple settings (i.e., at school, after school, with peers), children are more likely to sense that their parents are committed to the goal of restricting certain misbehaviors. Conversely, if children have already internalized parents' prosocial values and beliefs (an unlikely scenario for many aggressive children), then the need for parental supervision may actually decrease. Steinberg (1986) found evidence for this kind of buffering effect in his study of "latch-key" children. Authoritative parenting seemed to guard children against susceptibility to deviant peer pressure, particularly in that group of children who were poorly supervised and were hanging out with peers after school. Because children with authoritative parents are more likely to internalize parents' values and beliefs, Steinberg reasoned that such children are less easily influenced by peers with deviant norms. One implication of the work by Steinberg and others on children's susceptibility to peer pressure is that measures of parental monitoring may indirectly assess a child's level of internalized prosocial beliefs or committed compliance (Kochanska, 1995). If true, this would offer greater support to the argument that the construct of monitoring derives its predictive value not from its reflection of what parents are doing but from its reflection of what children are doing and what children believe about what they are doing.

Given Forgatch's (1991) findings that most parents in her treatment study failed to improve their monitoring, it seems prudent to proceed cautiously when trying to promote these skills in parents whose children are aggressive. One approach would be to familiarize parents with the concept of monitoring and its importance and then brainstorm with them all the ways they can increase their level of supervision. By pointing out the challenge of altering this aspect of parenting while simultaneously fostering a creative, collaborative approach to generating possible solutions, practitioners offer help to parents who can readily improve their monitoring and avoid offending parents who are unlikely to improve their level of monitoring. Given the multidimensional nature of this construct, practitioners can also point out to parents the connections between monitoring and the other aspects of parenting that are part of the overall RPT model (e.g., acceptance, structure, self-care).

7

Prosocial Values

As a child, the values of my family were solidly prosocial, a mix of principles and beliefs flavored by the culture of our South Louisiana, Roman Catholic heritage. There were times, however, as a teenager when I strayed from my family's values. I did not stray far or long, but I certainly knew that I had strayed. I knew because there was little ambiguity in my family about what was considered right or wrong, moral or immoral, honorable or profane. My parents made it a point to share their values with us. My mother, a junior high school teacher, was particularly adept at weaving into our lives the simple truths of an ethical, moral life. Some of her more unusual efforts are now part of family lore, which gets told and retold when we gather together. She once pinned to the wall of our breakfast room a picture of a starving child from a developing country. She felt the picture would help us better appreciate the riches of our own repast. When we were older and started going out with friends at night, she began a ritual that persists to this day. Before we would drive off, she would hold us close, make the sign of the cross on our forehead and say, "I'm putting you in the Lord's hands. Remember who you are and whose you are. Use good judgment and a light foot on the accelerator!" Together my mother and father made clear their beliefs about the way to treat others, the value of work and education, and the importance of faith and family.

All families transmit values (prosocial or antisocial) to their children. Prosocial values are a necessary complement to acceptance and containment in those parent–child relationships capable of socializing aggressive children. Aggressive children in relationships marked by an absence of prosocial values or an abundance of deviant values are at risk for later antisocial behavior. Recent studies offer support for an empirical link between conduct problems in children and deviancy in parents (Frick & Jackson, 1993; Tapscott, Frick, Wootten, & Kruh, 1996). These findings are often interpreted as support for the genetic transmission of antisocial tendencies. However, the data also allow for the possibility that parental modeling and reinforcement of deviant behavior is a contributing factor. That is not to say that all parents of aggressive children are criminals who routinely endorse antisocial behavior. But such parents do exist. One 10-year-old boy my colleagues and I worked with would accompany his father, who was addicted to crack-cocaine, on outings in which they stole goods that were pawned for drug money. Cases such as this one (which required reporting the father to child protective services) are easily recognized as examples of parental guidance gone awry. Less obvious examples are those families in which parents are doing very little to model or endorse a prosocial lifestyle even though theirs is a nondeviant system of values.

Empirical studies that directly examine the extent to which parents of aggressive children actually endorse prosocial or antisocial beliefs are lacking. The bulk of the work in this area has generally emphasized the modeling of aggressive behavior when parents discipline children (e.g., Eron, 1987; Weiss, Dodge, Bates, & Pettit, 1992). Attempts to assess parents' values, beliefs, and behaviors beyond the parent–child context are less obvious (cf. Frick & Jackson, 1993; Pettit et al., 1988). In fact, the term *values* is rarely invoked by investigators who study family process or treatment outcome. Researchers and practitioners in this field have been appropriately skittish about imposing our own values on others, but we have been excessively avoidant when considering the values of our research participants and therapy clients. This trend may be shifting, however, as we broaden our theoretical and methodological lenses and begin to recognize the important role that values play in the lives of individuals and families. For example, a recent study found that parents' values regarding alcohol use influenced the relation between parenting practices and adolescents' reports of substance use (Bogenschneider, Wu, Raffaelli, & Tsay, 1998). The relation between fathers' monitoring and adolescent substance use was stronger among adolescents whose fathers held more disapproving views of adolescent alcohol use. In *multisystemic therapy* (Henggeler et al., 1997), which is an empirically validated treatment for working with troubled families, one of its nine guiding principles of treatment is to promote *responsible* behavior in both children and parents. As researchers become more comfortable with the study of values, a number of interesting and important questions can be answered. For example, to what degree do parents' prosocial values predict parenting behavior over and above their specific beliefs about parenting? What is the relation between parents' prosocial values and their children's values and behavior? If practitioners target deficiencies in parenting, can treatment gains lead to improvement in prosocial beliefs and vice versa? Under what circumstances do explicit verbalizations about prosocial beliefs add significantly to parents' efforts to model prosocial values and behaviors? And finally, how can practitioners effectively assist parents whose prosocial values are ill formed or poorly endorsed?

In this chapter, I discuss the task of promoting parents' active endorsement of prosocial values. I begin by discussing reasons why parents may not perform this critical role. I then offer guidelines for helping parents endorse a coherent system of prosocial values. I close the chapter with a discussion of what I call the *third option*, a parenting technique that was first discussed in chapter 5. Conceptually, the third option falls midway between acceptance and containment, and it represents an opportunity for parents to endorse specific prosocial beliefs. Throughout this chapter, I use the phrase *endorsing prosocial values* to mean both the modeling of prosocial actions and the direct verbalization of prosocial beliefs.

Why Parents Fail to Endorse Prosocial Values

One can imagine several reasons why parents may fail to endorse a strong, prosocial set of values for their children. The reasons discussed here are derived primarily from my clinical experience, as I am unaware of systematic research on this topic.

Parents Have Adopted Deviant Values

As mentioned previously, most parents with aggressive children do not embrace a system of beliefs and values in which rules and the rights of others are routinely ignored or dismissed. Unfortunately, some parents do hold such deviant beliefs, so practitioners should be mindful of that possibility, particularly among those parents with a history of criminal involvement or drug dependence. There may also be parents who endorse a specific belief or action that can be considered deviant. For example, parents often encourage children not to let others hurt or take advantage of them. Some parents, however, may go so far as to coach their children to use an aggressive response in such instances (e.g., "It's ok to fight if somebody else starts it"). Another example is when aggressive children are told that they have to obey only their parents, not the teachers at school or any other adults. This scenario may arise when, for example, children from racial and ethnic minority groups have parents who regard non-minority group teachers as bigoted. These two examples also illustrate how children could overinterpret parents' comments and actions as an endorsement of deviant values. Some parents may be unaware that children are interpreting their views on assertiveness or their concerns about biased teachers as an endorsement of deviant values. Most parents will promptly back away from behaviors that lead to such misinterpretations, although others may defend their child's interpretation, further jeopardizing their child's hold on a prosocial set of values.

Parents Are Trapped in a Destructive or Deviant Lifestyle

I have worked with a number of parents, typically single mothers, who espoused prosocial values and could point to a time when they were prosocial, but who were currently caught in a deviant pattern of behavior. Parents who are financially destitute, battered, chemically dependent, or mentally ill are not necessarily antisocial in their orientation, but they may be susceptible to engaging in maladaptive and deviant patterns of behavior. Some parents feel so hopeless and alienated that common beliefs and mores no longer seem applicable to their lives. Others may fall prey to deviant lifestyles (e.g., illicit drug use, prostitution, check fraud) because abusive partners coerced them or because they may have lacked sound judgment as a result of severe emotional disturbance or substance use. The task for the practitioner is to make sense of the factors that led to and that maintain this antisocial way of life. In the case of the 10-year-old boy mentioned previously, his mother was an effective model for prosocial behavior as long as her husband, who was addicted to crack-cocaine, was not living in the home. Under his presence, however, any benefits derived from her guidance and modeling were lost because she tended to defer to the father and to his more deviant system of values.

There is evidence from laboratory studies of young, nonaggressive children that behaviors and beliefs are more likely to be imitated (and perhaps internalized) if modeled by powerful adults (e.g., Grusec, 1971). *Power*, in these studies, is typically operationalized as having control over desired resources. This research has also found evidence that models who are simply nurturing are far less effective than models who are powerful. One implication of this work is that powerful but deviant parents may loom as more influential than parents who are nurturing and prosocial but who lack power. The example of the family with the father who was addicted to crack-cocaine certainly supports that view. An important caveat to this hypothesis is that children may be less influenced by powerful but deviant parents if the relationships lack acceptance and containment. Deviant adults may monitor children too sporadically to be containing or may be too dictatorial to be accepting. Children who feel accepted and somewhat contained but who are free to act in a number of deviant ways are likely to be the most vulnerable. In fact, the promise of this kind of relationship is likely what attracts many children to join street gangs.

Parents Have Poorly Formed Value Systems

Some parents fail to endorse prosocial values, not because they hold deviant beliefs, but because they lack any system of well-articulated beliefs. One can imagine, for example, very young parents who started having children before they formed a stable and mature sense of identity. Their beliefs and actions are likely to vary greatly from one year to the next and from one relationship, job, or neighborhood to the next. If they are fortunate enough to have an involved and prosocial network of support, they are likely to embrace and model prosocial behaviors. A concerned neighbor, an inspiring religious leader, a wise grandparent are each examples of individuals who may guide (at least temporarily) these often rudderless parents. The well-known film, *It's a Wonderful Life*, uses this kind of theme to weave its tale about a man whose life touches the lives of others in significant ways. Although perhaps a difficult phenomenon to study empirically, I have observed families who experience major changes in their lives (good and bad) when seemingly insignificant events occur. Examples of such events include a different supervisor at work, a new family in the neighborhood, or a family physician that moves away. Rudderless parents are also vulnerable to the impact of stressful events (e.g., divorce, unemployment). All else being equal, parents who have stable, well-integrated value systems should be better able to cope with life's unpredictable demands.

Parents' Values Are Prosocial but Dormant

I have worked with a number of parents who are hard-working, responsible citizens but whose children seem adrift on a valueless sea. Sometimes these parents need assistance with and reminders about containment or supervision, and sometimes they need assistance with self-care (see chapter 9, this volume). But there are other parents who perform adequately many of the skills of parenting except that they do not make well known their prosocial values. One young mother with whom I worked had strong prosocial beliefs about work, philanthropy, and her own spirituality. Unfortunately for her children, she was emotionally private and generally too busy to reflect on or openly endorse these values. Because she was a single mother with numerous financial concerns, she had few opportunities to model any behavior except being at work. For this mother and for parents like her, an adequate system of prosocial values was too hidden for her children to appreciate. The task for practitioners is to determine the obstacles that are preventing a more illuminated expression of parents' values. Is the parent extremely quiet and reserved? Did the parent lack models for how parents commonly provide explicit guidance and salient examples? These parents may benefit also from help with structuring skills, particularly those that enhance family rules, routines, and rituals (see chapter 8, this volume).

Helping Parents Endorse Prosocial Values

The challenge of helping parents endorse prosocial values can vary tremendously depending on the extent to which parents currently ascribe to a prosocial way of life. Parents who are actively criminal or who have little concern over the possible ills that their deviant behaviors cause their children are unlikely to be persuaded by practitioners. On the other hand, parents who hold prosocial values but are currently engaged in a destructive and deviant lifestyle may well benefit from practitioners' efforts. Practitioners can, for example, help parents by targeting their repertoire of self-care skills or helping them obtain access to more focused intervention programs (e.g., a women's shelter, chemical dependency treatment center). Parents who fail to make their prosocial values explicit are most likely to benefit from a focus on family structure. Whether the failure to endorse prosocial values is due to family stress and disorganization or to parents' inhibitions about being more open with their beliefs, revamping current structures (e.g., routines, rituals) is a practical way to promote a family's prosocial identity. Practitioners can help parents identify those aspects of family structure that can be reflections of parents' prosocial values. For example, to what degree are family rules reflective of prosocial principles? Is there room in a family's daily or weekly routine for explicitly prosocial activities? What beliefs and values underlie the family's rituals? Activities that affirm a family's values range from civic duties such as recycling cans and bottles to checking on an elderly, homebound neighbor. Family rituals such as exchanging gifts during holidays and making annual trips to a loved one's gravesite can become special events that foster a prosocial orientation. Parents who want to advance greater caring among family members can institute rituals that encourage thoughtful, altruistic behaviors (e.g., planning a sibling's birthday celebration). Parents who struggle to articulate their spiritual beliefs may benefit by regularly involving their family in structured religious activities. Dosick's (1995) *Golden Rules: The Ten Ethical Values Parents Need to Teach Their Children* provides parents many ideas for activities that can illuminate prosocial values and beliefs. These include visiting the elderly, volunteering, taking a child to work, donating, returning library books, not yelling at umpires, voting, visiting sick friends, demonstrating, giving blood, paying taxes, praying and reading sacred texts, and visiting the cemetery.

The Third Option

In chapter 5, I described how parents who tacitly accept their child's unbecoming behavior could still speak openly about that behavior without sacrificing a posture of acceptance. Parents often disagree with many of the decisions their children make, and they find many of the behaviors in which their children engage undesirable. Compared to parents, school-age children can have very different ideas about clothes, food, music, language, and a host of other things. When the discrepancy between the views of children and parents becomes too great, parents may want to offer their views and the reasons for their views. If voiced in a way that leaves children with a choice about how to act, parents' views can be a form of tacit acceptance that I call the *third option*.

Recall from chapter 5 the example of a girl whose description of her deviant friend included a number of erroneous facts. I suggested there that parents who challenge erroneous beliefs about deviant peers might inadvertently inoculate children against the very arguments they are making. A better approach for her mother would be to voice her own views about her daughter's friend, as long as she makes it clear to her daughter that these views are not held up as absolute or ultimate truths. Assuming that access to or involvement with this friend was not an urgent issue, the mother could say

> I know you like her and that she can be really nice, but I get a bad feeling about her. And I know you think she's a good person, but I worry about some of the things she's done and the kids she hangs around. I guess I worry that her values may change your values.

The third option involves giving children clear messages that a given behavior or belief is at odds with family norms and values, even though it may not require parental intervention. Essentially, the third option means making explicit parents' prosocial beliefs and values in a way that children are most likely to hear. The third-option technique provides children with a clear understanding of parents' perspective without the risks of failed control efforts and without the ambiguity of passive acceptance. When children speak or act in ways that are ill advised but require no immediate intervention, parents may feel they have to bite their tongues in silence. And yet, if parents say nothing, children may assume that parents endorse whatever they are choosing to do or say. To the extent parents provide an overall atmosphere of acceptance for their children, the third option can provide a useful way to guide and educate children without being overly controlling. I use the term *third option* because behaviorally it falls midway between active acceptance and strict containment. Conceptually, the same can also be said of the strategy of endorsing prosocial values. When parents are unsure if it is better to be accepting or containing, they always have the option of making their values explicit. By positioning prosocial values in this way, parents who are familiar with the Responsive Parent Therapy (RPT) triangle (see the middle position of Figure 3.1, this volume) and feel stuck between acceptance and containment may be able to recall the third option.

For children, the benefit of this third option is that they can learn about their parents' perspective without being forced to adhere to that perspective. Empirical support for parents clearly communicating their values and opinions comes from recent studies suggesting that the most aggressive children have inaccurate and inflated views of self and others (Edens et al., 1999; Hughes et al., 1997). However, the conditions under which aggressive children can process information that corrects these distorted views are unclear (Zakriski & Coie, 1996). In one study, giving children with ADHD positive feedback (supposedly from a child play partner) resulted in a lowering of their inflated self-views (Diener & Milich, 1997). In RPT, the assumption is that a sustained relationship in which the child feels accepted and contained is needed before a child will be open to the lessons imparted by the adults in that relationship. However, I am unaware of research that has directly examined the benefits of training parents to use a technique like the third option. For example, it is unknown whether aggressive children and their parents can distinguish between opinions issued for consideration and comments meant to be harsh and criticizing. As is the case with other parenting techniques, the context in which the third option is used (e.g., quality of the parent–child relationship, level of stress in the family) is likely to be a significant moderator of its impact. Until such research is done, practitioners who introduce the third option should proceed cautiously, especially with parents whose remarks to children are generally negative.

Besides being a vehicle for advancing parents' prosocial values, the third option can also be used to deflect or diffuse children's verbally coercive behaviors. As reviewed in chapter 6, Patterson (1982) observed that parents in nonreferred families tend to overlook or deflect a child's verbally coercive behavior. If parents can succeed in stating their values without adding unnecessary threatening or inciteful comments, then the third option could be a useful mechanism for deflecting negative remarks made by children. Consider, for example, the act of swearing. As a practitioner, I often caution parents about targeting children's verbalizations because of the difficulty involved in containing what children say. So it is with swearing. Parents can choose to insist on no swearing, and they may be successful in their efforts to contain it. But if parents elected not to contain swearing—either because they are not that concerned about it or because they worry about the costs of enforcing a no-swear rule—then the third option may be helpful. The third option can be used to convey tolerance for the child's decision to swear while openly disagreeing with that decision. For example, a mother may say to her son "I don't like swearing in my house. I know you think it's okay, but I don't like it" or "If you want to swear, that's your business, but I really don't like it." In these examples, the mother stated very clearly her views about swearing. If mother and son enjoy a satisfying relationship and he is invested emotionally in that relationship, then his mother's views on swearing will matter to him. He may still swear, but he may be less likely to do it in her presence. If he continues to swear in her presence, it is with full knowledge that his mother disapproves; one day that information may become more salient to him. Of course, this lesson is all the more powerful if it is coupled with a consistent example of parents' not swearing. Practitioners should recognize, however, that views expressed by parents may come across as parental nattering even if not meant as such. Simple phrases that clarify parents' intent are helpful. Such phrases include "We see things differently. I think . . ."; "You may think I'm off my rocker, but I believe . . ."; and "For what it's worth, I feel. . . ."

Summary

The degree to which parents of aggressive children actively endorse a system of prosocial values is an important but seldom-studied research question. As a result, most practitioners are unlikely to consider parents' beliefs and values as reasonable targets of intervention. Instead, prosocial values are treated more as a background text that sets the upper limit on a child's successful socialization. In this chapter, I discussed a number of factors that can lead parents to eschew prosocial guidance and modeling in their home. For some, the failure to endorse a system of prosocial values is best addressed as an issue of poor parental self-care. For others, attention to family structure may offer insights into how prosocial values can be modeled and made more explicit. Perhaps the most direct way for parents to endorse prosocial values is to use what I have called the third option. Conceptually and pragmatically, the third option falls roughly midway between acceptance and containment. With this technique, parents can share their values while neither endorsing nor restricting their child's behavior.

8

Family Structure

Following the work of Salvador Minuchin (1974) and other proponents of structural family therapy, the Responsive Parent Therapy (RPT) approach to working with parents of aggressive children places particular emphasis on how families are structured and organized. This emphasis is based on the view that a child's sense of acceptance and containment is derived not only from parents' use of dyadic skills, but also from parents' ability to enhance family-wide structure and organization. Parents can use structuring skills to establish appropriate roles and boundaries and to develop and maintain adaptive rules, rituals, and routines. In this chapter, I offer a set of clinical guidelines that practitioners can use when targeting parents' ability to structure their homes and families. I begin, however, with a brief discussion of why practitioners should go beyond dyadic parent–child interactions and address aspects of family structure.

The Case for Attending to Family Structure

The empirical link between parental stress and child behavior problems is well documented and generally indicates that stress acts to disrupt parenting practices (Abidin, 1990). Researchers have identified a number of factors that can enhance parents' ability to respond to stress, including effective coping skills, a stable marriage, and reliable support network (Abidin, 1990). Unfortunately, parents of aggressive children often lack these resources, especially those parents who are least responsive to parent intervention—single mothers who are economically disadvantaged, socially isolated, and emotionally distressed (Dumas & Wahler, 1983; Webster-Stratton, 1990). The tendency for their homes and families to be unstructured and disorganized makes matters worse for these multiply stressed parents, thereby generating even more stress. In RPT, family structure and organization are thought to buffer parents and children from the vagaries of stress. By enabling parents to meet children's needs for acceptance, containment, and prosocial values, family structures can greatly reduce the impact of stress and upheaval on children's lives. Moreover, structure in the home and family is considered particularly important for parents who are lacking in social support, marital harmony, and adequate coping skills. In RPT, therapists endeavor to teach parents about the value of structuring their family and train them to use specific skills to promote that structure.

The idea that family structure can buffer parent–child relationships from unexpected stress is not without empirical support. For example, several studies suggest a positive association between child adjustment and firm generational boundaries (Sroufe, Jacobvitz, Mangelsdorf, DeAngelo, & Ward, 1985), organization in the home (Gorman-Smith & Tolan, 1998; Radke-Yarrow, Richters, & Wilson, 1988), stable routines (Brody & Flor, 1997), and regular family rituals (Constantin & Cavell, 1999a; Wolin, Bennett, & Noonan, 1979). Radke-Yarrow et al. (1988) found that positive mother–child relationships were associated with higher rates of child compliance, but only in stable families. Negative mother–child relationships were associated with mothers' use of harsh punishment, but only in chaotic families. Brody and Flor (1997) learned that family routines directly predicted parenting effectiveness and indirectly predicted child functioning in a sample of African American mothers who were single and living in a rural area. There have also been studies that fail to find support for the protective role of family structure. For example, in another study that involved African American single mothers, family routines failed to predict parenting effectiveness (Kotchick et al., 1997). However, these mothers lived in an urban setting and all were HIV positive, suggesting that extreme levels of stress exceeded the potential benefits of family structure. Similarly, Gorman-Smith and Tolan (1998) found that family structure could offset the toxic effects of neighborhood stress and violence, but only when the level of stress and violence was not extreme.

Available studies suggest a mixed picture regarding the extent to which structure and organization can protect families from the debilitating effects of stress. There is, however, another reason for promoting parents' use of structure and organization. The effective use of family structure can help parents who stray from their parenting goals because of changes in mood, errors in judgment, or poor skills implementation. Consider the recent study by Johnson, Cowan, and Cowan (1999) in which family organization was found to be an important predictor of children's externalizing problems. These investigators observed families engaged in a structured task and rated them with respect to parental leadership, strength of the marital subsystem, and family cohesion. Also rated were the following dyadic variables: parental warmth, negative affect, quality of instruction, and limit setting. As hypothesized, the composite measure of family organization predicted teacher-rated externalizing behaviors one year later. More importantly, the variance accounted for by family organization was above and beyond that predicted by the dyadic data. These findings suggest that interventions that focus exclusively on family dyads (e.g., mother–child) are likely to be less effective than those that focus on the family as a whole. Family structures provide a vehicle by which parents can codify successful parenting practices. Because parents with aggressive children are often inconsistent, practitioners who directly address family structure will help these parents preserve the relationship conditions necessary for socialization (i.e., acceptance, containment, and prosocial values). Chapter 6 discussed the value of parents developing and using containment scripts. Similarly, parents of aggressive children benefit when effective parenting practices are established beforehand, and these structures are allowed to do the work when parents are not at their best.

Promoting Parents' Use of Structure

I generally introduce the concept of family structure by discussing its role during times of stress and upheaval. Although parents may possess the skills needed to convey a sense of acceptance, containment, and prosocial values, they are cautioned that unexpected or prolonged stress can disrupt their ability to perform these skills. I suggest to parents that adaptive family organization can help in a couple of ways. First, organized families tend to generate less stress in their lives, whereas disorganized families often create crises where none existed before. Consider something as simple as taking out the garbage. If someone puts the trash out a day late and dogs spread the refuse throughout the neighborhood, the neighbors probably would complain to the police about the mess. It would be easy to miss the fact that poor family organization—not bad luck or cranky neighbors—was the original contributory factor. Second, adaptive family structures can reduce the number of decisions a parent has to make under stress. Because stress can impair parents' judgment, a previously established system of structure and organization can take over until parents are more settled.

Before practitioners suggest changes in a family's structure, it is important to learn about parents' current view of family structure. I suspect few parents give much thought to how their family is organized and structured, owing perhaps to the tendency for individuals to think linearly rather than systemically (Nichols & Schwartz, 1998). Fewer still seem to regard their family's structure as a reasonable target of change. The way a family is structured and how its members' lives are organized are often treated as a given and not as an aspect of family functioning that one readily changes. Because of the inertia that is associated with these concepts, an open discussion about family structure and organization is often helpful. Once parents are open to the possibility that they can change the way their family is organized, practitioners can help them form new structures that better reflect their family's needs and priorities. In RPT, training to promote parents' use of structure is organized around the 4 Rs of family structure: *roles, rules, rituals*, and *routines*.

Roles

In discussing containment skills training (chapter 6, this volume), I placed considerable emphasis on parents' ability to fulfill the role of authority figure. When skills training involves family structure, the task of assuming an authoritative parenting role is addressed head-on. Parents' ability to maintain clear generational boundaries, to avoid damaging role rever-sals, and to prevent the formation of unhealthy alliances is critical to par-ents adopting the role of authority figure. For many parents, this ability is acquired naturally and usually reflects a strong, healthy sense of self and a mature understanding of interpersonal relationships (see chapter 9, this volume). Not all parents are so fortunate. Some parents are unaware of the need for generational boundaries, they cannot recognize when par-ent and child roles are reversed, or they seem unwilling or unable to limit unhealthy subsystem alliances. Therefore, much of the training on family roles involves educating parents about adaptive versus maladaptive roles.

One way to achieve this is to revisit the myths about parenting listed in Exhibit 4.2 (this volume). Going over this list can be an effective re-minder of the vertical nature of the parent–child relationship. Parents may need help understanding and accepting that (a) the burden of making the relationship work rests largely with them, (b) they should not expect to get from children as much as they give, and (c) these truths may not have been appreciated by their own parents. Another way to promote par-ents' understanding of adaptive roles is through a discussion of how power is distributed in the family. By asking "Who's the boss at your house?" practitioners can learn the extent to which parents are viewed as persons of authority by themselves and their children. It is also helpful to have parents draw an organizational chart for the family. Practitioners may need to demonstrate this by depicting the organizational structure of an ideal family, one in which parents are the CEOs and children hold less power and answer to parents' authority.

This exercise is also a good lead-in to another important concept re-lated to family roles, that of boundaries. *Boundaries* are defined as psy-chological and behavioral barriers that enhance and protect the integrity of individuals and relationships. Using their depiction of family organi-zation, parents can illustrate the quality of the boundary that separates parents and children and the presence of any subgroups or alliances that exist within the family. For example, a mother and her daughter may be recognized as being very close, or two brothers who are close in age may be grouped together by parents. Parents committed to the process of iden-tifying maladaptive boundaries and alliances can also benefit from the inventory shown in Exhibit 8.1. When parents are asked to comment on issues ranging from children's teeth to parents' heartaches, they begin to appreciate in tangible ways the value of both personal and generational boundaries. They may also see more clearly the oddness, if not the danger, of role reversals and the parentification of children. Another way to illus-trate the concept of boundaries is to ask parents about rather outlandish scenarios that depict what life may be like in families with no boundaries. For example, I may ask parents to imagine what it would be like if every-one in their home were of the same size and age or if there were no doors or walls in their home. Once parents are clear on the concept of bounda-ries, it helps to reexamine the family's organizational chart and the Whose Business Is . . . ? inventory (Exhibit 8.1). Practitioners can then help par-ents identify areas that need modification.

Exhibit 8.1.   Questions That Promote Discussion of Adaptive Roles and
Boundaries

Whose "business" is . . .? (circle all that apply)				
1. Parent's hair style	child	parent	sibling	grandparent
2. Child's teeth	child	parent	sibling	grandparent
3. Monthly bills	child	parent	sibling	grandparent
4. Parent's romance	child	parent	sibling	grandparent
5. Child's misbehavior	child	parent	sibling	grandparent
6. Child's school work	child	parent	sibling	grandparent
7. Child's punishment	child	parent	sibling	grandparent
8. Parent's heartaches	child	parent	sibling	grandparent
9. Child's room	child	parent	sibling	grandparent
10. Child's grades	child	parent	sibling	grandparent
11. Parent's anger	child	parent	sibling	grandparent
12. Parent's clothes	child	parent	sibling	grandparent
13. Child's friends	child	parent	sibling	grandparent
14. Parent's work	child	parent	sibling	grandparent
15. Children's hobbies	child	parent	sibling	grandparent
16. Child's hairstyle	child	parent	sibling	grandparent
17. Parent's teeth	child	parent	sibling	grandparent
18. Child's heartaches	child	parent	sibling	grandparent
19. Parent's friends	child	parent	sibling	grandparent
20. Parent's room	child	parent	sibling	grandparent

There is little research to guide practitioners who want to teach parents specific skills for promoting healthy roles and boundaries. This may be due to the fact that concepts like roles and boundaries are fairly abstract and hard to measure. However, I suspect a more significant reason has to do with how these concepts are traditionally used in therapy. Typically, it is the therapist who assumes responsibility for identifying ill-defined boundaries, unhealthy alliances, and maladaptive roles. And it is the therapist who devises plans for improving family structure. Therapists use directives, enactments, and reframes to orchestrate the realignment of family structure (Minuchin, 1974). These structural changes are usually made without attending to what families will do if family structure shifts maladaptively at some point in the future. Family therapists generally do not train parents to use skills that can establish and maintain adaptive roles and healthy boundaries. In some cases, parents may not even be told the purpose behind the therapist's efforts. I prefer to assume that parents can benefit when therapists combine information about family roles and boundaries with specific suggestions that parents can use on their own. The suggestions presented in Exhibit 8.2 focus on specific behaviors that serve boundary-making and boundary-keeping strategies.

Rules

As defined here, household rules are guidelines used primarily to help children with situations that are too demanding or dangerous. Rules are

Exhibit 8.2. Suggestions for Promoting Family Boundaries

---

10 Ways to Make and Keep Boundaries in Your Family

1. Respect children's privacy and insist on them respecting your privacy.
2. Make it a rule to knock on doors before entering rooms.
3. Close (and lock) your door to maintain privacy. Allow children to do the same, as long as they are safe and do not abuse the privilege.
4. Do not discuss with children issues that are inappropriate or overwhelming for them (e.g., concerns over finances, romantic partners).
5. Make necessary although unpopular decisions on behalf of the whole family.
6. Do distinctively different things that are special with each of your children.
7. Comment on positive characteristics that set a child apart from parents and siblings.
8. Guard well a time each day or week when you are by yourself. Announce it often.
9. Guard well a time each week or month for you and your partner to be alone together. Announce it often.
10. Guard well at least one personal hobby or interest. Announce it often.

---

more formal than parental instructions, which are in effect all the time and not just when parents utter them. Examples of typical household rules include "no playing in the street," "no toys in the kitchen," and "no hitting or pushing." Household rules have long been considered an important aspect of effective child management. For example, Cunningham (1989) recommended that parents identify "hot spots" that frequently engender misbehavior in their children, such as when a parent is on the telephone. By establishing rules for these situations, children will know how to manage them more effectively (e.g., "When parents are on the telephone, children should either watch television or play in their room"). Cunningham (1989) also suggested that parents introduce the rule apart from the situation but then ask children to restate the rule each time the situation presents itself. Children who know the rule can be praised and those who do not know can be reminded. Holden (1983) found empirical support for this kind of proactive parenting in his naturalistic study of mothers and toddlers in the supermarket. Children whose mothers used proactive strategies (e.g., "Your job is to help Mom watch for the things on our shopping list") displayed less disruptive behavior than children whose mothers reacted only after their child had misbehaved.

Given the overlap between household rules and parents' use of instructions, a focus on rules is a valuable complement to containment skills training. Like other kinds of limits imposed by parents, rules work best when used sparingly but firmly. In fact, the short list of five or fewer target behaviors that parents generate during containment skills training (see chapter 6, this volume) is a useful set of household rules. A good set of rules can also reduce parents' tendency to natter their children. For example, if a child is constantly nagged about getting dressed in the morning, a succinct and well-defined rule (e.g., "Out of bed by 6:30 a.m." or "No television until you're dressed") may enable parents and children to get through the situation more efficiently and agreeably. The process of creating and implementing a new rule is similar to the formation of a behavioral contract. Thus, rules are not imposed hastily but after parents have engaged in careful observation, reflection, and planning. New rules often come from parents observing that their child routinely mishandles a given situation. For example, a mother may see that her daughter is having trouble completing her homework in the evening. On reflection, the mother may realize that this has been a recurring problem and that it seems to be made worse when her daughter does her homework in her room instead of at the kitchen table. The mother's plan for helping her daughter may involve a rule requiring all homework be done at the kitchen table. In this way, the demands of the homework situation do not exceed the child's capabilities. Because most household rules are designed to assist children in some way, parents may also want children's input on the new rule. Rules that reflect a child's input should invite less reactivity than rules designed solely by parents. Of course, parents should remain the final arbiters regarding any household rules.

The following is an example of a poorly established rule. A mother takes her two children to the park and later gets angry when they refuse yet again to leave when it is time. She then announces that there is a new family rule: "No more trips to the park." This rule has been set hastily, angrily, and without input from her children. Also, eliminating trips to the park will not solve the problem of how to structure her children's transition from the park to home. Later, she may find it difficult to enforce this rule, or she may ignore it because it does not fit her own needs. This same scenario can be used to illustrate a more effective approach to establishing rules. First, assume the mother recognized that her children were having difficulty leaving the park because of the demands of transitioning from play to nonplay settings. The mother could describe the family's problem of being delayed by play time that lasts too long. Depending on the age of her children, she may seek their input when devising the rule (for older children), or she may decide for herself what the rule is but ask them to comment on it (for younger children). She may suggest, for example, that on future trips to the park, she will warn them 5 minutes and 1 minute before it is time to leave but that they must leave the park after that. Her children may like this rule but have ideas about how they will be warned. Even though the mother devised the rule, her children can still feel a part of what was decided. In this way, the rule becomes a family or household rule and not just "Mom's rule" or "the thing Mom says when she gets mad at us at the park." The children could even give the rule a name (e.g., "The rule about how we quit playing"), further establishing it as a household fixture. Exhibit 8.3 presents a set of guidelines for establishing and implementing rules that may be useful as a handout.

Rituals

Chapter 5 discussed how parental acceptance could be enhanced when parents are trained to use child-directed play skills and reflective listening

Exhibit 8.3.   Guidelines for Establishing and Implementing Household Rules

When you establish and implement rules in your household, it may be helpful to consider the following:

1. *Is there a situation or a place that is too hard or too dangerous for your child to handle?* Here are several "hot spots": when (a) your child is crossing the street, getting ready for bed, getting dressed, brushing teeth or bathing, riding in the car, is at someone else's house, is out in public, and so on, or (b) you are cooking, talking on the telephone, entertaining visitors, and so on.

2. *What do your children need to better this situation?* Is it clear what you expect of the children? Can they remember what is expected from one time to the next? Is the situation so overwhelming or confusing that they cannot control their behavior without some help?

3. *Think of a rule that tells your children what to do in this situation.* Some of the best rules use *if–then* phrases. For example, a good rule for children who get angry and hit each other might be "If you are angry, then use your words."

4. *State the rule in a simple way.* Do not use too many words, and try using rules that are easy to say. (e.g., "We don't hurt in this family.")

5. *Try not to include punishment as part of the rule.* The goal of any rule should be to help children with hard-to-handle situations. For example, if chores were not done because children are watching television, it would make sense to make this rule: "If chores are not done, the television goes off." However, if watching television is not part of the problem, do not make it part of the rule.

6. *Have a family meeting to discuss the rule.* Start by describing the situation causing the problems. Tell everyone your idea for a new rule. Try not to sound as though your rule is the only rule that will work. Listen for ways to make the rule better.

7. *Remember that it is okay if your children do not like the rule.* You can say "I wish we had a better rule, but I guess this one will have to do."

8. *Ask your child the rule beforehand, if you know when a hot spot or other situation is coming up.* For example, if the telephone rings, say "Now what's the rule when I'm on the telephone?" Remind them of the rule if necessary.

---

skills. Some parents who are equipped with these skills may not use them, however. Overwhelmed parents of aggressive children may not be in the mood to play or listen to their troubling child, or they may regard these kinds of interactions as unnecessary, unnatural, or undeserved. Other parents may have the motivation to be accepting but lack the skills and scripts to be accepting. For parents who struggle to convey an ongoing message of acceptance, family rituals offer a convenient alternative. In the same way that rules help parents with containment, rituals can help parents with acceptance. If rules are "standing orders" for how children should behave, rituals are "standing invitations" to be a part of the family. As used here, *rituals* are regularly observed events that promote a child's sense of acceptance and enhance family stability and cohesion. Parents who have a regularly scheduled play time with their child have, in essence, created a family ritual. But scheduled play sessions generally fade over time as children get older and pursue other interests. If families have other rituals in place, then the loss of play time is not so critical. However, if there are no other rituals, then parents may need to continue their home play sessions or be assisted in developing new family rituals.

Family rituals need not be grand and elaborate. Some rituals occur fairly often and are built into a family's routine (see below). I refer to these as common or minirituals. Minirituals are usually the kinds of activities that all families must do each day or each week, but they are done in ways that make them special and beneficial to family members. Examples include dinnertime, bedtime, car rides, and trips to the grocery store. Other minirituals are enjoyable activities that a family incorporates into its daily or weekly routine. Examples include a reading time, bedtime prayers, a make-your-own-pizza night, a family video night, a weekly family meeting, a family board game night, a Saturday night slumber party in the den, a weekly trip to grandmother's, or weekly dining at a favorite family restaurant. Changing or creating new minirituals must take into account a family's routine (e.g., the amount of time between dinner and bedtime) and should not be scheduled in a way that disrupts that routine.

There are also rituals that take families out of their routine and are regarded as very special. I refer to these as uncommon or *major rituals*. Major rituals are less frequent and more formal than minirituals and are often used to mark important transitions or accomplishments in the life of a child or a family. Births, birthdays, funerals, weddings, religious and patriotic holidays, graduations, and extended trips or moves are all opportunities for major rituals. Most of these events generate strong emotions, sometimes more than can be reasonably dealt with by the persons involved. Major rituals can help by providing family members with certain scripts and activities that allow them to navigate these tough emotional waters (Constantin & Cavell, 1999a). Changing or creating a major ritual can require extensive planning and either creativity or creative borrowing. The success of family rituals depends upon making children feel valued and building a more cohesive sense of family. Parents should keep these goals in mind when planning the ritual activities and scripts.

Some family rituals are little more than elaborate affairs that cost a lot of time and money but fail to provide children with a sense of acceptance or family cohesion. For example, on Thanksgiving day in this country families fill their homes with relatives and friends and prepare large amounts of tasty food. But what makes for a "successful" Thanksgiving dinner? Some may point to the quality of the food and drink, but I suspect most will say the quality of the interactions with those present. If that is true, then the next question is how much preparation is put into this aspect of the Thanksgiving ritual versus the preparing of food and drink?

Exhibit 8.4.   Suggestions for Changing or Creating Family Rituals

1. Rituals are either special ways that families do ordinary things (like mealtime or bedtime) or special events that happen only once a year or less (like graduation). Rituals are an opportunity for children to feel accepted by parents and to feel close as a family.
2. Changing a family ritual or starting a new ritual can feel strange, but it can also be fun. Try the new ritual before deciding to keep it.
3. Talk with other families about their rituals and borrow the parts of their rituals that you like.
4. Any ritual—no matter how small—can be a success if the mood is warm and pleasant. How family members treat each other during a ritual is most important.
5. Any ritual—no matter how large or fancy—can be a failure if the mood is cold or hostile. Sometimes a major ritual can feel like a major disaster. It is better to keep it small and meaningful.
6. Keep these questions in mind when changing or creating a family ritual:
   (a) What is the main focus or activity of the ritual? (e.g., bedtime, birthdays, making and eating pizza)
   (b) Who does what and when in the ritual?
   (c) How often will the ritual occur? (e.g., daily, weekly, monthly, yearly)
   (d) What will we name the ritual?
   (e) What will make the ritual special for my child? (e.g., What will I do? What will I say? What material things, if any, will be used?)
   (f) What do I want the ritual to mean to my child and me?
7. Do not start too many rituals. The best rituals fit in your schedule and are not hard to maintain.

I would bet that many families do very little. Others may promote this aspect of the ritual in creative, memorable ways. Some may have an annual touch football game, others may allow each person present to give their own special thanks before the meal. The point is that rituals are rich in their potential to promote acceptance and cohesion, but they can also be barren of such properties if parents fail to keep these goals in mind. Exhibit 8.4 is a list of suggestions that parents can use when changing or creating rituals.

Routines

A family's *routine* is its daily, weekly, or monthly schedule of who does what, when, and where. Whether the activity is the evening meal, the Sunday dinner with grandparents, or the monthly meeting for parents, families operate best when they have some knowledge of what will happen and when. A routine can also indicate what is important to the family and how well organized the family is. In families that are relatively healthy, daily tasks (e.g., getting up and getting dressed, doing homework, taking a bath), weekend activities (e.g., time at the park), and monthly events (e.g., paying bills) are predictable and structured. Children who have a structured routine will know how to behave and will feel safer and less anxious about each new event or activity. Parents who have a structured routine are more likely to remain calm and make good decisions when stressful events could easily overwhelm them. In other families, the daily and weekly schedules are unpredictable and disorganized. Changes happen quickly and often. Priority may be given to activities (e.g., watching television) that disrupt a child's school performance or interfere with family functioning. Little attention is given to activities (e.g., dinnertime, study hour, family time) that are important to children's health and well-being and that lead to a greater sense of family.

When addressing the issue of family routines, practitioners may find it is useful to give parents the assignment of writing a summary of their current daily and weekly schedules. These summaries can be used to explore with parents the question of whether the family's routine is serving them well or should be altered in some way. Helpful questions to ask include (a) "Was it a difficult task to list your schedule?" (b) "Did you learn anything about your family by listing your daily schedule?" and (c) "Do you feel your daily and weekly schedules are a good reflection of your family's values and priorities?" If parents are ready to discuss making changes in their family's routine, practitioners can share the handout in Exhibit 8.5 with parents and discuss it in a step-by-step fashion.

Exhibit 8.5.   Steps to Improving Family Routines

Determine whether your family's routine needs to be changed. Do your days and weeks seem disorganized and unpredictable? Do you worry that your routine does not reflect your family's values?

1. **Begin by changing only one thing at a time.** Family routines are hard to change. Go slow, and do not try to overhaul the whole schedule at once: Your family will revolt!
2. **Change that part of your routine that will have the largest "ripple" effect.** Three things to keep in mind are (a) dinnertime, because it is the start of the evening; (b) the sheer number of activities or organizations in which parents and children are involved; and (c) the number of nights and hours that the television is turned on.
3. **Be realistic and do not overschedule.** Both parents and children need time to shift from one activity to the next, and family members need some time to be alone and to rest. This goal is often lost when families fill their schedules with many activities. Some activities may work better if scheduled once or twice a month and not daily or weekly.
4. **Every so often, "realign" the routines.** Families have a way of slipping into old, unwanted routines. Families also need to change their routines as children get older and their needs and interests change.
5. **Have fun and be creative.** Remember, you do not have to keep the same schedule because it is the way you have always done something. The television does not have to be on every night. Some household chores can be done every other day or week. Evening meals do not always have to be hot. And bath time does not have to be at night.

Summary

A family's structure is that set of tacitly understood rules that function to organize the way family members relate to one another. How families are organized and structured are important issues in family therapy, but family therapists typically do not train parents in skills that would allow them to make structural changes on their own. Parent training programs emphasize skill-building exercises but rarely cover systemic issues related to family structure. In RPT, the goal is to combine strategies that enhance dyadic relationships with strategies that improve family functioning and family structure. In this chapter, family structure was discussed in light of 4 Rs—roles, rules, rituals, and routines. These four types of family structure can be used to create a supportive infrastructure for parents who are vulnerable to stress, inconsistency, and emotional lability. For many parents with aggressive children, the decision to target family structure can create therapeutic opportunities that would otherwise not exist.

9

Parental Self-Care

Parenting an aggressive child is hard work from which parents rarely get a break. This is especially true for single parents who may not have the option of regularly relinquishing child care duties to a trusted coparent. At a conference symposium I organized on the topic of parent training, a panelist commented afterward on the insights that researchers and practitioners gain from our own experiences as parents. This panelist compared such insights to the kind of secrets one learns when joining a select club. We all agreed, although I wondered if an even more select club was that group of parents composed of single mothers. Parents who have the benefit of a reliable partner should respect and admire the Herculean tasks these women face, especially when they are socially isolated and financially burdened. Extant research continues to show that this group of parents is distinct, both in terms of their therapeutic needs and their potential to benefit from parent training (see chapters 2 and 3, this volume). To the degree single mothers are experiencing other risk factors (e.g., living in violent neighborhoods), their needs only increase and their responsiveness to treatment only decreases.

The importance of encouraging and assisting parents in their efforts to refuel so they can return to the task of managing a difficult child is among the many insights to come from the qualitative research of Spitzer and Webster-Stratton (Spitzer et al., 1991; Webster-Stratton & Spitzer, 1996). The importance of addressing the health and well-being of parents of difficult children is also reflected in programs that target marital dissatisfaction (Dadds, Schwartz, & Sanders, 1987), interpersonal distress (Webster-Stratton, 1994), and social support (Dadds & McHugh, 1992) in addition to parenting skills. For example, Webster-Stratton (1994) provided parents with 14 training sessions designed to improve family communication, problem solving, and coping skills. Parents participated in these sessions after completing a 12-week parent-training protocol. The results were mixed in that mothers improved significantly in their communication and problem-solving skills, but these skills added little to their parenting success or to their child's short-term functioning. However, similar improvements in fathers' communication and problem-solving skills did lead to improved parenting and to significant gains in children's use of prosocial strategies. Practitioners should not overlook studies such as this one that address the important issue of parental self-care.

Parental self-care can be defined as parents' ability to promote their own strengths and well-being so that they can continue the job of parenting. Unfortunately, the empirical literature on this topic is both limited and mixed. Yet the issue of parental self-care is still a critical one to address in parent therapy. It is one thing for practitioners to recognize the risk factors that portend disrupted parenting and a poor response to parent therapy; it is quite another to generate effective strategies for countering parental distress, fatigue, isolation, and burnout. I begin my discussion of parental self-care by reviewing empirical studies like that of Webster-Stratton (1994). I then offer an expanded view of parental self-care that encompasses three primary goals. I also discuss specific strategies that parents can use when attempting to change or cope with the burden of parenting an aggressive child.

Empirical Efforts to Promote Parental Self-Care

Prinz and Miller (1991) suggested that standard approaches to parent training need to be adapted or expanded to meet the needs of parents who face significant stress and instability. One of the first studies to assess the role of adjunctive therapies for parents of children with conduct problems was done by Dadds et al. (1987). They looked at whether *partner support training* (PST) would enhance the skills that parents acquired in parent training. PST focused on strategies (e.g., communication, problem solving) that parents could use to enhance the supportive nature of their marital relationship. Results showed that nondiscordant couples were unaffected by PST, but discordant couples showed significant gains when offered the added PST sessions. In a related study, Dadds and McHugh (1992) assessed the impact of an adjunctive treatment called *ally support training* (AST). Unlike the previous study by Dadds et al. (1987), this one involved single parents who were attempting to manage without a marital partner. Allies recruited by parents were trained to use a number of relationship-supporting skills (e.g., active listening) with the target parent. Both AST and parent-training-only groups improved, but no additional gains were found for the AST group. However, treatment responders from both groups were more likely to report high levels of social support from friends. Another option available to practitioners is to refer parents to individual therapy. Although I am unaware of such studies with parents of aggressive children, one study used this approach with high-risk mothers and their infants (Korfmacher, Adam, Ogawa, & Egeland, 1997). Mothers had opportunities for more intensive therapy, including insight-oriented therapy, but few mothers took advantage of these resources. Only 5 out of 55 mothers chose to engage in insight-oriented therapy at any time during the intervention. Mothers preferred supportive or problem-focused forms of assistance that addressed immediate needs and not past issues.

Each of these studies attempted to enhance parents' contacts with supportive others. A different strategy is to work directly with parents to improve their ability to cope and adapt on their own. Wahler and colleagues (Wahler, Cartor, Fleischman, & Lambert, 1993) used a procedure known as *synthesis training* to counter the tendency for insular mothers to have biased perceptions of their child's behavior. Therapists looked for occasions when parents confused stressful interactions with their child with stressful interactions with others. Although parent training combined with synthesis training did not lead to significant gains at posttreatment, follow-up assessments revealed improvements in both child aversive behavior and maternal consistency. Prinz and Miller (1994) used a similar modification in parent training, which they labeled *enhanced family treatment* (EFT). In EFT, standard behavioral parent training was combined throughout with efforts by therapists to elicit from parents their concerns about nonparenting issues. Compared to standard parent training, EFT led to significantly fewer dropouts, especially among high-adversity families. Pfiffner and her colleagues used a different approach to working directly with parents on issues of self-care (Pfiffner, Jouriles, Brown, Etscheidt, & Kelly, 1990). These researchers trained parents to use a series of problem-solving steps to address nonchild-related issues. Compared to parents who received only standard behavioral parent training, these parents reported significantly greater decreases in children's externalizing symptoms at follow-up.

Collectively, the studies reviewed here offer support for efforts to improve parents' self-care. Many questions remain, however, including which is the best way to proceed with parents in need? One tentative conclusion is that efforts to assist parents with *intra*personal coping skills may be more effective than approaches that rely on *inter*personal skills. The fact that parents of aggressive children are already struggling with one relationship (viz., the parent–child relationship) suggests they are at risk for other relationship difficulties (Webster-Stratton, 1990). In the following discussion, I offer an expanded view of parental self-care that builds on extant research and attempts to generate additional recommendations and testable hypotheses about practitioners' role in this area.

The Goals of Parental Self-Care

The framework for viewing parental self-care offered here subsumes and expands conceptually on previous work in this area. In line with the theme of this book, my aim is to address the principles that underlie specific self-care strategies and tactics. By adopting this framework, practitioners and parents can generate customized self-care plans and techniques based on specific needs and circumstances. In this expanded view of parental self-care, the focus is on three primary goals: energy, strength, and commitment. The metaphorical nature of these concepts is not well suited for research purposes but lends itself to clinical application.

Energy

I use the term *energy* to refer to parents' capacity to sustain their efforts from moment to moment, day to day, week to week, and so on. Like automobiles, parents can have plenty of "horsepower," a well-tuned engine, and a clear direction on where to go, but unless they have the fuel or energy to sustain themselves, little is accomplished. The lack of parental energy is often seen in parents who are depressed, overwhelmed, over-worked, and insular. The value of framing parenting problems as poten-tially a lack of sufficient energy is reflected in Webster-Stratton's (Webster-Stratton & Herbert, 1994; Webster-Stratton & Spitzer, 1996) observation that parents of aggressive children need refueling opportunities as well as skills training.

I recently worked with a family in which an 8-year-old boy was begin-ning to show signs of covert antisocial behaviors (e.g., lying, stealing). My assessment revealed that his mother had a fairly negative perception of him and often engaged in excessive correcting and criticism. In our work together, I focused on the importance of recognizing the role of her son's temperament and the benefits of having more realistic expectations of him. We also did skills training that focused specifically on her use of parental acceptance. After 4 to 6 sessions, things began to improve markedly for this family, but I felt the gains were due more to self-care issues than to other treatment efforts. I had learned in an early session that this mother was feeling depressed, distant from her husband, and overwhelmed by her weekly schedule. A second job as a waitress that she did on weekend nights was contributing to the strain of her schedule. What impressed me most about this mother was that soon after sharing my impressions of how drained she must feel, she quit her second job. This impressed and sur-prised me because she had offered seemingly good reasons for keeping the job. This mother began to respond beautifully to her son's needs after she no longer worked Friday and Saturday nights. In my view, she now had the energy to do the job of parenting this challenging boy.

Strength

The concept of parental strength is akin to a vehicle's horsepower: A fully fueled car may not be up to the task if it lacks sufficient horsepower. In lay language, parental strength can be thought of as character or personal integrity. Psychologically, *parental strength* is a summary term to describe the quantity and quality of parents' repertoire of skills. As parent trainers, we add to parents' strength each time we teach them a new parenting technique or assist in their construction of an effective parenting script or family structure. But parental strength can also be influenced by person-ality variables, such as security of attachment and ego strength. In the context of parenting an aggressive child, *strength* refers to parents' ability to execute the right parenting strategy despite the interference of opposing forces—both external and internal.

External forces include the child's protests and counterattacks, the doubts and criticisms of other adults, and the competing demands of a parents' life. Internal forces include parents' own doubts and self-criticisms, as well as the emotional costs that arise when they carry out unpopular executive decisions. The vertical nature of the parent–child relationship is one factor that makes parental strength such a pivotal determinant of a child's successful socialization (Hartup, 1989). Unlike the give-and-take of horizontal, adult–adult relationships, the parent–child relationship cannot be used as a reliable resource for renewing parental strength. The parent–child relationship is also typically not self-perpetuating, particularly when the child is hard to like and aggressive. Therefore, parental strength must be renewed by sources operating outside the parent–child system. Common sources of strength are parents' adult–adult relationships, but other sources of strength may also be available. The availability of these other sources is often a function of the degree to which parents have adaptive and stable self-systems. To the extent parents have a maturely developed sense of who they are, are satisfied with their sense of self, and have a range of effective coping skills, their ability to extract rewards and renewal from their environment is greatly enhanced. Conversely, to the extent they lack an adaptive self-system, parents are more likely to generate additional stress in their lives. The task for practitioners is to keep these possible sources of strength in mind when working with parents who typically lack adaptability and stability in their self-system and in their adult–adult relationships. The wholesale remaking of parents' self-systems and support networks is not likely, but efforts to enhance parents' self-care skills are still justified. With a goal as fundamental as parental strength, such factors as parents' developmental history, their innate abilities, and their current life circumstances will constrain but not define what can be achieved through better self-care.

Commitment

Parents who suffer emotionally, interpersonally, or economically may struggle to sustain the level of commitment that is needed to parent an aggressive child. Note that I make a distinction between parents' beliefs and goals about parenting and their commitment to those beliefs and goals. This is a subtle distinction, but its implications affect how one works with struggling parents of difficult children. The most important implication is that parents who lack a strong commitment to the role of parenting can still have reasonable and positive beliefs about parenting. Many parents who are overwhelmed by and who withdraw from the demands of parenting continue to believe in the goals of socialization. However, their experiences and perceptions have resulted in their concluding that they personally cannot affect their child's outcome. A second implication is that efforts to improve parental self-care should lead generally to greater commitment by parents to their children. Without directly challenging parents, practitioners can promote commitment to the job of parenting by addressing the obstacles to better self-care. In this way, practitioners reduce the risk of heightened resistance that often follows directly confronting parents (Patterson & Forgatch, 1985).

The notion that parents can more fully commit to meeting their child's needs when their own needs are addressed must be qualified, however. Because of the vertical nature of the parent–child relationship, children are more dependent on parents and are generally less capable of promoting their own self-care. Parents cannot reasonably expect to have their needs met completely and immediately when children are relying on parents to meet their needs. Unfortunately, there are some parents whose emotional needs are great and whose capacity to defer those needs is limited. These parents are typically those who were maltreated or poorly parented by their own parents. Parents who are emotionally labile or aloof may not be able to manage the demands of a vertical parent–child relationship. Indeed, their children may function more like age mates or may even assume a parentified role in which the children assume the duties of caring for their parents' emotional needs. Children who are parentified are especially at risk for hostile, self-destructive behavior when their parents combine emotional neediness with frequent criticism and demands (Kerfoot, 1979). Such children are intensely frustrated by a parent who is both negative and fragile. To counterattack a nattering, needy parent means that one is jeopardizing an already fragile attachment relationship. In my clinical experience, children living under these conditions are more explosive and unpredictable than most other children. Also, their parents are unlikely to benefit from self-care efforts unless parental psychopathology is addressed via psychotherapy, medication, or a combination of the two.

The reader may recognize similarities between factors thought to compromise parents' endorsement of prosocial values (see chapter 7, this volume) and factors thought to interfere with commitment to the job of parenting. It would be difficult to imagine actively prosocial parents who are also not committed to caring for their children. On the other hand, workaholic parents or parents who assume inordinate levels of autonomy and competence in their children may seem lacking in their commitment to the role of parenting. One mother with whom I worked had become pregnant with her oldest child before she finished high school. Now at the age of 30, with three children and no co-parent, she decided to resume her adolescent dream of a college education. Although in many respects this was an admirable goal, she made a number of decisions that suggested she was abdicating her role as parent in an effort to pursue this dream. She moved away from a supportive extended family and from nearby colleges to attend a larger university in a community where she knew virtually no one. She also worked full-time, often in excess of 40 hours per week, for reasons that seemed to go beyond financial need. She also joined a service fraternity, whose members were much younger students, and she devoted time to projects and meetings when her children desperately needed her. As a result, her children were often unsupervised, and her position as the adult in charge quickly dissolved. She seemed to believe that her children were now old enough to fend for themselves (the two youngest were 10 and 12 years of age). She also believed that extended family members and former husbands should assume more of the responsibility for child care, but this arrangement was never solidified. Much of the work we did together centered on the loss of this mother's youthful dreams and on strategies that could help her succeed in furthering her education while remaining committed to raising her children.

Self-Care Strategies

Before I describe specific self-care strategies, I should note that many parents, even those who face significant emotional, interpersonal, and financial burdens, may reject practitioners' efforts to discuss this topic. Typical obstacles include feelings of hopelessness, distrust, and limited experience with the concept or pursuit of self-care. The following dialogue offers an example of how one might discuss self-care with a reluctant parent:

> *Practitioner:* It doesn't sound like you have any time to yourself—time when you can stop, catch your breath, and collect your thoughts.
> *Parent:* Are you kidding? I don't have time to go to the bathroom!
> *Practitioner:* Do you think it would help if you had some time off? A lot of parents with difficult children tell me it does help, especially if they know when the breaks will happen, and they don't have to wait too long for the next one.
> *Parent:* Oh, I'd love to go to a movie, or to the mall, or just watch TV without being interrupted every 5 seconds, but it's not going to happen.
> *Practitioner:* Is that because it would be impossible to make it happen or because you would feel too guilty doing it, or both?
> *Parent:* I might feel a little guilty, but mainly it would be that my kids and my schedule won't allow it.
> *Practitioner:* So you're stuck then.
> *Parent:* That's right. Trapped!
> *Practitioner:* How do you do it then? How do you keep going day in and day out with all you have to do?
> *Parent:* Beats the hell out of me! Some days I can't do it. I might call in sick to work or if I do go to work I might be so tired and so mean at the end of the day that I know I can't be helping my kids.
> *Practitioner:* And I would bet on the weekend you're exhausted and your kids need you.
> *Parent:* That's right. In fact, sometimes I think I get more rest at work than at home!
> *Practitioner:* Who knows how rough it is for you?
> *Parent:* No one, really. Maybe my mom and my sister, but they've got their own problems, and half the time all they do is tell me what I'm doing wrong. I don't need that.
> *Practitioner:* No, you don't. Do they ever help out?
> *Parent:* Every once in a while, if I'm desperate, I might ask my mom to keep the kids, but it's usually not worth the hassle.
> *Practitioner:* Is your time at work rewarding at all? Is it a break from the demands of parenting or just another source of stress?
> *Parent:* I have some good days at work and I get along with a couple of the women who work there. But it's a long day and we don't get many chances to rest. It's hard.

Practitioner: Do you see it getting better any time soon, or do you think it will be a while before you'll have some time to yourself and a less stressful life?

Parent: I don't expect it to change right away unless I win the lottery! Otherwise, I'm stuck with waiting till the kids get older and stay out of trouble or they get locked up because they finally went too far with all their stuff.

Practitioner: Will you make it until then?

Parent: I'll have to.

Practitioner: But how? Is there something about you as a person or as a parent that keeps you going?

Parent: Well, I do love my kids, and I want them to have a better life than I did. But it's hard.

Practitioner: You've certainly convinced me of that! In fact, I'm not sure if your goal of making things better for your children is possible unless things improve for you first. Does that sound crazy for me to say that?

Parent: I guess not, but I don't see how it can happen.

Practitioner: Well, I think you're right: Whatever changes you make to take better care of yourself are probably not going to be very big and won't be easy—at least at the start. But I'm still wondering if you even think it makes sense that "If I help myself, I help my children"?

Parent: I'm not sure.

Practitioner: The idea is based on the tendency for children to look up to, to respect, and to take after those adults in their life who are strong and caring. I'm suggesting that one of the best ways to help your kids is to be the healthiest, most confident person you can be. I've seen your ability to be caring, but I think your kids also need you to be strong and healthy. That means taking care of yourself physically, emotionally, interpersonally, and for some parents, spiritually.

So you see, we're talking about more than an occasional break to go shopping; we're talking about the possibility of changing the way you take care of yourself, the way you see yourself and, eventually, the way your children see you.

Parent: I don't know about all that.

Practitioner: Let me give you examples of what I've seen other parents do to take better care of themselves. Some of these won't fit with your situation, but you'll have a better idea of what I'm talking about. For example, one mother. . . .

This hypothetical script illustrates a number of points. The first is that a useful beginning posture blends a large dose of support and validation with a dash of curiosity. I gradually became more curious as the mother became more hopeless. Probes that asked if anyone knew about her struggle and what it was about her that kept her going were pivotal. These probes allowed the mother to stop deflecting and to be more candid about her struggles. It was then that I processed with her the potentially foreign idea that helping herself would be an effective way to help her children. It would have been a mistake to assume this mother would immediately agree to that point. By practically encouraging her to reject it as crazy, I set the stage once again for her to respond in an open and productive manner. Finally, my approach to educating her about various self-care strategies is also tentative, offered as a set of examples that may or may not fit.

In the sections that follow, I describe several strategies that parents can pursue in their attempts to promote parental energy, strength, or commitment. These strategies include approaches to self-care that go beyond improving parents' reactions to stress. Coping with stress is but one part of a stable and adaptive self-system. Proactive strategies that help parents to prevent the occurrence of stress and that promote greater psychological growth are also needed. Not all of these strategies are feasible for parents. Also, the specifics of how parents pursue these strategies can vary greatly from one family to the next.

Time Off

A popular exercise in high school classes designed to prepare students for the demands of parenting is to assign the task of caring for a single raw egg. The primary lesson students should learn from this exercise is the nearly unremitting sense of responsibility that parents face. Of course, the younger and the more dependent the child, the greater the continuity of responsibility. As children become more independent and better able to care for themselves, parents will enjoy longer and more frequent respites from this responsibility. The picture is more complicated, however, for parents of highly aggressive children. The pace with which their children demand attention is intensified, and the years devoted to vigilant monitoring and prolonged worry are likely to stretch well beyond adolescence. In short, these parents are working harder and longer than most other parents. In this respect, they are little different from parents whose children suffer from serious developmental delays, physical impairments, or chronic medical illnesses. Social services agencies designed to help children and families-at-risk recognize the insidious impact of stress-filled parenting, and some have begun to offer respite opportunities to parents who are desperate for a break.

Unfortunately, not all parents of aggressive children are served by such progressive agencies. Many parents cannot easily create their own respite opportunities because of financial constraints or because they lack a supportive partner or social network. However, I have also been struck by the number of parents who could have access to breaks from parenting but either fail to take such breaks or use them in ways that limit their refueling potential. The reasons parents give for not taking time off vary, but most seem to underestimate both their need for and the benefits of time off. In my experience, the tendency to downplay the need for a break from parenting is more common among married couples, and it is usually the father who is less likely to require respite from parenting. A likely explanation is that fathers are less often in the parenting role (even when mothers also work outside the home) and thus have less need for a departure from it.

The task of increasing parents' time off from the role of parenting can present the practitioner with a host of obstacles. Practitioners must not only be creative in assisting parents who desire time off and persistent in encouraging parents who fail to see the value of time off, they must also be wise in how they advise parents to use their time off. Questions about when and how to schedule time off from parenting are difficult to answer. There is a lack of empirical research on the parameters of effective refueling. For example, is it better for parents to take short breaks that occur fairly often or long breaks that happen sparingly? Is it more beneficial for parents to take spontaneous, unpredictable breaks or planned, regular breaks? Should parents use time off to engage in exciting, fun-filled recreational or entertainment activities, or should parents pursue quiet reflection? Are parents better served by activities that bring them into contact with other adults (some of whom are parents), or is it more advantageous to seek solitude (or time just as a couple, for those with partners)? Undoubtedly, parents will differ in the degree to which they benefit from quiet solitude versus stimulating social gatherings. Parents are also likely to differ over time in their refueling preferences. Still, if the primary purpose of time off is to reinvigorate one's self as a parent, then practitioners may want to guide parents toward the activities that best perform that function.

In one of the few studies to address the issue of time off from parenting, Colleta (1981; cited in McLoyd, 1990) assessed the benefits of refueling for low-income adolescent mothers. These mothers were found to be warmer and less rejecting toward their preschool children when their continuous interaction was interrupted by a break of more than 2 hours. This finding suggests that brief, regular breaks might pay greater dividends to needy parents than extended breaks or vacations that occur infrequently and unpredictably. I generally recommend this combination, based on this research and my own experiences as a practitioner and a parent. For distressed parents with difficult children, knowing that at predictable intervals (e.g., weekly, biweekly) they will be able to enjoy a brief (e.g., 2 hours) recess from the job of parenting can feel like a life jacket to a drowning person. These eagerly anticipated breaks might be the only thing that keeps them afloat. One difficulty with this kind of recommendation, however, is that parents may view time off as something they do only if they feel overwhelmed. I suggest that time off is more beneficial when used as a regular prophylactic against possible stress than as an antidote to current and excessive stress. Building parenting breaks into one's schedule is hampered when parents view time off as a significant detour from their routine and as a major investment of their time. Therefore, practitioners may need to propose the use of time off on a trial basis only.

It should be noted that time off from parenting does not have to mean time away from parenting. It is certainly easier for parents to refuel when they can more fully depart from their caregiving role, but many parents do not have the luxury of regular time away. Instead, these parents may need to search for creative ways to find time off while home. Many single mothers will attest to the fact that time behind a locked bathroom door can hold great appeal when their children are making one demand after another. Other parents might establish their bedroom (if they do not have to share it with children) as sacred ground—off limits to children or an occasional retreat. Some working parents may create a daily ritual in which they take a brief, isolated pause before they begin their evening caregiving duties. For parents who work and come home immediately afterward, collapsing on the floor or couch ("vegging out") before assuming the evening duties or enforcing an earlier bedtime for all children may be useful options. As one can see, there is a necessary overlap between parental self-care and a family's structure, especially the use of routines and rituals. Unless parents build into their schedule a break from parenting that is protected and that occurs regularly, it is unlikely that they will be able to sustain their self-care plans. Few parents have the resources to take time off whenever they need it and at a moment's notice; instead, most parents require time off to be a permanent fixture in their schedule to make it sustainable. Even parents who come to appreciate the value of time off can fail to recognize that its predictable occurrence is an important aspect of refueling.

Many families lead busy, active lives, and those who do not can always use television as an easy escape that requires no prior planning. Strong desires to take time off can evaporate in the face of poor planning. Parents who have a partner also need to find a time in their schedule for time off and team building. Deciding who takes responsibility for planning the time together is an important task for parents with partners. One couple with whom I worked complained about never finding time to speak at length with each other without being interrupted by one thing or another. Each seemed to expect the other to plan time off. I had identified this couple's lack of coordination and mutual support as an important contributor to their child's defiant and aggressive behavior. To emphasize how strongly I believed in the value of their taking time off together, I insisted on not meeting with them until they had engaged in a least one parenting break. For these parents, the diffusion of responsibility affected more than their scheduling of time off; it also affected their overall approach to parenting.

The strategy of time off from the caregiving role is fundamental to parents' self-care. It is a prerequisite to refueling and is an important component when pursuing other self-care goals. If parents do not have regular, predictable opportunities to attend to their own needs, either as individuals or as a couple, they risk an erosion of their energy, strength, and commitment.

Instrumental Support

For a lot of parents, particularly for single mothers, successfully procuring assistance with the duties and demands of parenting can be a highly rewarding form of self-care. Instrumental support can take many forms, including help with finances, chores, household maintenance, transportation, children's health care, and of course child care itself. What role can or should practitioners play in helping parents pursue this self-care strategy? Very rarely, I submit, should practitioners be the direct providers of this type of assistance to parents. Even practitioners who conduct regular home visits with parents should be cautious about the extent to which they are viewed as providers of instrumental aid. The therapeutic scope and time-limited nature of our work fits better with a goal of empowering parents to obtain their own instrumental support directly or through an available service agency. That is not to say that practitioners cannot use instrumental assistance to facilitate parents' participation in an intervention program. Many parent training groups offer complimentary food and child care to parents who would not otherwise come. Some well-funded programs even provide transportation and monetary compensation to participating parents. Such generous inducements are impractical in most settings, but practitioners should strive to be creative when seeking to ease the burden of parents' participation in an intervention.

Assisting parents in their efforts to procure greater instrumental support usually means educating them about where and how to access available resources. In my own community, we are fortunate to have an agency whose sole purpose is to help parents identify and take advantage of the many service agencies and organizations that exist locally and federally. Whether the need is for immediate food, shelter, or clothing or whether the goal is job training or debt consolidation, this agency can make the necessary connections. It is still important for practitioners to apprise themselves of the resources available, but agencies such as this one are typically more informed and more efficient than most practitioners.

The task of the practitioner is to identify the critical needs parents have that can be addressed through existing resources. Parents may not be aware of resources, the steps to follow to access these resources, or the significant impact such resources can have on their family's functioning. Therefore, the more familiar practitioners are with human services agencies and charitable organizations, the more informative they can be to parents in need. One of the best ways to stay informed and connected to such agencies and organizations is to develop positive relationships with members of their staff. Treating agency staffers as competent professionals and being grateful for their assistance are essential, but practitioners may also consider assisting with fundraising efforts, public awareness campaigns, or advisory boards. Sometimes parents in need can benefit from not only what you as a practitioner know but who you know. Indeed, introducing parents to a friendly, helpful staff person can be one of the more valuable roles a practitioner can play. If the service agency is layered in bureaucracy and red tape, such a connection may even be a necessary prerequisite to gaining the help parents desire.

Emotional Support

Research on the subject of social support indicates that perceptions of others' support are more predictive of adjustment and maladjustment than are more "objective" measures of others' support (Cohen & Syme, 1985). In other words, how supported a parent feels can often be more critical than the actual support they receive. It is not surprising, therefore, to find that perceptions of emotional support are more strongly associated with adjustment than are perceptions of instrumental support (Cohen & Wills, 1985). Parents of aggressive children may find that their social circle can quickly shrink when their children are hurtful, destructive, and extremely disruptive. In fact, as their number of positive social contacts decreases, their exposure to negative social contacts often increases (Dumas & Wahler, 1985). Dirty, doubtful looks in the supermarket, sneers from neighbors, and complaints from teachers may be the only acknowledgment from others that one is parent to a difficult child. Even family members can second guess and not support a struggling parent. The odds of this happening seem to increase when there are strong child effects. Children who are extremely hyperactive and impulsive or who are temperamentally fearless and strong willed may not respond to the same parenting strategies that worked with other children. Thus, what seems like a fairly simple issue for outsiders is actually a complex, demanding, and chronic challenge for parents. For someone to appreciate fully and without criticism the nature of their dilemma can be a powerful source of support for parents of aggressive children (Szykula, Mas, Turner, Crowley, & Sayger, 1991). Practitioners should be careful, however, not to equate social contacts with social support. As Wahler & Fox (1981) have shown, parenting effectiveness can actually deteriorate when insular mothers experience social contacts that are negative. Similarly, a study of young Latina mothers found that support provided by grandmothers was inversely related to the sensitivity that mothers showed with their infants (Rhodes, Contreras, & Mangelsdorf, 1994).

Because emotional support and understanding is often a critical feature of effective self-care, I routinely ask single parents of aggressive children if anyone is aware of their struggle (see sample dialogue above). By acknowledging the possibility of their feeling alone and misunderstood, I thus begin my own effort to be emotionally supportive. This interaction may also serve to model for parents the value inherent in accurate emotional understanding. Unfortunately, many parents may be unable to obtain similar kinds of support outside of intervention unless practitioners specifically target this aspect of their self-care. For parents with partners, a reasonable place to begin is with their efforts to support each other. As suggested by the studies reviewed earlier (Dadds et al., 1987; Webster-Stratton, 1994), enhancing parents' ability to communicate effectively and to problem-solve together can be a useful adjunct to standard parent-training interventions. Some parents may not be willing to commit to such lengthy adjunctive treatments, and some practitioners might feel that an explicit focus on the marital relationship is beyond their expertise. In these instances, practitioners may want to focus more narrowly on the goal of mutual support for parenting rather than on the marital relationship generally. By limiting the focus in this way, practitioners stay closer to parents' manifest agenda while providing skills and scripts that can reduce marital distress and enhance relationship satisfaction. Also, if parents learn to resolve conflicts and be supportive when it comes to issues of parenting, these skills might generalize to other issues. The hazard of taking parents in a direction they had not intended to go and the risk of focusing on marital issues that could derail the work of parent therapy are thus avoided.

I am reluctant to push parents toward greater instrumental support for one another until I have some confidence that their respective struggles as parents are mutually understood and appreciated. My reluctance is based on my assumption that parents' current level of instrumental assistance is a function of their perceptions of what is fair and equitable. For example, a father who offers little or no child care assistance on evenings and weekends may feel so entitled because of his wage-earning efforts. A mother may feel justified in spending beyond the family's means because she has few breaks from her caregiving role. Both may feel they deserve help from the other, but each is unlikely to offer help to the other if it means that person would be at a disadvantage to the other. I can imagine at least three reasons why parents may do an inadequate job of supporting each other emotionally. The first is that a larger and more serious set of marital concerns is interfering with the job of parenting. More common is the possibility that parents have yet to establish regular opportunities for positive and meaningful communication. Few parents can convey and receive messages of emotional support while also doing household chores, unwinding from work, and responding to interrupting children. As noted earlier, time off from parenting is often directly related to parents' success at being emotionally supportive. A third reason for a lack of emotional support between parenting partners has to do with task requirements that are specific to emotional support. For some parents, the task of being emotionally supportive may be too difficult or too costly for them personally.

To be minimally supportive, parents must be able and willing to listen to their spouse's parenting concerns without refuting or trivializing these concerns (Gottman, 1994). Unfortunately, even if nothing at all needs to be said in response, the task of remaining in such a situation may be overwhelming for some parents. Parents who are uncomfortable in the face of their partner's distress or who tend to avoid any potential conflict are likely to struggle during an emotionally supportive interaction. A study conducted by one of my students (Welch, 1996) supports the notion that individuals differ in their ability to be emotionally supportive. In this study, male and female college students were asked to soothe a female confederate who acted as if she were in an emotional crisis. Participants knew that confederates were in a role but were told that the study was a way to learn more about how to manage crisis hot-line calls. As expected, women were judged to be more effective soothers than men. Also, participants who scored higher on the Avoidance dimension of the Adult Attachment Questionnaire (Simpson, Rholes, & Phillips, 1996) were less effective at soothing than more securely attached participants. The work of Simpson, Rholes, and Nelligan (1992) also supported the influence of attachment style on emotional soothing. In their study, college students in a dating relationship participated in a laboratory exercise that involved inducing stress in the female partner. As expected, avoidant women tended to withdraw from their partners, and avoidant men became angry if their partners displayed emotional distress. Together these studies suggest that some mothers and fathers may be unable to tolerate the emotional arousal that can arise during a supportive exchange. Therefore, it is incumbent on the practitioner to recognize these individual differences in parents. As Gottman (1994) has shown in his study of stable marriages, some couples achieve relationship stability by avoiding emotional conflict, whereas others derive their stability from engaging in conflict. What seems most critical is that the particular strategy used is acceptable to both parties.

Practitioners who attend to these individual differences in emotional regulatory skills are more likely to find a suitable strategy by which parents can feel supported by their partners. My usual manner of framing this task is to ask parents under what conditions they can imagine hearing —without criticism or challenge—the emotional concerns their partner has about parenting. Many parents need nothing more than a span of uninterrupted time off from parenting. For them, the chance to huddle together and affirm their commitment to be a parenting team is enough. Other parents need greater assurances that this time of emotional sharing will be safe and tolerable for them personally. Parents will need help identifying the conditions that meet these criteria. Practitioners should consider such factors as the setting, the likelihood of being distracted or interrupted, the ground rules governing the interaction, and the mode by which messages are conveyed. The parents with whom I have worked have identified a range of possible conditions. One mother preferred late evening drives with her husband; one father preferred to rely primarily on written messages between himself and his wife. Another couple would retreat to their bedroom for 15 minutes each afternoon while their teenage daughter supervised the younger children. Another couple combined nightly strolls with the rule that one could talk without interruption on the way out and the other could do the same on the way in. Again, the key here is to explore with parents the conditions that would enable both of them to endure the discomforts of potentially strong emotion. The less comfortable parents are with the display of emotional distress, or the greater the potential for supportive interactions to disintegrate into unresolved conflict, the more parents will need extensive skills training or highly structured, team-building rituals. And the most feasible of these, it seems, is the use of rituals that guide parents during those occasions when they need to respond in uncomfortable but emotionally supportive ways toward their spouse.

In describing the goals of such rituals to parents, I suggest that huddling together should allow parents an opportunity to learn that each is working hard and that neither is free from worry or concern: I frequently comment that "nobody is winning." I remind parents that a shared emotional burden is usually less daunting than one carried alone: "Parents who worry in isolation can fall prey to any number of stressors, but parents who worry together can weather most any storm." I strongly suggest that learning about each other's concerns is often all that is needed or possible. Although working together to eliminate the source of concern or resolving a long-standing debate are admirable goals, these may not be realistic. A more practical goal is for parents to make a sincere effort to understand each other's struggle as a parent. Pursuing the goal of resolving all conflicts may needlessly compromise the primary goal of emotional support and understanding. That is not to say that team-building rituals cannot also be used to enhance marital satisfaction, to coordinate the week's parenting efforts, or to just take a break from parenting. However, these goals should not substitute for emotional support.

The task of identifying potentially supportive persons can truly be difficult for parents without partners or those who cannot rely on their partners for consistent emotional support. Because other people may be less invested in the relationship than one's coparent, practitioners must also carefully consider strategies for obtaining adequate emotional support. As with the procurement of instrumental support, practitioners will need to be familiar with resources that offer individual counseling, support groups, home visitors, or volunteer mentors. Parents may also benefit from supportive relationships with helpful teachers, understanding school counselors, concerned clergy, and trusted neighbors. Adult family members (e.g., grandparents, aunts, uncles, siblings) can also be potential sources of emotional support. When considering where to go or with whom to visit, practitioners should let parents know that advice and expertise can be helpful, but emotional support will likely depend on the other person's ability to listen and understand their parenting dilemma. Indeed, other parents with difficult children are one possible source of emotional support. Interactions with parents who know well the struggle of parenting an aggressive child and who remain somewhat humbled by the experience can be an ideal resource for parents in need of emotional support. However, even well-meaning parents may falter at the job of being supportive. Persons who are willing to play a supportive role may need the parent to direct them in their efforts. Practitioners can help by coaching the parent in how to request emotionally supportive responses from others. Phrases such as "I need to bend your ear for a few minutes," "Can I tell you what happened today?" and "I need you to tell me I'm not crazy or a bad parent" can be wonderful entrées to emotionally supportive exchanges.

Before ending the discussion of emotional support, I should point out that parents may *not* need to voice their concerns to another person for emotional support. Some parents may feel safer and may experience greater relief if they express their parenting worries by writing in a diary or a journal. Letters to distant friends or relatives that are not mailed, visits to the graves of deceased loved ones, and moments of quiet prayer can give parents a sense of having freely expressed their frustrations and fears without the risk of being questioned or attacked. For some parents, this may be the only option possible; for others it may be the approach that is most accessible and available.

Nonparental Interests and Activities

This particular self-care strategy assumes that parents whose lives are narrowly restricted to the demands of parenting may eventually suffer reductions in their levels of energy, strength, and commitment. Conversely, to the extent parents lead multidimensional lives with pursuits that extend beyond parenting, they may actually bolster their levels of energy, strength, and commitment. Although somewhat paradoxical, these assumptions are reflected in many of the strategies designed to prevent professional burnout. Individuals with multiple and diverse sources of support, satisfaction, and accomplishment are less vulnerable to fatigue and apathy. One mother with whom I worked found that gardening helped to soothe her and refuel her. However, she had no other interests, and she struggled as a person and as a parent when the weather did not permit gardening activities. Therefore, one method of promoting parental self-care is to assist parents in identifying ways in which they can expand the scope of their lives. This may entail rediscovering lost interests or beginning new pursuits.

Admittedly, there are some parents for whom such advice seems ludicrous. But nearly all parents have access to parks, libraries, television and magazines, and a place of worship. The fact that parents value themselves enough to engage in something other than parenting is more important than what they actually do besides parenting. Parents who cannot fathom having interests and activities outside of parenting—even when parenting is demanding and tiring—are unlikely to portray the strength and self-confidence necessary to earn children's respect. Parents who are overly concerned with and overcommitted to the task of parenting are at risk of hurting themselves and not helping their children. I sometimes ask parents to identify things about which they are passionate. This provocative question is designed to shift their self-views from one dimension (i.e., parenting) to multiple dimensions. Parents tell me they are passionate about music, movies, books, travel, or any number of things, but they also realize that they seldom have stopped to consider the possibility that their passions can coexist with parenting.

Health and Personal Integrity

This last self-care strategy is the most global and ambitious of all of those presented. The idea here is that self-care should have as its ultimate goal improving the overall level of parents' adjustment. To adopt this strategy can mean many things, but each entails a commitment to and a valuing of the self. Whether the issue is promoting a healthier lifestyle (e.g., better diet, exercise), attending to one's medical needs (e.g., adhering to medical regimens), furthering one's education, seeking greater spirituality, or giving back to one's community, the self-system is expanded and enriched by them all.

For many parents of aggressive children, this last strategy is too ambitious. Some parents, however, could benefit from this broad-based approach to self-care. As parents grow wiser and healthier, their capacity to let go of minor parenting concerns increases, as does their ability to stand resolutely on parenting issues of major concern. Such parents lead full, productive lives that include, but are not solely defined by, their role as parents.

Self-Care Skills and Tactics

This section begins by discussing a number of issues that practitioners should keep in mind as they help parents select the self-care skills and tactics that suit them best. Although the focus here is on skills and tactics that are specific to parental self-care, one can recognize in this discussion many of the features associated with adaptive coping in general (Lazarus & Folkman, 1984; Moos & Billings, 1982). One model that is particularly useful for practitioners distinguishes among *problem-focused, appraisal-focused*, and *emotion-focused coping*. Each part of this tripartite model is useful, but all have their limitations. Some of the stress that parents face is appropriately handled when parents focus on the problem and act instrumentally to eliminate or reduce its impact. At other times, parents can benefit by altering their appraisal of the stressful event. When done adaptively, parents may find a way to accept and understand their limited control over an event or the time-limited nature of its impact. At other times, parents are best served by dealing directly with the emotional fallout produced by a stress event. If the stressful event is not a problem that can be fixed, adaptive coping means lowering one's overarousal directly (e.g., relaxation exercises) but in ways that do not create their own problems (e.g., alcohol abuse). There are times, of course, in which parents will need to rely on a mix of coping strategies. Some stressful events (e.g., loss of a job) may cause such emotional upset that problem-focused strategies may be ineffective unless appraisal and emotion-focused coping is used first. Knowing the differences among these three kinds of coping strategies, although at times blurred, is helpful because of the variety of stressful events that parents face.

Parents can also differ in the ways they would prefer to cope. Some parents eschew emotion-focused coping strategies, emphasizing instead approaches that directly target the presence or severity of the stressor. Other parents follow a different course, rarely engaging in problem-focused coping and concentrating primarily on lessening their negative arousal or reappraising the meaning of the event. Relying on a limited repertoire of coping skills can be hazardous when the skills do not match the task demands or when parents execute the skills poorly. Some methods of emotion-focused coping, for example, may produce short-term gains but long-term problems. Regular use of alcohol, tobacco, or other drugs to modulate one's affect is a common example of maladaptive, emotion-focused coping. Although parents who use such maladaptive ways of coping may require more than parent therapy, they can still benefit from information and training in alternative ways to cope. For example, exercise, deep breathing, and prayer or meditation are all common forms of adaptive, emotion-focused coping. Practitioners must realize, however, that coping styles are often overlearned responses to threatening events. Therefore, parents' willingness to shift from one coping strategy to another may exceed their abilities to make that shift. Indeed, it may be easier for some parents to shift from maladaptive to adaptive forms of coping within a particular coping mode (i.e., problem- or emotion-focused) than it is to shift between modes.

The difference between interpersonal and intrapersonal coping strategies is another useful distinction to keep in mind when addressing parents' self-care skills. Support for this distinction comes more from the study of adult attachment (Simpson & Rholes, 1998) than it does from the traditional coping literature. Clinically, I find this distinction to have considerable usefulness. It allows practitioners to apply relevant findings from the study of adult attachment to the goal of enhancing parental self-care. Some parents—those who present as more avoidant or dismissive of close relationships—tend to select coping strategies that are intrapersonal in nature. When they are under stress, they prefer to rely on their own resources rather than to depend on another's kindness or competence. Parents who show a strong preference for *intrapersonal coping*—for going it alone—may not be open to learning about coping strategies that involve others. Practitioners will be more successful if they seek to expand parents' coping repertoire within their preferred mode.

Parents who are more ambivalent or preoccupied in their attachment style tend to prefer *interpersonal coping*. Under stressful conditions, these parents are more comfortable sharing their burdens than they are going it alone. This preference may involve seeking others' help to reappraise or solve a problem or may lead to reliance on others for emotional soothing. Because interpersonal modes of coping require a responsive, helpful other, parents who prefer this mode are at great risk if their lives are filled with stress but devoid of supportive and available adults.

It is also not uncommon for parenting partners to differ in how they prefer to cope with stress. For example, I recently worked with a family in which the father was very effective and reliant on his own set of skills to deal with stress, whereas his wife preferred to seek the proximity of significant others when feeling overwhelmed. On one particularly stressful evening when all seemed to be going wrong for the entire family, the father wanted nothing more than to be by himself, drinking a beer. His wife, meanwhile, wanted nothing more than to be at his side, hearing his reassuring words! Fortunately for this couple, most of the stress they encountered did not affect them simultaneously. Therefore, the father's preference for emotional distance and the mother's preference for emotional closeness did not overly tax their combined set of coping skills. On the other hand, escalating coercion on the part of their 7-year-old child forced them to reexamine their ability to work together as a parenting team. Much of my work with them focused on their divergent styles of coping

Fix the problem by yourself	Think differently about the problem by yourself	Feel less distressed by yourself
Fix the problem with other's help	Think differently about the problem with other's help	Feel less distressed with other's help

Figure 9.1. Styles of coping.

and how they could support each other despite these important differences.

Parents' preferences for interpersonal versus intrapersonal coping and for problem-focused, appraisal focused, or emotion-focused coping can inform practitioners who are hoping to promote more adaptive self-care skills. Practitioners can use Figure 9.1 with parents to identify their preferred modes of coping and to educate parents about underused strategies. Practitioners should not avoid efforts to expand parents' coping beyond preferred modes. Detailed coping scripts that run counter to parents' preferences (e.g., standard problem-solving steps used by a parent who overuses emotion-focused coping) can be a valuable resource. However, failing to acknowledge preferred modes of coping may invite parental resistance and treatment failure.

Exhibit 9.1.   Opportunities and Pitfalls for Parental Self-Care Worksheet

---

Do These Help or Hinder Your Job as a Parent?

Your physical health and well-being
Your emotional or psychological health and well-being
Your spiritual health and well-being
Your marriage or romantic relationships
Your relationships with other adult family members
Your relationships with neighbors
Your relationships with coworkers
Your relationships with adult friends
Your relationships with adult members of any organizations to which you belong
Your hobbies and leisure time
Your entertainment activities
Your recreational or exercise activities
Your work outside the home
Your chores in the home
Your financial situation
Your home or apartment
Your neighborhood
Your city
Your family
Your children
Your partner

Table 9.1. Tactics and Skills for Parental Self-Care

Category	Tactic or skill
Coping skill	Relaxation
	Breathing
	Exercise
	Help-seeking
	Appraisal
	Prayer
Coping tactic	Daily or weekly rituals
	Paid help
	Simplified schedule
	Medication
	Scheduled breaks
Change skill	Problem solving
	Assertiveness
	Organizational improvement
	Financial problem solving
	Occupational problem solving
	Interpersonal conflict resolution
Change tactic	New romantic partner
	New neighborhood
	New community
	Financial assistance
	Agency help

To illustrate the various self-care options available to parents, Exhibit 9.1 offers a list of life domains. Practitioners and parents can jointly review this list and assess which domains reflect opportunities and which domains reflect pitfalls. Table 9.1 categorizes different self-care efforts based on whether the goal is to cope with the stressor or to change it. This is not an exhaustive list of skills and tactics but one that may be used to spur parents' own search for better ways to self-care. This list distinguishes between self-care *skills* that parents can acquire and use in a variety of situations and self-care *tactics* that are typically used to deal with a single situation or circumstance.

Summary

I have attempted in this chapter to provide a sense of how important it is to attend to parents' ability to care for themselves. Parents of aggressive children seldom enjoy the task of socialization and, compared to most other parents, they need more support for, assistance with, and time off from parenting. If they fail to recognize these needs or if they are unsuccessful at meeting these needs, then both they and their children are likely to suffer. I argued here that effective self-care should target three fundamental goals. These are parents' energy, strength, and commitment. I also discussed a set of self-care strategies that may be helpful for practitioners and parents to keep in mind, ranging from time off from parenting to advancing one's own health and personal integrity. I also offered a typology of skills and tactics that can be used to cope with or change directly the issues and events with which parents struggle. The efforts of practitioners and the information they have to offer will not benefit parents, however, if parents do not recognize that their health and well-being—physical, emotional, interpersonal, and spiritual—is also a gift to and an example for their children.

10

School-Based Parent Intervention

Parent training programs that target oppositional–defiant children and children with conduct disorder have traditionally been offered in clinic settings. Recently, however, researchers who develop and evaluate treatment programs for aggressive children have begun to conduct programs that extend beyond the clinic. My own research program is reflective of this trend. When I began my parenting research it was in a clinic setting, and the families with whom I worked were able and willing to come to the clinic. I continue to work with parents in my clinical practice, but my research efforts are now focused primarily on interventions that take place outside the clinic setting. Why has this shift occurred? Why are researchers expanding their focus and going into homes and schools to conduct their investigations? There appear to be several reasons.

One reason is that empirical support for parent training has reached a level of documented efficacy that justifies attending to issues of real-world effectiveness and treatment dissemination. Although some questions regarding treatment efficacy and generalizability persist (see chapter 2, this volume), there is enough data documenting what works to warrant taking parent training out of the clinic and "on the road." Perhaps the best example of this trend is the work of Matt Sanders in Australia. He has been successful in developing parenting programs that reach entire communities—some in very isolated areas—via television or through a combination of mailings and telephone contact (e.g., Connell, Sanders, & Markie-Dadds, 1997). A second reason for the shift from the clinic is that a significant number of parents do not access clinic-based programs (Cavell & Hughes, in press; Dumas, 1996). Moreover, parents who do not or cannot take advantage of clinic-based programs are often some of the neediest of parents. They are likely to be single, poor, socially isolated, and members of an ethnic minority group (Cavell & Hughes, in press). Thus, by leaving the clinic and going into the community, researchers and practitioners can potentially help a greater number of serious, at-risk families.

Parenting work conducted in a clinic setting is not exactly "preaching to the choir," but it is often a very different experience from community-based family intervention. Programs that target and actively recruit at-risk families tend to involve a greater number of parents who may resist intervention efforts. Because these parents did not seek assistance on their own, they are often less apt to believe that something is wrong with their parenting practices (Cavell & Hughes, in press; Kumpfer & Alvarado, 1995). When targeted families have little choice in whether they participate or not, their level of resistance is even greater. For example, I supervise doctoral students who conduct parenting groups for parents of juvenile delinquents. These parents are ordered by the court to attend the group while their children participate in a military-style boot camp program. When a student of mine held the first one of these groups, neither she nor I were prepared for what happened. The parents were already angry at the juvenile justice system for its seeming indifference to the concerns of parents. They were particularly bothered by the requirement to take their child to boot camp each weekday morning at 6 a.m. and to attend mandatory parenting "classes." Because the classes seemed to imply that parents were at fault for their child's misdeeds and because an apparent representative of the juvenile service system was leading the class, these parents unloaded on my student. Once we overcame this hurdle, we were able to make many useful changes in how we work with this population of parents. Essentially, we have tried to distance ourselves from the juvenile service system itself, and we emphasize that our role is to help in ways that are relevant to parents.

The point of this example is to illustrate that both the process and the content of parenting work can change dramatically when practitioners shift from the clinic to the community and from parent-initiated to program-recruited or program-required participation. For practitioners who work exclusively with families in a clinic setting, the move to a community-based program can be both rewarding and challenging. But unless practitioners can adapt to the demands of community-based work, the rewards will be few. This chapter offers several guidelines to aid practioners in conducting work in school-based settings.

School-Based Parent Interventions

Practitioners who work in or with schools are well positioned to assist families with aggressive children. Such practitioners have more opportunities to identify aggressive children and perhaps greater access to the parents of these children. There are two ways to view the concept of school-based intervention. One way is as a descriptor of the point of service delivery. In other words, *school-based interventions* are those interventions delivered at school. This rather narrow use of the term, however, fails to capture the range of interventions that could be seen as school based. Indeed, if setting were the only difference between clinic-based and school-based parent work, I doubt that I would be devoting an entire chapter to the topic. A second perspective is one that views school-based interventions as those targeting children in schools. As mentioned previously, targeting and actively recruiting a school-based sample of aggressive children can significantly affect both the process and content of parenting work.

Types of School-Based Service Delivery

Large, Structured Parenting Programs

One type of parent program that can be delivered in a school setting is a curriculum-focused intervention designed to serve a large number of parents simultaneously. Most of these are better labeled *parent-education programs*. In the parlance of prevention science, these programs are primary or universal prevention efforts: Most of the families participating have yet to evince any appreciable risk. The purpose of school-based parent-education classes is broad coverage of a limited service. The assumption is that if large numbers of parents had even minimal information about effective parenting, then the community as a whole should experience lower levels of delinquency and related problems.

There are several advantages to conducting parent-education classes in a school setting. One is the tendency of parents to see school-related activities as less stigmatizing than professional therapy. Second, parents may imbue programs sponsored by local school districts with greater credibility than those offered in clinics. Another advantage to school-based parenting classes is the lower costs to the community. Finding and paying for the physical space that is usually required for large parenting classes is prohibitive unless schools make available their cafeterias, assembly rooms, or gymnasiums. School-based parent-education classes also benefit from the opportunity to take advantage of the school district's system of communicating with parents. Announcements about forthcoming parenting classes can be placed in school newsletters, in school-related newspaper columns, in flyers sent home to parents, on recorded telephone messages, or on web pages.

Although large, structured parenting programs may not specifically serve families who are at risk, it does not mean that at-risk parents may not benefit from attending. For example, Cunningham and his colleagues (Cunningham, Bremner, & Boyle, 1995) developed school-based parent training programs designed to aid a broad range of parents, including a subset identified because of their child's emergent problem behavior. With this approach, involvement by a large number of parents may actually enhance the attendance and the level of engagement of at-risk parents. In my own community, parents identified as abusive have, as part of their agreement with child protective services, an obligation to attend parent-education classes sponsored by the local school district. Although some parents may be resistant, the opportunity to see other parents trying to improve their parenting may be informative and inspirational. Of course, not all at-risk parents will attend a structured parenting program simply because classes are at school and are open to all. Parents most in need may not attend or, if they do attend, they may be inadequately served by the curriculum and by the heavily didactic nature of the classes. Parents of severely aggressive children generally need much more than parent-education classes.

Small, Structured Parenting Groups

The structured parent training groups offered in most clinic settings can be readily transported to the school setting. These groups are designed to accommodate about 6 to 10 parents, their content is curriculum driven, and they generally run for 8 to 12 sessions. Because of the structured curriculum and the small number of participants, groups such as these are some of the easiest to conduct. If practitioners are working from a detailed, step-by-step manual supported by ready-made handouts, scripted exercises, or even videotaped models (e.g., Webster-Stratton, 1987), then their task is easier. Small parent training groups are also rewarding for practitioners, assuming that the number and type of parents served do not overwhelm the group leaders. When both parents and practitioners actively value the group training experience and when the costs of participating in a well-organized program are not excessive, working with parents in a school setting makes a great deal of sense. Practitioners will have to address a number of logistical issues, however, such as the costs of materials and supplies, parents' child care needs, and perhaps the provision of refreshments. Often these concerns are best managed with input and assistance from parents themselves, and none are hugely prohibitive.

The primary disadvantage to this format is that many parents of aggressive children will not take advantage of the opportunity to learn better parenting. As with large parenting classes, school setting and sponsorship will attract some parents, but not necessarily those parents who need help. Free child care, refreshments, little or no fees, and the appeal of small-group camaraderie can all help, but these factors may not be enough to overcome some parents' distrust or inertia. One option is to offer school-based interventions only to certain at-risk families. Using specific screening criteria (see example below), practitioners can ensure that they are targeting parents whose children are clearly at risk. This approach to parenting work is known as *selected* or *secondary prevention*. Secondary prevention programs create new challenges for practitioners, not the least of which is how to get parents of at-risk children to participate in an intervention they did not seek.

Parent Intervention in the Home

One way to help parents who are unlikely to either start or sustain their involvement in a parenting program at school is to visit them in the home. Again, the school-based nature of this strategy is the locus of screening and not the point of service delivery. This approach to parent intervention is currently being used in a number of school-based prevention trials (e.g., Conduct Problems Prevention Research Group [CPPRG], 1992). One of these is a 5-year, National Institute on Drug Abuse-funded project called *PrimeTime*, which is codirected by Jan Hughes and myself. An exciting aspect of codirecting this project is the opportunity to visit with other prevention researchers and hear them describe similar challenges to working with parents of aggressive children. Researchers differ in their response to these challenges, which perhaps results from the particular features of their target sample or the nature of their prevention model. Programs also differ in the extent to which they rely exclusively on in-home parent work or whether they combine it with a structured training group that meets at school. Most prevention trials also combine parent-focused interventions with treatments targeting children's social problem-solving skills and academic success. Prevention trials vary in the age of the children targeted, pace and length of their work with parents, incentives offered to parents, and the degree to which therapists follow a structured curriculum. Despite all of these differences, prevention researchers generally agree that practitioners who work with community samples of at-risk families must be prepared to work harder, longer, and more creatively than they would if their only contact with parents occurred when families come into the clinic.

The PrimeTime Approach to School-Based Consultation

To provide readers with a more tangible example of school-based parenting work, I describe here the PrimeTime approach to parent intervention. I discuss the goals of PrimeTime practitioners' work with parents and then describe a number of specific suggestions that other practitioners can use when working with parents of aggressive children from a school-based sample. These suggestions are not so much empirically supported treatment techniques as they are strategies derived from our many experiences with PrimeTime parents.

The PrimeTime program is a secondary prevention trial that targets aggressive children in Grades 2 and 3. The intervention spans a period of about 18 months. Target children are nominated by teachers and then screened for level of aggression. Children are eligible to participate if their score on the Aggressive Behavior subscale of Achenbach's (1991) Teacher Report Form (TRF) is at least 1 standard deviation above the mean (60T) and their peer-rated aggression is above the mean. Children may also qualify if either the TRF or Peer-related Aggression score is at least 2 standard deviations above the mean. The aim of the program is to lower the incidence of adolescent delinquency and substance abuse in this at-risk sample. The name *PrimeTime* is essentially a triple *entendre* in that PrimeTime practitioners (a) intervene at a prime or significant point in the lives of children; (b) provide them with prime or high-quality socializing relationships, in the form of a therapeutic mentor and improved parent–child and teacher–child relationships; and (c) use these relationships to prime or prepare children motivationally for their subsequent involvement in a problem-solving skills training (PSST) group.

Conceptually, PrimeTime is an extension of the Responsive Parent Therapy (RPT) model presented here in this volume. To the degree that aggressive children participate in long-term relationship with prosocial adults from whom they sense both acceptance and containment, they are less likely to display a pattern of antisocial behavior. However, because many severely aggressive 2nd- and 3rd-grade children have parents who struggle tremendously with the tasks of socialization, other treatment components are needed. These other components are designed to jump start or propel aggressive children in a prosocial direction long and far enough to begin a series of positive transactional exchanges between them and their environment. Therefore, in addition to their parent interventions, PrimeTime also provides teacher consultation, therapeutic mentoring, and PSST.

Case Managers (CMs) are the heart of the PrimeTime service delivery model. CMs are responsible for 8 to 10 families each, consult with parents and teachers, co-train and supervise mentors, and lead PSST groups. One advantage to using the case manager model is that CMs have opportunities to provide direct service to aggressive children in PSST while working closely with each child's parent, teacher, and mentor. Our CMs are doctoral students in school, clinical, or counseling psychology programs who have had prior experience working with at-risk families. They take courses in system consultation, family therapy, and child psychopathology. They assist in training mentors, and they participate in a tutorial in which they learn to implement the PSST component. They also receive weekly supervision from one of the project's directors and participate in a weekly staffing and in-service meeting. They receive a 20-hour per week graduate stipend for serving as CMs to between 8 and 10 families.

PrimeTime staff has now recruited and begun treating a third and final cohort of aggressive children. My PrimeTime colleagues and I will follow the first cohort for three years post-treatment and plan to request additional funding that will extend the follow-up assessment into high school. Our immediate outcome variables include parent, teacher, and peer reports of aggression, and our impact variables focus on level of criminality and substance use. We are also collecting data on hypothesized mediator (social cognitions, quality of mentoring) and moderator (child's level of self-inflation and idealization, adult-rated psychopathology, and perceived acceptance and containment) variables. We assess a range of parenting practices (harshness, inconsistent discipline, monitoring) with both self-report instruments and raters' impressions. We also assess the quality and structure of the home environment using a modified version of the Home Observation for Measurement of the Environment (HOME) (Caldwell & Bradley, 1984). Parents also complete a survey that assesses their criminal and substance use history, as well as current level of depression and history of maternal rejection. Extensive sociodemographic information is also gathered on each family.

We refer to our parenting work as *parent consultation*. We do so for a number of reasons. First, parents of severely aggressive children often do not display the capacity to effectively socialize their children, so we were unsure of the extent to which we could rely on significant gains in parenting. Because our intervention is not parent-initiated and we meet with parents in their homes, we wanted to assist those parents who could benefit from consultation, while also devoting sufficient therapeutic time, energy, and expertise to other strategies when parents were not responsive. The term *consultation* also reflects the fact that our contact with parents may occur only every 3 to 4 weeks, although with some families and at some times the frequency of contact can rise to weekly or twice weekly. Because our CMs consult with teachers, often with the goal of meeting with parents, the term *consultation* also highlights our view that both parties are important players in the child's life. Finally, a consultative stance is also more in line with the fact that our parenting work seldom resembles structured parent training. Instead, we typically work with parents in a manner that is theory-driven and problem-focused but always responsive to parents' level of engagement. Although we aim and are prepared for the opportunity to conduct specific skills training, we also recognize that much of our parenting work will be consultative and not didactic.

Goals

CMs pursue three primary goals in their parenting work. The first of these partly reflects the research nature of the PrimeTime project. CMs are responsible for recruiting parents into the project and for ensuring that parents follow through with their assessment tasks. CMs possess both the expertise and the level of contact to meet the demands involved in recruiting and assessing this sample of parents. A second goal is to enhance the socializing qualities of the parent–child relationship. This is the most commonly pursued goal of parent intervention, but in PrimeTime, our focus is on parents' ability to convey acceptance, containment, and a belief in prosocial values. It is this theoretical perspective, supported by the other features of the RPT model (see chapter 3, this volume), that guides and informs consultation on issues of parenting or family functioning. The final goal is to improve the communication between the home and school systems. Rather than working in opposition or in isolation, CMs work to increase the overlap in how these two systems approach the job of socialization (and education). Often this means paying attention to how well parents and teachers recognize and understand each other's efforts. Perhaps most importantly, it means increasing children's sense that parents and teachers have shared expectations for prosocial behavior and academic success.

Consultative Tips and Tactics

This section contains specific recommendations that have emerged from the PrimeTime parent consultation work. These clinical tidbits are not broad strategies to pursue but instead are potentially helpful tips and tactics that have served us well in our work. I have organized the discussion according to the intervention goal or strategy that it is most likely to serve.

When the purpose is recruitment or assessment. Ethical guidelines concerning informed consent largely dictate our procedures for recruiting families into the project. Nonetheless, there remains some latitude in how we recruit parents and solicit their cooperation with assessment. Exercising this latitude usually means clarifying and reminding parents of the benefits of participation, most of which are spelled out in the consent forms. We remind parents that their child will have a college student mentor for a span of nearly 18 months, that they will be compensated for completing any assessment instruments, and that the program is designed to promote their child's school success (behaviorally, academically). We also point out that the services the child will receive will be free. Also implicit in the information we give to parents is that they are not required to attend any project-related events outside the home. We have also learned ways to facilitate the task of having parents complete their questionnaires. In setting up times to administer or pick up these measures, we let parents know that CMs will arrive with the compensation money. We have also learned that some parents cannot complete the measures unless we assist them. For some, this means reading the items to them, and for others it means assisting with child care while they read and respond to the items.

When the purpose is to enhance the therapeutic alliance. Chapter 4 noted the importance of a strong working alliance to the process of effective parent therapy. When practitioners go into parents' homes to offer them a service they did not ask for, establishing an alliance can dominate the consultative process. One advantage that we enjoy in PrimeTime is that our intervention lasts for 18 months and CMs meet with parents two or three times before treatment starts. Therefore, CMs can move more slowly than would practitioners who operate with a 10–12-week limit. This added time gives us an opportunity to show that we can fulfill our service obligations (e.g., weekly mentor visits, contact with teachers). It also allows us to learn more about the perspectives and concerns of parents. Because PrimeTime staff identifies target children on the basis of teacher and peer reports, there are some parents in the program who perceive few problems with their child at home. Other prevention programs have included parents in the screening process and are thus less apt to encounter this situation. Because our screening criteria are known to be reliable indicators of children's at-risk status, we are willing to work with parents who initially see little need for intervention. Sometimes their ratings prove to be an accurate prediction of their child's progress; more often, however, parents come to recognize that their child is showing a significant pattern of deviant behavior, at least at school.

In line with chapter 4 recommendations regarding the processing of parents' cognitions and emotions, our general posture toward reluctant parents is to be responsive but curious. PrimeTime staff members attend to and honor their wishes regarding participation, but we ask parents to educate us about their decisions. Of course, this must be done genuinely and with the firm belief that parents often know things about their child that is lost on teachers and practitioners. This is particularly likely when children respond better to one socialization style (e.g., a mother's) than to another (e.g., a teacher's). Practitioners strengthen their alliance with parents when they treat as legitimate the following question: "Why is my child viewed as having problems at school?" Despite extensive efforts by CMs to be responsive, move slowly, and process openly parents' view of things, there will continue to be some parents who do not engage fully in the consultative process. Prevention programs that work with parents for more than 2 years (e.g., CPPRG, 1992) can continue to adopt a "wait-and-see approach." Some well-funded prevention trials also have the capacity to pay parents for their participation in treatment. In PrimeTime, we are compelled to pursue other methods if we want to access parents and help target children. Sometimes this means that CMs shift some of their time and energy to other PrimeTime treatment components (i.e., teacher consultation, mentoring, PSST). Temporarily backing away from parent consultation may be necessary if CMs are to be responsive and sustain a fragile alliance. This can present a dilemma for CMs who are supposed to be helping parents improve their socializing skills and who must also meet the expectations of PrimeTime supervisors. At times like this, CMs and their supervisor need to be understanding and inventive.

One option that is fairly low risk but often quite helpful to the therapeutic process is to rely on one-way communiqués. If consultation is slowed, PrimeTime CMs are encouraged to provide parents with written notes or telephone messages updating them about significant events involving their child's teacher or mentor. CMs also provide parents with a series of newsletters describing the current focus of their child's PSST group. It is also not uncommon for CMs who perceive a rupture in the working alliance to mail cards or letters to parents. The advantage to using one-way communiqués is that they are less intrusive and demanding than two-way exchanges. Also, CMs can use aspects of the written weekly summary described in chapter 4 with these written letters and notes. As discussed in chapter 4, written messages that document a practitioner's efforts to be supportive can be more meaningful than many spoken messages. In sum, the use of one-way communiqués allows for continued documentation of support while honoring parents' current wishes for minimal participation.

With some parents, their willingness to participate in consultation is hard to assess. They may sound eager to meet with CMs and be quite willing to schedule a visit while rarely participating in an actual face-to-face meeting. Thus it is unclear whether they are being avoidant or whether their lives are simply too chaotic to allow for scheduled visits. Regardless of the reasons, it is clear that these parents need a different approach to consultation. For some, a shift to unscheduled, drop-in visits works well. Ideally, such visits have been broadly agreed to by parents beforehand. Some of the parents with whom we work are comfortable with this approach, perhaps because it is in keeping with their usual manner of meeting with visitors. On other occasions, CMs have used unscheduled drop-in visits to determine whether parents have been avoidant or unavailable for previously scheduled but missed appointments. When CMs arrive for scheduled visits, they may get no answer to their knocks or be told that parents are asleep, out, or otherwise and suddenly unavailable. Thus CMs may make an unscheduled visit, at a time they are sure that parents are at home, in order to learn if parents are willing to meet if the proper arrangements can be made. Even then, it may be unclear whether CMs should back off or try harder. Some parents may directly state their wishes, and others may be too uncomfortable to do this. Often CMs are left wondering if they are too pushy or not flexible enough. Sometimes they are both.

In other words, CMs may need to persist but do so in a different way than they have been. For example, some parents are uncomfortable meeting with CMs in their home but are willing to meet outside the home. Some prefer to meet at the school, and others prefer visits conducted over a cup of coffee at a fast-food restaurant. Parents differ in their reasons for not wanting to meet in the home. Some may be embarrassed by their meager living conditions, and others may be concerned over the behavior of a difficult family member. Alcoholic or drug-abusing spouses and abusive partners can be significant impediments to parent consultation. Other parents may feel uncomfortable with neighbors knowing that a service provider is visiting them. Sometimes parents have concerns about the gender or ethnicity of the CM. White men, in particular, seem to find the going tough when working with African American or Latina mothers. Furthermore, parents who work outside the home may prefer meeting briefly during their work break. Sometimes CMs offer to buy these parents lunch if they can meet during lunch time. One mother worked in a retail department store and occasional (albeit brief) contacts with her were possible if the CM was actually shopping (or at least seemed to be shopping). Another CM attended the target child's softball games in an effort to meet with parents. Each of these alternative visitation formats provided the CM with greater access to parents. Despite the value of one-way communiqués, it is virtually impossible to have a productive working alliance unless one can actually meet periodically with parents. PrimeTime staff, when generating alternative visitation formats, also strive to minimize the overall costs to parents in time, money, and emotional discomfort. More demands may be made of parents later on, but initially the goal for reluctant parents is any kind of contact that is perceived positively by parents. Our thinking here is in keeping with Wahler's (Wahler and Fox, 1981) findings on insular mothers. He found that a majority of their nonfamilial contacts were rather aversive in nature. Therefore, if given a choice about such contacts, these mothers do the logical thing and pass.

How can CMs alter their contacts in ways that appear to be more positive to parents? What changes would be compelling enough that parents would suddenly find time to meet? Because we do not pay parents to participate in consultation, we have few options. One is to offer to bring dinner (e.g., pizza) to the home visit so that parents will not have to buy or prepare dinner and children may even be occupied with a treat while parents meet with CMs. A different tact is to frame the purpose of meetings exclusively in terms of a child-focused goal. For example, CMs may find that access to families is increased when the purpose of the home visit is to have that target child complete a form or questionnaire, meet briefly with both the CM and the mentor, or read an individualized note from the teacher. It may not be essential to meet with the child in the home for these and other similar reasons, but these child-focused tasks can often serve as a CM's only ticket into the home. With greater access, CMs should find it easier to demonstrate their willingness to work for and not against parents. If this happens, then CMs will be able to resort less often to child-focused visits to gain access.

When the purpose is to orient parents toward more reasonable socialization goals. Given that parents may not share the same concerns about their child's behavior that teachers and peers have reported, CMs are occasionally confronted with parents who see little need for consultation. As mentioned earlier, it is important to recognize the possibility that parents have a more accurate view of their child's level of risk. In our experience, this is most likely to occur when a PrimeTime target child is the only or one of the few minority-group-member children in a classroom with a majority-group teacher and mostly majority-group students. Because in-group cultural norms can bias teacher perceptions of appropriate behavior, some target children may be inaccurately labeled as aggressive. CMs often assist such parents by consulting with other teachers who know the child (e.g., previous teachers, music and art teachers) and by directly observing the child's behavior at school. With this added information, parents can better determine their child's level of risk. More often than not, however, it seems that parents who have little concern about their child's school behavior either (a) experience a different pattern of behavior at home or (b) have yet to appreciate the potentially hazardous nature of their child's aggression. I am not aware of studies that have explored the reasons for actual (vs. perceived) differences between a child's aggression at school versus home. My clinical experience suggests that parents who effectively contain their child's use of coercion in the home but who fail to convey adequately a sense of acceptance may have children who are aggressive only at school. Such children are also more likely to engage in covert anti-social behaviors at home and at school. Items on the Delinquency scale of Achenbach's (1991) Child Behavior Checklist (CBCL) that assess children's guilt over misdeeds and their lying and stealing may be helpful in understanding these types of cases. Another possibility is that parents are containing and accepting effectively except in the area of sibling conflict. Children who lack opportunities to learn to resolve sibling conflict because parents routinely intervene may feel parents are never on their side and may be prone to using aggression with peers at school (see chapter 6, this volume).

Parents whose own perceptions lead to a minimization of their child's risk status are perhaps most challenging for CMs. Some parents have incredibly high levels of tolerance for rambunctious or coercive child behavior. They may see little need to counter these tendencies, preferring to just go along with the status quo. CM efforts to illustrate the child's risk status are helpful here. Profile sheets from Achenbach's (1991) CBCL scales can provide parents with useful graphic images and with percentile scores that are more easily understood by parents. Explaining what percentile scores mean and clarifying the importance of certain cut-off points (e.g., 70T) can also help parents appreciate how uncommon their child's level of aggression is. Procedures for making productive use of such feedback sessions have been shown to be a useful adjunct to parenting work (see chapter 4, this volume). This type of feedback may also help parents who recognize their child's aggression as excessive but believe it is a temporary phase with few developmental consequences.

For parents who believe their child's aggression is a problem but feel incapable of doing anything about it, data-based feedback may provide a temporary spark of motivation, but probably not enough to sustain a lengthy consultative relationship. Instead, CMs must be able to frame the task of socialization as one that is realistic for parents. The minimal-treatment approach discussed in chapter 4 is useful here. Consultants ask parents to generate a short list of prohibited behaviors that are then discussed in consultation. Parents who are struggling to gain control over their child's behavior can find it difficult to focus their disciplinary efforts on a more limited set of misdeeds. Also, their short list may include behaviors that have little relevance for their child's later adjustment (e.g., bathing every day vs. every other day) or prohibitions that are nearly impossible for them to enforce (e.g., no arguments between siblings). This exercise can be instructive, however, in that parents and CMs can discuss the list of target behaviors not in terms of parents' goals or children's needs but as realistic, achievable outcomes. By emphasizing a list that contains only behaviors on which parents can reliably insist, CMs guide parents toward a much simpler and practical socialization plan.

When the purpose is to teach specific parenting skills. Although home visits may yield frequent and predictable contacts between CMs and parents, they are no guarantee that parents will be open to systematic skills training. In fact, because gaining access to and developing an alliance with parents often requires extreme flexibility and responsiveness on the part of CMs, a skills-training agenda may seem at times like an odd appendage to the consultative process. Of course, parent-skills training may be precisely what some parents are seeking from consultation. However, this is seldom a prominent sentiment among PrimeTime parents. Therefore, other means by which CMs can introduce parents to more adaptive parenting practices are needed. In keeping with the child-focused approach mentioned earlier, CMs may have success by modeling skills they use directly with children. For example, parents whose children are struggling academically may benefit from occasional tutoring sessions in which the CM demonstrates specific ways to assist the child. CMs who use this kind of home visit should meet first with the child's teacher. In this way, CMs will not only be better informed about how to assist the child academically, but teachers will also be aware that an effort is being made by parents to assist them in their goals. By engaging with children in this kind of academic task, CMs can model important skills with the target child in the home. Thus, skills training is promoted in a way that is unlikely to threaten parents.

But what about parenting skills that are not academically related? How can CMs model these skills when parents have shown a strong reluctance to discuss or be trained in specific skills? As before, CMs can model these skills during child-focused home visits. Visits that follow a well-planned agenda that will shape the goals and activities of the children are needed to enable CMs to respond with the specific skills being targeted. For example, if CMs want to model the important use of household rules, they can plan a home visit that involves making signs for household rules, similar to those often found in classrooms. CMs arrive with plenty of art supplies and poster paper so that children find the activity engaging. The CMs can suggest they make the signs and post them in a prominent place in the house (e.g., on the refrigerator).

Of course, the task of making signs about house rules begs the question "Are there house rules?" In my experience, aggressive children rarely are able to articulate a clear set of family rules. Given this likelihood, CMs can suggest that parents hold a family meeting. The transition to this topic creates an opportunity to model even more parenting skills. Also, a family meeting addressing family rules should ideally have a parent present. Therefore CMs and children can together request a parent's presence at this meeting. Extending the process even further, CMs can suggest that the first task should be to plan the family meeting. Children and parents, with assistance from CMs, can decide the time and day of the meeting, which room will be used, and smaller details like whether the television will be on. CMs can offer to serve as recording secretary and suggest that parents officially call the meeting to order. CMs can also offer to provide drinks and snacks for the meeting so that it can be both fun and helpful. CMs can even use the time prior to the official family meeting to check with parents about the kinds of rules they want to include on the list of household rules. This tactic of checking in with parents beforehand will further convey to parents that they are considered in charge and are the final arbiter of family rules. Parents who are asked to assist with family meetings should be less resistant to a discussion about rules than parents who are approached more directly on the need for rules and who may feel their parenting skills are being questioned. By carefully planning and implementing a family meeting in this way, CMs create a pleasant opportunity for parents to gain some helpful information in organizing their family and asserting their authority. Parents can also gain valuable information about the kinds of rules their children need, and they will witness the process of discussing rules in a way that engenders greater child cooperation and investment. The family should emerge from this series of visits with important products, including child-made signs listing the family's rules and a greater level of family structure. Going through this collaborative and goal-oriented process is also likely to enhance the alliance between parents and CMs.

There are other, less elaborate methods of steering consultation toward specific skills training. Some parents are more willing to indulge CMs if CMs have first taken the time to visit with them and hear their concerns (see Prinz & Miller, 1994). One PrimeTime CM in particular is especially adept at this, perhaps because she is Hispanic and bilingual like many of the parents with whom she works. Also, her manner of interacting is supportive, positive, and interested. She is also patient and she times well the introduction of her own agenda. She tends to do this in an offhand way, beginning with such phrases as "By the way, do we have time to talk about _____" or "Oh, before I forget, I'm supposed to ask you about _____ today. My supervisor has been bugging me about it." This tactic of placing blame on one's supervisor can help preserve the therapeutic alliance even if parents are resistant to the training per se. John Reid, of the Oregon Social Learning Center, identified this approach as one frequently used by therapists in their prevention work (personal communication, June 1998). A related tactic is to leave parents with handouts and other materials about parenting that they can peruse at their leisure. For parents who are reluctant to have consultations focus on their parenting skills, these materials should probably be offered more as parting gifts than as assignments for parents. CMs can describe the materials as something they found interesting or as routine handouts given to all parents with whom they work. This low-key approach is an effort to balance the risk of having little effect on parents' use of better parenting practices with the risk of having a negative impact on the therapeutic alliance.

Maintaining a supportive and productive consultative relationship with PrimeTime parents can be a daunting task for staff. Using these visits to pursue a skills-training agenda only adds to the challenge. The most successful CMs will be those who are flexible, patient, and creative. Effective CMs will also keep their focus on the socializing aspects of the parent–child relationship (i.e., acceptance, containment, prosocial values) even though parents may not always see the need to focus on these goals. Supervisors can play a valuable role by backing CM efforts and redirecting CMs if efforts to be responsive to parents lead to excessive drift from the goals of socialization.

When the purpose is to promote home–school communication. An integral part of parent consultation in PrimeTime is increasing the degree to which teachers and parents work toward the same goals. As more practitioners and researchers shift their focus from the clinic to the schools, the home–school interface becomes an important intervention arena. When my colleagues and I first piloted PrimeTime, we envisioned regular conjoint meetings with parents and teachers that followed a standard series of problem-solving steps. We have since modified our aims to reflect the fact that neither parents nor teachers actually initiated the consultative process. Our original plans for consultation were feasible only if both parents and teachers had significant concerns, each agreed on what these concerns were, and each viewed consultation as a reasonable strategy for addressing these concerns. Because these conditions were rarely met, we now emphasize communication rather than coordination and collaboration. Our CMs are less concerned with developing intervention plans that rely on parents and teachers working in concert; instead, they strive (a) to make parents and teachers aware of each other's efforts and concerns and (b) to make children aware that parents and teachers share the same broad socialization and academic goals. These two goals are more amenable to the kind of consultation that takes place with PrimeTime parents and teachers. The pursuit of these goals does not depend on a carefully crafted plan for linking home and school, nor does it depend on parents and teachers agreeing on how each should do their part in socializing the target child. It does not even depend on actual face-to-face meetings, although these can be very helpful. Although the original expectations for PrimeTime consultations have been scaled back, they are not unimportant. Mutual respect between parents and teachers can be powerful sources of influence, especially insofar as children witness it. Parents who respect teachers are more likely to endorse academic goals and less likely to undermine teachers' efforts. Teachers who respect parents are more likely to seek parent input and less likely to become overly punitive or indifferent toward the target child. Finally, children who face a common set of expectations at home and school are likely to be better monitored and more consistently contained.

PrimeTime CMs have developed a number of procedures that have proven helpful in trying to advance the communication between home and school. A commonly used procedure is one we call *shuttle diplomacy*—a term normally used by a country's state department. In PrimeTime consultations, *shuttle diplomacy* is the process of meeting separately with parents and teachers in an iterative fashion until establishing conditions for a successful conjoint meeting. In other words, CMs do not rush into arranging joint meetings unless they are fairly sure it will be a positive experience for both parents and teachers. The role of CM in this process may resemble that of a diplomat, but more often it is akin to that of a translator. We have found that in brief, poorly planned conjoint meetings, parents and teachers rarely sense that their positions have been well articulated and understood. Therefore, CMs engage in a fair amount of preparatory work to learn what each party would want the other to know. CMs may need to make multiple visits before they can ascertain a parent's or teacher's concerns and wishes. They may need to make additional visits to learn how a given message is likely to be received and to coach the senders on how best to package their message. Equipping parents with useful scripts, informed by previous consultation visits, can make a tremendous difference in the process and the outcome of a conjoint meeting.

Parents in particular may need CMs to be aware of their concerns if they are to have a voice at a conjoint meeting. Therefore, CMs often function more as parent spokespersons than as impartial consultants. We lean in this direction because a meeting with a teacher at school about a troubling son or daughter is generally not a level playing field. Therefore, parents (and ultimately children and teachers) are better served when CMs assist parents in stating their concerns and wishes. To offset perceptions by teachers that their views are being discounted, CMs use prior visits to inoculate teachers against this viewpoint. Teachers are brought in as professional allies who are asked to understand that parents must be heard by teachers if they are to be open to hearing from teachers. Teachers may also benefit from knowing that when CMs give voice to parental concerns and wishes, they do not necessarily endorse those views. If parents feel supported as they speak their mind, then they may be more open to seeing the school as a safe place that has their child's best interests at heart. Many PrimeTime parents have never been or only rarely been to the school campus or visited with teachers. Parents from racial or ethnic minority groups may be convinced that teachers are prejudiced or that a visit to school can only be a negative experience. Many parents with whom we work had poor school experiences as children and may fear more of the same. Others may be doubtful that they can play a constructive role in helping their child, especially academically. Some parents are so avoidant that CMs need to insist on offering them a ride to the school when a conjoint meeting is scheduled.

There are occasions, of course, when PrimeTime parents and teachers, perhaps with assistance from the CM, generate a very detailed and coordinated plan to solve a specific problem. The most common example of this is some type of contingency management plan based on notes sent between home and school. Given that PrimeTime goals are focused predominantly on enhanced communication, CMs sometimes discourage teachers from sending home notes that elicit parent-delivered punishments. We are especially concerned about teacher reports of misbehavior that did not lead to school-based consequences or that carry the expectation that parents should punish children again once they get home. The first issue flies in the face of our conceptual model and the notion that children are unlikely to experience socializing effects from a relationship in which the containment is out-sourced, in this case to parents. The second issue is of concern because punishing children a second time at home could represent unnecessary damage to the parent–child relationship. Less damage, and perhaps greater gains, may follow efforts by parents to talk with children about their misdeeds at school. If children are adequately contained at school, parents may be more effective if they adopt a somewhat but not completely neutral position about what happened and offer to problem-solve with the child in ways to avoid future school sanctions. This approach does not undermine the teacher, but it can be an important way to help the child. Unfortunately, some parents are so reactive and punitive when they get bad news from their child's school that CMs discourage teachers from sending home any reports except those that are mandatory.

Summary

Practitioners who work with aggressive children in school settings or through a school-based intervention project are engaged in a challenging and important psychological enterprise. The developmental risks associated with severe school-age aggression are well documented and serious. But working with parents of severely aggressive children can be demanding and frustrating in several areas. When parents reject the help—because they never asked for it or do not trust it—practitioners face even greater challenges. No single or simple program of parent training will suffice. Practitioners must have a clear and stable vision of the principles guiding their intervention, while also exercising considerable flexibility, patience, and creativity with how those principles are to be pursued. I hope that the lessons learned from PrimeTime described in this chapter will serve as a useful guide for school-based practitioners who face these challenges.

Epilogue

Aggression in children can be an unyielding characteristic that is often repeated from one generation to the next. Children who exhibit disruptive and aggressive behavior make up nearly one half of all child referrals for psychological services (McMahon & Forehand, 1988). The failure to effectively treat childhood aggression can lead to tremendous social costs, including economic loss resulting from aggressive and antisocial acts, the costs of containing and rehabilitating delinquent and criminal adolescents and adults, and the human suffering that is part of life in a violent community. There is also evidence to suggest that aggressive acts committed by children and adolescents are increasing dramatically (Lykken, 1995).

Who Shall Intervene?

Part of the impetus for writing this book was the growing problem in American society of youth crime and violence. The increased incidence of violent crimes committed by young people suggests that early intervention should be a high priority. Aggressive children—a group clearly at risk for later delinquency—represent an easily identified population to target for selective prevention programs. Unfortunately, under current models of health care delivery, many aggressive children do not receive the kinds of services their behavior warrants. Which system of care is most likely to intervene on behalf of aggressive children? More importantly, which system of care is prepared to offer the kind of intervention that is reflected in a relationship-based model of socialization?

The Education System?

The child who behaves aggressively at school and meets diagnostic criteria for conduct disorder may be placed in special education classes for children with severe emotional disturbances. More likely, however, the child will be viewed as socially maladjusted, which is not considered a disability under current federal guidelines. Therefore, these children are unlikely to receive services that are available to children who do meet special education guidelines. Even if aggressive children qualify for special education services, mental health and other related services are rarely provided, and

existing service arrangements are rarely state-of-the-art and are thus unlikely to address the multidetermined nature of children's aggression
(Duchnowski, 1994).

The Health Care System?

Too many children, particularly economically disadvantaged children, do
not have access to mental health services in the private sector. Those who
do have access—either through private-payor systems or government-
sponsored programs such as Medicaid—are likely to be inadequately
served by a health care delivery system that construes intervention too
narrowly to benefit a severely aggressive child. Common restrictions on
the number of sessions, the types of services (e.g., no family therapy), and
the locus of intervention (e.g., a clinic office) are at odds with many of the
trends that characterize up-to-date, research-based intervention programs.

The Social Services System?

Family and individual therapy, parent training, and other mental health
services are often available from social services and child protection agencies; however, these services are usually not available to families with
aggressive children unless there is evidence of pathological parenting (viz.,
abuse or neglect). And again, the quality of services provided often falls
short of the needs such families have. In many communities like my own,
the only parent training that is available to families through child protective services is a series of monthly parent-education lectures sponsored by
the local school district.

The Juvenile Justice System?

By the time children enter the juvenile justice system, the window of opportunity for instituting a targeted prevention program will likely have
closed. Some children may enter the system earlier, but their access comes
at the cost of having started their criminal activity earlier and having a
more serious prognosis. Also disconcerting is the fact that juvenile justice
interventions typically involve the aggregation of aggressive youth into a
common setting. Recent work by researchers in Oregon suggests that this
practice may produce iatrogenic effects (Dishion & Andrews, 1995) that
could be avoided if such grouping did not occur (Chamberlain & Reid,
1998).

Our society can ill afford to ignore aggressive children. And yet, we
do not have a coordinated effort for dealing with these at-risk youth. Instead, services currently provided by education, health care, juvenile justice, and welfare agencies are often difficult to access or poorly designed
to offset the downward trajectory of aggressive children. Recent campaigns

and programs promoting health care reform, school reform, and crime prevention offer some promise (Hughes & Cavell, 1995). If schools continue to assume a greater role in the coordinated delivery of children's health care services, then psychologists, counselors, and others who operate in schools may be able to work more closely with the parents of children in need, including the parents of aggressive children. However, it must be recognized that the problem of childhood aggression is embedded within a larger social, political, and economic matrix and that interventions may not succeed unless these broader issues are also addressed (Kazdin, 1993).

Implications of a Relationship-Based Model of Socialization for Parents' Involvement in Treating Aggressive Children

In this book, I have asserted that aggressive children are unlikely to benefit from interventions that do not involve their long-term participation in what I have called *socializing relationships*. According to this conceptualization, aggressive children will continue in their negative trajectory unless they experience a stable relationship with an adult who provides them with a sense of acceptance, containment, and prosocial values. This book is an effort to describe how practitioners can use this conceptual framework when working with parents of aggressive children. Throughout, I have tried to paint a realistic picture of the challenges parents and practitioners face. I have also tried to emphasize therapeutic principles that are not only supported empirically and theoretically, but that also make practical sense to parents and the practitioners who work with them. As I stated in the first chapter, the main task for practitioners is to help find that combination of acceptance, containment, and prosocial guidance that is most realistic and sustainable given both the parent and the child. I believe our ability to help families with aggressive children will be greatly enhanced if practitioners come to view our helping role in this way.

Sadly, however, there will be some parent–child dyads for whom this kind of relationship is not possible. Despite our best efforts, some parents will be unable to establish and maintain an emotionally positive relationship with their child while attending to the added goals of containing coercive behavior and modeling prosocial behavior. For some of these parents, the task may have been possible with a different child or at a different time in their life. Ineffective parents are not so ineffective with a child who is less demanding and impulsive or later in life, when parents are older and wiser. How often have we as practitioners worked with grandparents who as guardians seem to possess considerable skills as caregivers even though they struggled earlier in life to care for their own children?

When adult members of a dyad find their relationship is no longer viable, one or both can decide to end it. Of course, the decision to end a marriage or some other close relationships is too often premature and preventable, but the option to end such a relationship is not considered an unreasonable course of action. Our society has established laws that govern the process by which couples end their relationship through separation and divorce: The legal status of adult marital partners imbues them with the right to end a relationship they would regard as unworkable and unhealthy. The legal status of parent or child does not come with this same right. In fact, parents have a legal obligation to care for their children and to not harm them. The state may terminate a parent–child relationship if parents are severely abusive or neglectful, but this is a rather extreme criterion for ending an unhealthy relationship compared to that used with married adults. Older adolescents may on occasion seek legal emancipation from their parents, but this is hardly routine practice in our society. For most parent–child dyads stuck in a chronic and intractable pattern of coercive interaction, few options are available. Informal living arrangements with relatives and friends or formal placements in residential treatment facilities and group homes are common, but few of these options seem to hold great promise, given the relationship demands necessary for socializing aggressive children.

In the final chapter, I discussed efforts to implement a school-based intervention program that offers a mentoring component in addition to parent and teacher consultation and PSST. Mentors in the PrimeTime program are trained to provide the kind of socializing conditions (acceptance, containment, and prosocial values) that parents ideally would provide. In effect, these mentors are intended to function as surrogate socializing agents. Readers must recognize, however, that a 2-hour-per-week mentoring relationship with a college-age student is unlikely to meet the needs of all children whose parents are as yet unable to socialize them. These mentoring relationships do last for a year and a half, and the mentors are trained and supervised by experienced practitioners. However, our mentors are often young, middle- to upper-class White women and our target children are typically economically disadvantaged boys from racial and ethnic minority groups. To expect these relationships to be transforming in a fundamental, long-lasting sense may be too much to hope for.

To this end, programs and policies that recognize the gap between what is typically available in our society versus what is required to intervene effectively with aggressive children are needed. The Multisystemic Therapy program developed by Henggeler and Borduin (1990) and the treatment foster care program described by Chamberlain and Reid (1998) are excellent examples. Both of these models reflect inventive ways to address the problem of antisocial and aggressive youth. More programs like these, which are willing to break from old, worn ways of viewing the practitioner's role, are greatly needed. Also, needed, however, are policies and funding practices that allow for such innovation. My hope is that the RPT model will provide some guidance when these efforts involve working with the parents of aggressive children. Society should not give up too easily or quickly on these parents. Just as aggressive children may need mentors, so too may parents of aggressive children need therapeutic mentors in the form of sensitive and informed practitioners.

References

Abidin, R. (1983). *Parenting Stress Index Manual.* Charlottesville, VA: Pediatric Psychology Press.

Abidin, R. (1990). Introduction to the special issue: The stresses of parenting. *Journal of Clinical Child Psychology, 19,* 298–301.

Abikoff, H., Courtney, M., Pelham, W. E., & Koplewicz, H. S. (1993). Teachers' ratings of disruptive behaviors: The influence of halo effects. *Journal of Abnormal Child Psychology, 21,* 519–533.

Achenbach, T. M. (1991). *Manual for the Child Behavior Checklist and Revised Child Behavior Profile.* Burlington, VA: Author.

American Psychiatric Association. (1994). Diagnostic and Statistical Manual of Mental Disorders (4th ed.). Washington, DC: Author.

Arnold, J., Levine, A., & Patterson, G. R. (1975). Changes in sibling behavior following family intervention. *Journal of Consulting and Clinical Psychology, 43,* 683–688.

Asarnow, J. R., & Callan, J. W. (1985). Boys with peer adjustment problems: Social cognitive processes. *Journal of Consulting and Clinical Psychology, 53,* 80–87.

Axline, V. (1969). *Play therapy* (Rev. ed.). New York: Ballantine.

Bandura, A. (1969). *Principles of Behavior Modification.* New York: Holt, Rinehart, and Winston.

Barkley, R. A. (1987). *Defiant children: A clinician's manual for parent training.* New York: Guilford Press.

Baum, C. G., & Forehand, R. (1981). Long-term follow-up assessment of parent training by use of multiple outcome measures. *Behavior Therapy, 12,* 643–652.

Baumrind, D. (1967). Child care practices anteceding three patterns of preschool behavior. *Genetic Psychology Monographs, 75,* 43–88.

Baumrind, D. (1973). The development of instrumental competence through socialization. In A. D. Pick (Ed.), *Minnesota symposia on child psychology, Vol. 7* (pp. 3–46). Minneapolis: University of Minnesota Press.

Beelmann, A., Pfingsten, & Losel, F. (1994). Effects of training social competence in children: A meta-analysis of recent evaluation studies. *Journal of Clinical Child Psychology, 23,* 260–271.

Bernal, M. E., Klinnert, M. D., & Schultz, L. A. (1980). Outcome evaluations of behavioral parent training and client centered parent counseling for children with conduct problems. *Journal of Applied Behavior Analysis, 13,* 669–677.

Bierman, K. L., & Smoot, D. L. (1991). Linking family characteristics with poor peer relations: The mediating role of conduct problems. *Journal of Abnormal Child Psychology, 19,* 341–356.

Bierman, K. L., & Wargo, J. B. (1995). Predicting the longitudinal course associated with aggressive-rejected, aggressive (nonrejected), and rejected (nonaggressive) status. *Development and Psychopathology, 7,* 669–682.

Blechman, E. A. (1996). Coping, competence, and aggression prevention: II. Universal school-based prevention. *Applied & Preventive Psychology, 5,* 19–35.

Bogenschneider, K., Wu, M., Raffaeli, M., & Tsay, J. C. (1998). Parental influences on adolescent peer orientation and substance use: The interface of parenting practices and values. *Child Development, 69,* 1672–1688.

Bornstein, M., Bellack, A. S., & Hersen, M. (1980). Social skills training for highly aggressive children. *Behavior Modification, 4,* 173–186.

Bowlby, J. (1982). *Attachment and loss: Vol 1. Attachment* (2nd ed.). New York: Basic Books.

Brody, G. H., & Flor, D. L. (1997). Maternal psychological functioning, family processes, and child adjustment in rural, single-parent, African American families. *Developmental Psychology, 33,* 1000–1011.

Brody, G. H., Stoneman, Z., McCoy, J. K., & Forehand, R. (1992). Contemporaneous and longitudinal associations of sibling conflict with family relationship assessments and family discussions about sibling problems. *Child Development, 63,* 391–400.

Brown, S. (1988). *Treating adult children of alcoholics: A developmental perspective*. New York: Wiley.

Bugental, D. B., Blue, J., & Lewis, J. (1990). Caregiver cognitions as moderators of affective reactions to "difficult" children. *Developmental Psychology, 25*, 631–638.

Bugental, D. B., Brown, M., & Reiss, C. (1996). Cognitive representations of power in caregiving relationships: Biasing effects on interpersonal interaction and information processing. *Journal of Family Psychology, 10*, 397–407.

Bugental, D. B., Lyon, J. E., Lin, E. K., McGrath, E. P., & Bimbela, A. (1999). Children "tune-out" in response to the ambiguous communication style of powerless adults. *Child Development, 70*, 214–230.

Bukowski, W. M., & Hoza, B. (1989). Popularity and friendship: Issues in theory, measurement, and outcome. In T. J. Berndt & G. W. Ladd (Eds.), *Peer relationships in child development* (pp. 15–45). New York: Wiley.

Cairns, R. B., Cairns, B. D., Neckerman, H. J., Gest, S. D., & Gariepy, J. (1988). Social networks and aggressive behavior: Peer support or peer rejection. *Developmental Psychology, 24*, 815–823.

Caldwell, B. M., & Bradley, R. H. (1984). *Administration manual for the Home Observation for Measurement of the Environment*. Little Rock, AR: University of Arkansas at Little Rock.

Calvert, S. C., & McMahon, R. J. (1987). The treatment acceptability parent training program and its components. *Behavior Therapy, 18*, 165–179.

Campbell, S. B., Pierce, E., March, C., Ewing, L. J., & Szumowski, E. K. (1994). Hard-to-manage preschool boys: Symptomatic behavior across contexts and time. *Child Development, 65*, 836–851.

Capaldi, D. M., & Patterson, G. R. (1991). Relation of parental transitions to boys' adjustment problems: I. A linear hypothesis. II. Mothers at risk for transitions and unskilled parenting. *Developmental Psychology, 27*, 489–504.

Carifio, M. S., & Hess, A. K. (1987). Who is the ideal supervisor? *Professional Psychology: Research and Practice, 18*, 244–250.

Cavell, T. A. (1990). Social adjustment, social performance, and social skills: A tri-component model of social competence. *Journal of Clinical Child Psychology, 19*, 111–122.

Cavell, T. A. (1996, August). *Responsive parent training: A preliminary trial*. Paper presented at the 14th Biennial Meeting of the International Society for the Study of Behavioral Development, Quebec City, Quebec, Canada.

Cavell, T. A., (1999a). *Updating our approach to parent training. I: The case against targeting noncompliance*. Manuscript submitted for publication, Texas A&M University.

Cavell, T. A., (1999b). *Updating our approach to parent training. II: Acceptance as the prototypical form of positive parenting*. Manuscript submitted for publication, Texas A&M University.

Cavell, T. A., Constantin, L. P., Welch, J. S., & Kinnee, C. S. (1999). *Responsive parent training: A preliminary trial*. Manuscript submitted for publication.

Cavell, T. A., Frentz, C. E., & Kelley, M. L. (1986). Acceptability of paradoxical interventions: Some nonparadoxical findings. *Professional Psychology: Research and Practice, 17*, 519–523.

Cavell, T. A., & Hughes, J. N. (in press). Secondary prevention as context for assessing change processes in aggressive children. *Joural of School Psychology*.

Chamberlain, P., & Reid, J. B. (1987). Parent observation and report of child symptoms. *Behavioral Analysis, 9*, 97–109.

Chamberlain, P., & Reid, J. B. (1998). Comparison of two community alternatives to incarceration for chronic juvenile offenders. *Journal of Consulting and Clinical Psychology, 66*, 624–633.

Charlop, M. H., Parrish, J. M., Fenton, L. R., & Cataldo, M. F. (1983, August). *Long-term follow-up of a large scale parent training program*. Paper presented at the American Psychological Association Convention, Anaheim, CA.

Christian, R., Frick, P. J., Hill, N., Tyler, L. A., & Frazer, D. (1997). Psychopathy and conduct problems in children: II. Subtyping children with conduct problems based on their interpersonal and affective style. *Journal of the American Academy of Child and Adolescent Psychiatry, 36*, 233–241.

Cicchetti, D., Cummings, E. M., Greenberg, M. T., & Marvin, R. S. (1990). An organizational perspective on attachment beyond infancy. In M. T. Greenberg, D. Cicchetti, & M. Cummings (Eds.), *Attachment in the preschool years: Theory, research and intervention* (pp. 3–49). Chicago: University of Chicago Press.

Cohen, S., & Syme, S. L. (1985). *Social support and health.* New York: Academic Press.

Cohen, S., & Wills, T. (1985). Stress, social support, and the buffering hypothesis. *Psychological Bulletin, 98,* 310–357.

Cohn, D. A., Patterson, C. J., & Christopoulos, C. (1991). The family and children's peer relations. *Journal of Social and Personal Relationships, 8,* 315–346.

Coie, J. D. (1990). Toward a theory of peer rejection. In S. R. Asher & J. D. Coie (Eds.), *Peer rejection in childhood* (pp. 365–401). New York: Cambridge Press.

Coie, J. D., & Dodge, K. A. (1983). Continuities and changes in children's social status: A five-year longitudinal study. *Merrill-Palmer Quarterly, 29,* 261–282.

Coie, J. D., Dodge, K. A., & Kupersmidt, J. B. (1990). Peer group behavior and social status. In S. R. Asher & J. D. Coie (Eds.), *Peer rejection in childhood* (pp. 17–59). New York: Cambridge University Press.

Coie, J. D., & Kupersmidt, J. B. (1983). A behavioral analysis of emerging social status in boys' groups. *Child Development, 54,* 1400–1416.

Coie, J. D., Underwood, M., & Lochman, J. E. (1991). Programmatic intervention with aggressive children in the school setting. In D. J. Pepler & K. H. Rubin (Eds.), *The development and treatment of childhood aggression* (pp. 389–410). Hillsdale, NJ: Erlbaum.

Cole, D. A., & Carpentieri, S. (1990). Social status and the comorbidity of child depression and conduct disorder. *Journal of Consulting and Clinical Psychology, 58,* 748–757.

Colleta, N. (1981). Social support and the risk of maternal rejection by adolescent mothers. *Journal of Psychology, 109,* 191–197.

Conduct Problems Prevention Research Group. (1992). A developmental and clinical model for the prevention of conduct disorder: The FAST Track Program. *Development and Psychopathology, 4,* 509–528.

Connell, J. P. (1990). Context, self, and action: A motivational analysis of self-system processes across the life span. In D. Cicchetti & M. Beeghly (Eds.), *The self in transition: Infancy to childhood* (pp. 61–97). Chicago: University of Chicago Press.

Connell, S. L., Sanders, M. R., & Markie-Dadds, C. (1997). Self-directed behavioral family intervention for parents of oppositional children in rural and remote areas. *Behavior Modification, 21,* 379–408.

Constantin, L. P., & Cavell, T. A. (1999a). *Family rituals, parenting style, and the link to adolescent psychosocial development.* Manuscript submitted for publication.

Constantin, L. P., & Cavell, T. A. (1999b). *"Follow your child's lead": Training mothers to use child-directed play skills.* Manuscript submitted for publication.

Coufal, J. D. (1982). *An experimental evaluation of two approaches to parent skills training: Parent–child participation versus parents only.* Paper presented at the National Council on Family Relations, Washington, DC.

Coufal, J. D., & Brock, G. W. (1979). Parent-child relationship enhancement: A skills training approach. In N. Stinnett, B. Chesser, & J. Defrain (Eds.), *Building family strengths: Blueprints for action* (Vol. 1). London: University of Nebraska Press.

Crick, N. R., & Dodge, K. A. (1994). A review and reformulation of social information-processing mechanisms in children's social adjustment. *Psychological Bulletin, 115,* 74–101.

Crick, N. R., & Grotpeter, J. K. (1995). Relational aggression, gender, and social-psychological adjustment. *Child Development, 66,* 710–722.

Cummings, E. M., Ballard, M., El-Sheikh, M., & Lake, M. (1991). Resolution and children's responses to interadult anger. *Developmental Psychology, 27,* 462–470.

Cunningham, C. E. (1989). Training parents of language-delayed children with behavior problems. In C. E. Schaefer & J. M. Briesmeister (Eds.), *Handbook of parent training: Parents as co-therapists for children's behavior problems* (pp. 133–175). New York: Wiley.

Cunningham, C. E., Bremner, R., & Boyle, M. (1995). Large group community-based parenting programs for families of preschoolers at risk for disruptive behaviour disorders: Utilization, cost effectiveness, and outcome. *The Journal of Child Psychology and Psychiatry, 36,* 1141–1159.

Dadds, M. R., & McHugh, T. A. (1992). Social support and treatment outcome in behavioral family therapy for child conduct problems. *Journal of Consulting & Clinical Psychology, 60*, 252–259.

Dadds, M. R., Schwartz, S., & Sanders, M. (1987). Marital discord and treatment outcome in behavioral treatment of child conduct disorders. *Journal of Consulting & Clinical Psychology, 55*, 396–403.

Dangel, R. F., & Polster A. (1984). *Parent training: Foundations of research and practice.* New York: Guilford Press.

Deater-Deckard, K., & Dodge, K. A. (1997). Externalizing behavior problems and children revisited: Nonlinear effects and variation by culture, context, and gender. *Psychological Inquiry, 8*, 161–175.

Diener, M. B., & Milich, R. (1997). Effects of positive feedback on the social interactions of boys with attention deficit hyperactivity disorder: A test of the self-protective hypothesis. *Journal of Clinical Child Psychology, 26*, 256–265.

Dishion, T. J., & Andrews, D. W. (1995). Preventing escalation in problem behaviors with high-risk young adolescents: Immediate and 1-year outcomes. *Journal of Consulting and Clinical Psychology, 63*, 538–548.

Dishion, T. J., Andrews, D. W., & Crosby, L. (1995). Adolescent boys and their friends in adolescence: Relationship characteristics, quality, and interactional processes. *Child Development, 66*, 139–151.

Dishion, T. J., & Patterson, G. R. (1992). Age effects in parent training outcomes. *Behavior Therapy, 23*, 719–729.

Dishion, T. J., Patterson, G. R., Stoolmiller, M., & Skinner, M. L. (1991). Family, school, and behavioral antecedents to early adolescent involvement with antisocial peers. *Developmental Psychology, 27*, 172–180.

Dishion, T. J., Spracklen, K. M., Andrews, D. W., & Patterson, G. R. (1996). Deviancy training in male adolescent friendships. *Behavior Therapy, 27*, 373–390.

Dix, T. (1991). The affective organization of parenting: Adaptive and maladaptive processes. *Psychological Bulletin, 110*, 3–25.

Dix, T., & Lochman, J. E. (1990). Social cognition and negative reactions to children: A comparison of mothers of aggressive and nonaggressive boys. *Journal of Social and Clinical Psychology, 9*, 418–438.

Dodge, K. A. (1983). Behavioral antecedents of peer social status. *Child Development, 54*, 1386–1399.

Dodge, K. A. (1986). A social information processing model of social competence in children. In M. Perlmutter (Ed.), *Cognitive perspective on children's social and behavioral development* (pp. 77–125). Hillsdale, NJ: Erlbaum.

Dodge, K. A. (1993). The future of research on the treatment of conduct disorder. *Development and Psychopathology, 5*, 311–319.

Dodge, K. A., & Coie, J. D. (1987). Social information processing factors in reactive and proactive aggression in children's peer groups. *Journal of Personality and Social Psychology, 53*, 1146–1158.

Dodge, K. A., & Crick, N. R. (1990). Social information-progressing bases of aggressive behavior in children. *Personality and Social Psychology Bulletin, 16*, 8–22.

Dodge, K. A., & Frame, C. L. (1982). Social cognitive biases and deficits in aggressive boys. *Child Development, 53*, 620–635.

Dodge, K. A., Murphy, R. R., & Buschbaum, K. C. (1984). The assessment of intention-cue detection skills in children: Implications for developmental psychology. *Child Development, 55*, 163–173.

Dodge, K. A., & Newman, J. P. (1981). Biased decision-making processes in aggressive boys. *Journal of Abnormal Psychology, 90*, 375–379.

Dodge, K. A., Pettit, G. S., & Bates, J. E. (1994). Socialization mediators of the relation between socioeconomic status and child conduct problems. *Child Development, 65*, 649–655.

Dodge, K. A., & Somberg, D. R. (1987). Hostile attributional biases among aggressive boys are exacerbated under conditions of threats to the self. *Child Development, 58*, 213–224.

Dosick, W. (1998). *Golden rules: The ten ethical values parents need to teach their children*. San Francisco: Harper.

Duchnowski, A. (1994). Innovative service models: Education. Task force report on innovative models of mental health services for children, adolescents, and their families [Special issue]. *Journal of Clinical Child Psychology, 23*(Suppl.): 13–18.

Dumas, J. E. (1989). Treating antisocial behavior in children: Child and family approaches. *Clinical Psychology Review, 9*, 197–222.

Dumas, J. E. (1996). Why was this child referred? Interactional correlates of referral status in families of children with disruptive behavior problems. *Journal of Clinical Child Psychology, 25*, 106–115.

Dumas, J. E., & LaFreniere, P. J. (1993). Mother–child relationships as sources of support or stress: A comparison of competent, average, aggressive, and anxious dyads. *Child Development, 64*, 1732–1754.

Dumas, J. E., LaFreniere, P. J., Serketich, W. J. (1995). "Balance of power": A transactional analysis of control in mother-child dyads involving socially competent, aggressive, and anxious children. *Journal of Abnormal Psychology, 104*, 104–113.

Dumas, J. E., & Wahler, R. G. (1983). Predictors of treatment outcome in parent training: Mother insularity and socioeconomic disadvantage. *Behavioral Assessment, 5*, 301–313.

Dumas, J. E. & Wahler, R. G. (1985). Indiscriminate mothering as a contextual factor in aggressive-oppositional child behavior: "Damned if you do and damned if you don't." *Journal of Abnormal Child Psychology, 13*, 1–17.

Dunn, J. (1995). *From one to two*. New York: Ballantine.

Eardley, D. (1978). *An initial investigation of a didactic version of filial therapy dealing with self-concept increase and problematic behavior decrease*. Unpublished doctoral dissertation, Pennsylvania State University, State College.

Edens, J., Cavell, T. A., & Hughes, J. N. (1999). The self-systems of aggressive children: A cluster-analytic investigation. *Journal of Child Psychology and Psychiatry, 40*, 441–454.

Eisenstadt, T. H., Eyberg, S., McNeil, C. B., Newcomb, K. N., & Funderburk, B. (1993). Parent-child interaction therapy with behavior problem children: Relative effectiveness of two stages and overall treatment outcome. *Journal of Clinical Child Psychology, 22*, 42–51.

Emery, R. E. (1989). Family violence. *American Psychologist, 44*, 321–328.

Eron, L. (1987). The development of aggressive behavior from the perspective of a developing behaviorism. *American Psychologist, 42*, 435–442.

Evans, S. W., & Short, E. J. (1991). A qualitative and serial analysis of social problem solving in aggressive boys. *Journal of Abnormal Child Psychology, 19*, 331–340.

Eyberg, S. (1988). Parent-child interaction therapy: Integration of traditional and behavioral concerns. *Child and Family Behavior Therapy, 10*, 33–45.

Faber, A., & Mazlish E. (1980). *How to talk so kids will listen & listen so kids will talk*. New York: Avon.

Feldman, E., & Dodge, K. A. (1987). Social information processing and sociometric status: Sex, age, and situational effects. *Journal of Abnormal Child Psychology, 15*, 211–227.

Felson, R. B., & Russo, N. J. (1997). Parental punishment and sibling aggression. *Social Psychology Quarterly, 51*, 11–18.

Fergusson, D. M., Horwood, L. J., & Lynskey, M. T. (1995). The stability of disruptive childhood behavior. *Journal of Abnormal Child Psychology, 23*, 379–396.

Forehand, R., King, H. E., Peed, S., & Yoder, P. (1975). Mother–child interactions: Comparison of a noncompliant clinic group and a non-clinic group. *Behavior Research and Therapy, 13*, 79–84.

Forehand, R., & Long, N. (1991). Prevention of aggression and other behavior problems in the early adolescent years. In D. J. Pepler and K. H. Rubin (Eds.), *The development and treatment of childhood aggression* (pp. 317–330). Hillsdale, NJ: Erlbaum.

Forehand, R. L., & McMahon, R. J. (1981). *Helping the noncompliant child: A clinician's guide to present training*. New York: Guilford Press.

Forehand, R. & McMahon, R. J. (1984). Parent training for the noncompliant child: Treatment outcome, generalization, and adjunctive therapy procedures. In R. F. Dangel & A. Polster (Eds.), *Parent training: Foundations of research and practice* (pp. 298–328). New York: Guilford Press.

Forehand, R., Middlebrook, J., Rogers, T., & Steffe, M. (1983). Dropping out of parent training. *Behavior Research and Therapy, 21,* 663–668.

Forgatch, M. S. (1991). The clinical science vortex: A developing theory of antisocial behavior. In D. J. Pepler and K. H. Rubin (Eds.), *The development and treatment of childhood aggression* (pp. 291–315). Hillsdale, NJ: Erlbaum.

Frick, P. J., & Jackson, Y. K. (1993). Family functioning and childhood antisocial behavior: Yet another reinterpretation. *Journal of Clinical Child Psychology, 22,* 410–419.

Frick, P. J., Lahey, B. B., Loeber, R., Stouthamer-Loeber, M., Christ, M. G., & Hanson, K. (1992). Familial risk factors to oppositional defiant disorder and conduct disorder: Parental psychopathology and maternal parenting. *Journal of Consulting and Clinical Psychology, 60,* 49–55.

Garbarino, J. (1995). *Raising children in a socially toxic environment.* San Francisco: Jossey-Bass.

Gardner, F. E. (1987). Positive interaction between mothers and conduct-problem children. Is there training for harmony as well as fighting? *Journal of Abnormal Child Psychology, 15,* 283–293.

Ginott, H. G. (1976). *Between parent and child.* New York: Avon Books.

Ginsberg, B. G. (1984). Beyond behavior modification: Client-centered play therapy with the retarded. *American Psychology Bulletin, 6,* 332–334.

Ginsberg, B. (1989). Training parents as therapeutic agents with foster/adoptive children using the filial approach. In C. E. Shaefer & J. M. Briesmeister (Eds.), *Handbook of parent training: Parents as co-therapists for children's behavior problems* (pp. 442–478). New York: Wiley.

Gorman-Smith, D., & Tolan, P. (1998). The role of exposure to community violence and developmental problems among inner-city youth. *Development & Psychopathology, 10,* 101–116.

Gottman, J. M. (1994). *What predicts divorce?* Hillsdale, NJ: Erlbaum.

Gottman, J. M., Katz, L. F., & Hooven, C. (1996). Parental meta-emotion philosophy and the emotional life of families: Theoretical models and preliminary data. *Journal of Family Psychology, 10,* 243–268.

Gottman, J. M., Katz, L. F., & Hooven, C. (1997). *Meta-emotion.* Mahwah, NJ: Erlbaum.

Greenberg, M. T., & Speltz, M. L. (1988). Attachment and the ontogeny of conduct problems. In J. Belsky & T. Nezworski (Eds.), *Clinical implications of attachment* (pp. 177–218). Hillsdale, NJ: Erlbaum.

Greenberg, M. T., Speltz, M. L., DeKlyen, M. (1993). The role of attachment in the early development of disruptive behavior problems. *Development and Psychopathology, 5,* 191–214.

Greist, D. L., Forehand, R., Wells, K. C., & McMahon, R. J. (1980). An examination of differences between nonclinic and behavior problem clinic-referred children and their mothers. *Journal of Abnormal Child Psychology, 9,* 217–219.

Grusec, J. E. (1971) Power and the internalization of self-denial. *Child Development, 42,* 93–105.

Grusec, J. E., & Goodnow, J. J. (1994). Impact of parental discipline methods on the child's internalization of values: A reconceptualization of current points of view. *Developmental Psychology, 30,* 4–19.

Guerney, B. (1964). Filial therapy: Description and rationale. *Journal of Consulting Psychology, 28,* 304–310.

Guerney, B. (1977). *Relationship enhancement: Skill training programs for therapy, problem prevention, and enrichment.* San Francisco: Jossey-Bass.

Guerney, B. G., & Stover, L. (1971). *Filial therapy* (Final report on grant MH 18264-01). Bethesda, MD: National Institute of Mental Health.

Guerney, L. F. (1983). Introduction to filial therapy: Training parents as therapists. In P. A. Keller & L. G. Ritt (Eds.), *Innovations in clinical practice: A source book: Vol. 2* (pp. 26–39). Sarasota, FL: Professional Resource Exchange.

Guerney, L. F., & Guerney B. G. (1985). The relationship enhancement family of family therapies. In L. L'Abate & M. Milan (Eds.), *Handbook of family therapy* (pp. 506–524). New York: Wiley.

Guerney, L. F., & Guerney B. G., Jr. (1987). Integrating child and family therapy. *Psychotherapy, 24,* 609–614.

Guerra, N. J., & Slaby, R. G. (1989). Evaluative factors in social problem solving by aggressive boys. *Journal of Abnormal Child Psychology, 17,* 277–289.

Hanf, C. (1969). *A two-stage program for modifying maternal controlling during mother-child interaction.* Paper presented at the meeting of the Western Psychological Association, Vancouver, British Columbia, Canada.

Hanf, C., & Kling, J. (1973). *Facilitating parent-child interaction: A two-stage training model.* Unpublished manuscript, University of Oregon Medical School, Portland.

Harter, S., Marold, D. B., Whitesell, N. R., & Cobbs, G. (1996). A model of the effects of perceived parent and peer support on adolescent false self behavior. *Child Development, 67,* 360–374.

Harter, S., & Pike, R. (1984). The pictorial scale of perceived competence and social acceptance for young children. *Child Development, 55,* 1969–1982.

Hartup, W. W. (1989). Social relationships and their developmental significance. *American Psychologist, 44,* 120–126.

Hastings, P. D., & Grusec, J. E. (1998). Parenting goals as organizers of responses to parent-child disagreement. *Developmental Psychology, 34,* 465–479.

Hatcher, R. L., & Barends, A. W. (1996). Patients' view of the alliance in psychotherapy: Exploratory factor analysis of three alliance measures. *Journal of Consulting and Clinical Psychology, 64,* 1326–1336.

Hawkins, J. D., Catalano, R. F., & Miller, J. Y. (1994). Risk and protective factors for alcohol and other drug problems in adolescence and early adulthood: Implications for substance abuse prevention. *Psychological Bulletin, 112,* 64–105.

Hawkins, R. P., Peterson, R. F., Schweid, E., & Bijou, S. W. (1966). Behavior therapy in the home: Amelioration of problem parent-child relations with the parent in the therapeutic role. *Journal of Experimental Child Psychology, 4,* 99–107.

Hazan, C., & Shaver, P. R. (1994). Deeper into attachment theory. *Psychological Inquiry, 5,* 68–79.

Hembree-Kigin, T., & McNeil, C. B. (1995). *Parent-child interaction therapy.* New York: Plenum Press.

Henggeler, S. W., & Borduin, C. M. (1990). *Family therapy and beyond: A multisystemic approach to treating the behavior problems of children and adolescents.* Pacific Grove, CA: Brooks/Cole.

Henggeler, S. W., Schoenwald, S. K., Borduin, C. M., Rowland, M. D., & Cunningham, P. B. (1997). *Multisystemic treatment of antisocial behavior in children and adolescents.* Pacific Grove, CA: Brooks/Cole.

Henry, W. P., Schacht, T. E., Strupp, H. H., Butler, S. F., & Binder, J. L. (1993). Effects of training in time-limited dynamic psychotherapy: Mediators of therapists' responses to training. *Journal of Consulting and Clinical Psychology, 61,* 441–447.

Hess, A. K. (1987). Psychotherapy supervision: Stages, Buber, and a theory of relationship. *Professional Psychology: Research and Practice, 18,* 251–259.

Hinshaw, S. P. (1992). Externalizing behavior problems and academic underachievement in childhood and adolescence: Causal relationships and underlying mechanisms. *Psychological Bulletin, 111,* 127–155.

Hinshaw, S. P., & Anderson, C. A. (1996). Conduct and oppositional defiant disorders. In E. J. Mash, & R. A. Barkley (Eds.), *Child psychopathology* (pp. 113–149). New York: Guilford Press.

Holden, G. W. (1983). Avoiding conflict: Mothers as tacticians in the supermarket. *Child Development, 54,* 64–69.

Horne, A. M., & Patterson, G. R. (1980). Working with parents of aggressive children. In R. R. Abidin (Ed.), *Parent education and intervention handbook* (pp. 159–184). Springfield, IL: Thomas.

Huesman, L. R., Eron, L. D., Lefkowitz, M. M., & Walder, L. O. (1984). Stability of aggression over time and generations. *Developmental Psychology, 20,* 1120–1134.

Hughes, J. N., & Cavell, T. A. (1994). Enhancing competence in aggressive children. In G. Cartledge & J. F. Milburn (Eds.), *Teaching social skills to children: Innovative approaches* (3rd ed.). New York: Pergamon.

Hughes, J. N., & Cavell, T. A. (1995, August). *An integrated home-school prevention program for aggressive children.* Paper presented at the annual meeting of the American Psychological Association, Washington, DC

Hughes, J. N., Cavell, T. A. & Grossman, P. (1997). A positive view of self: Risk or protection for aggressive children? *Development and Psychopathology, 9,* 75–94.

Hughes, J. N., Cavell, T. A., & Jackson, T. (1999). Influence of teacher-student relationships on childhood conduct problems: A prospective study. *Journal of Clinical Child Psychology, 28,* 173–184.

Hughes, J., & Sullivan, K. (1988). Outcome assessment in social skills training with children. *Journal of School Psychology, 26,* 167–183.

Humphreys, L., Forehand, R., McMahon, R., & Roberts, M. (1978). Parent behavioral training to modify child noncompliance: Effects on untreated siblings. *Journal of Behavior Therapy and Experimental Psychiatry, 9,* 235–238.

Hymel, S. (1986). Interpretations of peer behavior: Affective bias in childhood and adolescence. *Child Development, 57,* 431–445.

Jacobson, N. S. (1992). Behavioral couple therapy: A new beginning. *Behavior Therapy, 23,* 493–506.

Jernberg, A. M., (1989). Training parents of failure-to-attach children. In C. E. Schaefer & J. M. Briesmeister (Eds.), *Handbook of parent training: Parents as co-therapists for children's behavior problems* (pp. 392–413). New York: Wiley.

Johnson, S. M., Bolstad, O. D., & Lobitz, C. K. (1976). Generalization and contrast phenomena in behavior modification with children. In E. J. Mash, L. A. Hamerlynck, & L. C. Handy (Eds.), *Behavior modification and families* (pp. 160–188). New York: Brunner/Mazel.

Johnson, S. M., & Lobitz, G. K. (1974). Parental manipulations in home observations. *Journal of Applied Behavior Analysis, 7,* 23–31.

Johnson, V. K., Cowan, P. A., & Cowan, C. P. (1999). Children's classroom behavior: The unique contribution of family organization. *Journal of Family Psychology, 13,* 355–371.

Kazdin, A. E. (1987). Treatment of antisocial behavior in children: Current status and future directions. *Psychology Bulletin, 102,* 187–203.

Kazdin, A. E. (1993). Treatment of conduct disorder: Progress and directions in psychotherapy research. *Development and Psychopathology, 5,* 277–310.

Kazdin, A. E. (1995a). Child, parent and family dysfunction as predictors of outcome in cognitive-behavioral treatment of antisocial children. *Behaviour Research & Therapy, 33,* 271–281.

Kazdin, A. E. (1995b). Scope of child and adolescent psychotherapy research: Limited sampling of dysfunctions, treatments, and client characteristics. *Journal of Clinical Child Psychology, 24,* 125–140.

Kazdin, A. E. (1997). Parent management training: Evidence, outcomes, and issues. *Journal of the American Academy of Child and Adolescent Psychiatry, 36,* 1349–1356.

Kazdin, A. E., Bass, D., Siegel, T., & Thomas, C. (1989). Cognitive-behavioral therapy and relationship therapy in the treatment of children referred for antisocial behavior. *Journal of Consulting and Clinical Psychology, 57,* 522–535.

Kazdin, A. E., Mazurick, J. L., & Bass, D. (1993). Risk for attrition in treatment of antisocial children and families. *Journal of Clinical Child Psychology, 22,* 2–16.

Kerfoot, M. (1979). Parent-child role reversal and adolescent suicidal behavior. *Journal of Adolescence, 2,* 337–343.

Kipling, Rudyard. (1982). Baa Baa, Blacksheep. In J. K. Gardner (Ed.), *Readings in developmental psychology* (2nd ed., pp. 346–361). Boston: Little, Brown, & Co.

Kochanska, G. (1993). Toward a synthesis of parental socialization and child temperament in early development of conscience. *Child Development, 64,* 325–347.

Kochanska, G. (1995). Children's temperament, mothers' discipline, and security of attachment: Multiple pathways to emerging internalization. *Child Development, 66,* 597–615.

Kochanska, G., Aksan, N., & Koenig, A. L. (1995). A longitudinal study of the roots of preschoolers' conscience: Committed compliance and emerging internalization. *Child Development, 66,* 1752–1769.

Korfmacher, J., Adam, E., Ogawa, J., & Egeland, B. (1997). Adult attachment: Implications for the therapeutic process in a home visitation intervention. *Applied Developmental Science, 1,* 43–52.

Kotchick, B. A., Forehand, R., Brody, G., Armistead, L., Morse, E., Simon, P., & Clark, L. (1997). The impact of maternal HIV infection on parenting in inner-city African American families. *Journal of Family Psychology, 11,* 447–461.

Kuczynski, L. (1984). Socialization goals and mother-child interaction: Strategies for long-term and short-term compliance. *Developmental Psychology, 20,* 1061–1073.

Kuczynski, L., & Hildebrandt, N. (1997). Models of conformity and resistance in socialization theory. In J. E. Grusec & L. Kuczynski (Eds.), *Parenting and children's internalization of values* (pp. 227–256). New York: Wiley.

Kumpfer, K. L., & Alvarado, R. (1995). Strengthening families to prevent drug use in multiethnic youth. In G. J. Botvin, S. Schinke, & M. A. Orlandi (Eds.), *Drug abuse prevention with multiethnic youth* (pp. 225–294). Thousand Oaks, CA: Sage.

Lahey, B. B., Hartdagen, S. E., Frick, P. J., McBurnett, K., Connor, R., & Hynd, G. W. (1988). Conduct disorder: Parsing the confounded relation to parental divorce and antisocial personality. *Journal of Abnormal Psychology, 97,* 334–337.

Lahey, B. B., Loeber, B., Hart, E. L., Frick, P. J., Applegate, B., Zhang, Q., Green, S. M., & Russo, M. F. (1995). Four-year longitudinal study of conduct disorder in boys: Patterns and predictors of persistence. *Journal of Abnormal Psychology, 104,* 83–93.

Lahey, B. B., Russo, M. F., Walker, J. L., & Piacentini, J. C. (1989). Personality characteristics of the mothers of children with disruptive behavior disorders. *Journal of Consulting & Clinical Psychology, 57,* 512–515.

Larzelere, R. E., (1996). A review of outcomes of parental use of nonabusive or customary physical punishment. *Pediatrics, 98,* 824–831.

Larzelere, R. E., Sather, P. R., Schneider, W. N., Larson, D. B., & Pike, P. L. (1998). Punishment enhances reasoning's effectiveness as a disciplinary response to toddlers. *Journal of Marriage and the Family, 60,* 388–403.

Lay, K., Waters, E., & Park, K. (1989). Maternal responsiveness and child compliance: The role of mood as a mediator. *Child Development, 60,* 1405–1411.

Lazarus, R. S., & Folkman, S. (1984). *Stress, appraisal, and coping.* New York: Springer.

Levant, R. F. (1983). Client-centered skills-training programs for the family: A review of the literature. *Journal of Counseling Psychologist, 11,* 29–46.

Lieberman, A. F., Weston, D. R., & Pawl, J. H. (1991). Preventive intervention and outcome with anxiously attached dyads. *Child Development, 62,* 199–209.

Lochman, J. E. (1992). Cognitive–behavioral intervention with aggressive boys: Three-year follow-up and preventive effects. *Journal of Consulting and Clinical Psychology, 60,* 426–432.

Lochman, J. E., & Curry, J. F. (1986). Effects of social problem-solving training and self-instructional training with aggressive boys. *Journal of Clinical Child Psychology, 15,* 159–164.

Lochman, J. E., & Dodge, K. A. (1994). Social–cognitive processes of severely violent, moderately aggressive, and nonaggressive boys. *Journal of Consulting and Clinical Psychology, 62,* 366–374.

Loeber, R. (1990). Development and risk factors of juvenile antisocial behavior and delinquency. *Clinical Psychology Review, 10,* 1–42.

Loeber, R., Farrington, D. P., Stouthamer-Loeber, M., & Van Kammen, W. B. (1998). *Antisocial behavior and mental health problems: Explanatory factors in childhood and adolescence.* Mahwah, NJ: Erlbaum.

Loeber, R., Stouthamer-Loeber, M., Van Kammen, W., & Farrington, D. P. (1991). Initiation, escalation and desistance in juvenile offending and their correlates. *The Journal of Criminal Law & Criminology, 82,* 36–82.

Loeber, R., Wung, P., Keenan, K., Giroux, B., Stouthamer-Loeber, M., Van Kammen, W. B., & Maughan, B. (1993). Developmental pathways in disruptive child behavior. *Development and Psychopathology, 5,* 103–133.

Long, P., Forehand, R., Wierson, M., & Morgan, A. (1994). Does parent training with young noncompliant children have long-term effects? *Behavior Research and Therapy, 32,* 101–107.

Lutzker, J. R. (1994). Referee's evaluation of "Assessment of a new procedure to prevent timeout escape in preschoolers by McNeil et al." *Child & Family Behavior Therapy, 16,* 33–35.

Lykken, D. T. (1995). *The antisocial personalities.* Hillsdale, NJ: Erlbaum.

Lyons-Ruth, K. (1996). Attachment relationships among children with aggressive behavior problems: The role of disorganized early attachment patterns. *Journal of Consulting and Clinical Psychology, 64,* 64–73.

Lytton, H. (1990a). Child and parent effects in boys' conduct disorder: A reinterpretation. *Developmental Psychology, 26,* 683–697.

Lytton, H. (1990b). Child effects—still unwelcome? Response to Dodge and Wahler. *Developmental Psychology, 26,* 705–709.

Maccoby, E. E. (1980). Comment and reply. In G. R. Patterson (Ed.), Mothers: The unacknowledged victims. *Monographs of the Society for Research in Child Development, 45* (5, Serial No. 186).

Maccoby, E. E. (1992). The role of parents in the socialization of children: An historical overview. *Developmental Psychology, 28,* 1006–1017.

Maccoby, E. E., & Martin, J. (1983). Socialization in the context of the family: Parent–child interaction. In P. H. Mussen (Series Ed.) & E. M. Hetherington (Ed.), *Handbook of child psychology: Vol. 4. Socialization, personality, and social development* (pp. 1–101). New York: Wiley.

MacKinnon-Lewis, C., Starnes, R., Volling, B., & Johnson, S. (1997). Perceptions of parenting as predictors of boys' sibling and peer relations. *Developmental Psychology, 33,* 1024–1031.

Main, M., Kaplan, N., & Cassidy, J. (1985). Security in infancy, childhood and adulthood: A move to the level of representation. *Monographs of the Society for Research in Child Development, 50*(1–2, Serial No. 209), 66–104.

Mash, E. J., & Dozois, D. J. (1996). Child psychopathology: A developmental-systems perspective. In E. J. Mash & R. A. Barkley (Eds.), *Child psychopathology* (pp. 3–60). New York: Guilford Press.

Mash, E. J., & Terdal, L. G. (1988). *Behavioral assessment of childhood disorders* (2nd ed). New York: Guilford Press.

McCord, J., & Tremblay, R. E. (1992). *Preventing antisocial behavior: Interventions from birth through adolescence.* New York: Guilford Press.

McLoyd, V. C. (1990). The impact of economic hardship on black families and children: Psychological distress, parenting, and socioemotional development. *Child Development, 61,* 311–346.

McMahon, R. J., & Forehand, R. (1984). Parent training for the noncompliant child: Treatment outcome, generalization, and adjunctive therapy procedures. In R. F. Dangel & A. Polster (Eds.), *Parent training: Foundations of research and practice* (pp. 298–328). New York: Guilford Press.

McMahon, R. J., & Forehand, R. (1988). Conduct disorders. In E. J. Mash & L. G. Terdal (Eds.), *Behavioral assessment of childhood disorders* (2nd ed., pp. 105–153). New York: Guilford Press.

McNeil, C. B., Clemens-Mowrer, L., Gurwitch, R. H., & Funderburk, B. W. (1994). Assessment of a new procedure to prevent time-out escape in preschoolers. *Child & Family Behavior, 16,* 27–33.

McNeil, C. B., Eyberg, S., Eisenstadt, T. H., Newcomb, K., & Funderburk, B. (1991). Parent-child interaction therapy with behavior problem children: Generalization of treatment effects to the school setting. *Journal of Clinical Child Psychology, 20,* 140–151.

Milich, R., Widiger, T., & Landau, S. (1987). Differential diagnosis of attention deficit and conduct disorders using conditional probabilities. *Journal of Consulting & Clinical Psychology, 55,* 762–767.

Miller, G. E., & Prinz, R. J. (1990). Enhancement of social learning family interventions for childhood conduct disorder. *Psychological Bulletin, 108,* 291–307.

Miller, P. A., & Eisenberg, N. (1988). The relation of empathy to aggressive and externalizing antisocial behavior. *Psychological Bulletin, 103,* 324–344.

Milne, D. (1986). *Training behavior therapists: Methods, evaluation and implementation with parents, nurses and teachers.* Cambridge, MA: Brookline Books.

Minuchin, S. (1974). *Families and family therapy*. Cambridge, MA: Harvard University Press.

Moffitt, T. E. (1993). Life-course persistent and adolescence-limited antisocial behavior: A developmental taxonomy. *Psychological Review, 100,* 674–701.

Moos, R. G., & Billings, A. G. (1982). Conceptualizing and measuring coping resources and processes. In L. Goldberger & S. Breznitz (Eds.), *Handbook of stress: Theoretical and clinical aspects*. New York: Free Press.

Morrison, G. M., Forness, S. R., & MacMillan, D. L. (1983). Influences on the sociometric ratings of mildly handicapped children: A path analysis. *Journal of Educational Psychology, 75,* 63–74.

Nichols, M. P., & Schwartz, R. C. (1998). *Family therapy: Concepts and methods* (4th ed.). Boston: Allyn & Bacon.

Olweus, D. (1979). Stability of aggressive behavior patterns in males: A review. *Psychological Bulletin, 86,* 852–875.

Olweus, D. (1991). Bully/victim problems among schoolchildren: Basic facts and effects of a school based intervention program. In D. J. Pepler & K. H. Rubin (Eds.), *The development and treatment of childhood aggression* (pp. 139–168). Hillsdale, NJ: Erlbaum.

Orgel, A. R. (1980). Haim Ginott's approach to discipline. In D. Dorr & M. Zax (Eds.), *Comparative approaches to discipline for children and youth* (pp. 151–184). New York: Springer.

Oxman, L. (1971). *The effectiveness of filial therapy: A controlled study*. Unpublished doctoral dissertation, Rutgers University, New Brunswick, NJ.

Panella, D., & Henggeler, S. W. (1986). Peer interactions of conduct-disordered, anxious-withdrawn, and well-adjusted black adolescents. *Journal of Abnormal Child Psychology, 14,* 1–11.

Parke, R. D., & Slaby, R. G. (1983). The development of aggression. In E. M. Hetherington (Ed.), *Handbook of child psychology: Vol. 4. Socialization, personality, and social development* (pp. 547–641). New York: Wiley.

Parker, J. G., & Asher, S. R. (1987). Peer relations and later personal adjustment: Are low-accepted children at risk? *Psychological Bulletin, 102,* 357–389.

Parker, J. G., & Asher, S. R. (1993). Friendships and friendship quality in middle childhood: Links with peer group acceptance and feelings of loneliness and social dissatisfaction. *Developmental Psychology, 29,* 277–287.

Parpal, M., & Maccoby, E. E. (1985). Maternal responsiveness and subsequent child compliance. *Child Development, 56,* 1326–1334.

Patterson, G. R. (1982). *Coercive family process*. Eugene, OR: Castalia.

Patterson, G. R. (1985). Beyond technology: The next stage in developing an empirical base for parent training. In L. L'Abate (Ed.), *Handbook of family psychology; Volume 2* (pp. 1344–1379). Homewood, IL: Dorsey.

Patterson, G. R. (1986). Performance models for antisocial boys. *American Psychologist, 41,* 432–444.

Patterson, G. R. (1997). Performance models of parenting: A social interactional perspective. In J. E. Grusec & L. Kuczynski (Eds.), *Parenting and children's internalization of values* (pp. 193–226). New York: Wiley.

Patterson, G. R., & Bank, L. (1986). Bootstrapping your way in the nomological thicket. *Behavioral Assessment, 8,* 49–73.

Patterson, G. R., & Brodsky, G. (1966). A behavior modification program for a child with multiple problem behaviors. *Journal of Child Psychology and Psychiatry, 7,* 277–295.

Patterson, G. R., Capaldi, D. M., & Bank, L. (1991). An early starter model for predicting delinquency. In D. J. Pepler & K. H. Rubin (Eds.), *The development and treatment of childhood aggression* (pp. 139–168). Hillsdale, NJ: Erlbaum.

Patterson, G. R., & Chamberlain, P. (1994). A functional analysis of resistance during parent training therapy. *Clinical Psychology: Science & Practice, 1,* 53–70.

Patterson, G. R., Chamberlain, P., & Reid, J. B. (1982). A comparative evaluation of a parent-training program. *Behavior Therapy, 13,* 638–650.

Patterson, G. R., DeBaryshe, B. D., & Ramsey, E. (1989). A development perspective on antisocial behavior. *American Psychologist, 44,* 329–335.

Patterson, G. R., Dishion, T. J., & Chamberlain, P. (1993). Outcomes and methodological issues relating to treatment of antisocial children. In T. R. Giles (Ed.), *Handbook of effective psychotherapy* (pp. 43–88). New York: Plenum.

Patterson, G. R., & Fleischman, M. J. (1979). Maintenance of treatment effects: Some considerations concerning family systems and follow-up data. *Behavior Therapy, 10,* 168–185.

Patterson, G. R., & Forgatch, M. S. (1985). Therapist behavior as a determinant for client noncompliance: A paradox for the behavior modifier. *Journal of Consulting and Clinical Psychology, 53,* 846–851.

Patterson, G. R., & Gullion, M. E. (1968). *Living with children: New methods for parents and teachers.* Champaign, IL: Research Press.

Patterson, G. R., Reid, J. R., & Dishion, T. J. (1992). *Antisocial boys.* Eugene, OR: Castalia.

Patterson, G. R., Reid, J. B., Jones, R. R., & Conger, R. E. (1975). *A social learning approach to family intervention. Vol. 1. Families with aggressive children.* Eugene, OR: Castalia.

Pepler, D. J., & Rubin K. H. (1991). *The development and treatment of childhood aggression.* Hillsdale, NJ: Erlbaum.

Perlman, M., & Ross, H. S. (1997). The benefits of parent intervention in children's disputes: An examination of concurrent changes in children's fighting styles. *Child Development, 64,* 690–700.

Perry, P. G., Perry, L. C., & Rasmussen, P. (1986). Cognitive social learning mediators of aggression. *Child Development, 57,* 700–711.

Pettit, G. S., Dodge, K. A., & Brown, M. M. (1988). Early family experiences, social problem solving patterns, and children's social competence. *Child Development, 59,* 107–120.

Pfiffner, L. J., Jouriles, E. N., Brown, M. M., Etscheidt, M. A., & Kelly, J. (1990). Effects of problem-solving therapy on outcomes of parent training for single-parent families. *Child & Family Behavior Thereapy, 12,* 1–11.

Pierce, E., Ewing, L. J., & Campbell, S. B. (1999). Diagnostic status and symptomatic behavior of hard-to-manage preschool children in middle childhood and early adolescence. *Journal of Clinical Child Psychology, 28,* 44–57.

Price, J. M., & Dodge, K. A. (1989). Peers' contributions to children's social maladjustment: Description and intervention. In T. J. Berndt & G. W. Ladd (Eds.), *Peer relationships in child development* (pp. 341–370). New York: Wiley.

Prinz, R. J., Blechman, E. A., & Dumas, J. E. (1994). An evaluation of peer coping-skills training for childhood aggression. *Journal of Clinical Child Psychology, 23,* 192–203.

Prinz, R. J., & Miller, G. E. (1991). Issues in understanding and treating childhood conduct problems in disadvantaged populations. *Journal of Clinical Child Psychology, 20,* 379–385.

Prinz, R. J., & Miller, G. E. (1994). Family-based treatment for childhood antisocial behavior: Experimental influences on dropout and engagement. *Journal of Consulting & Clinical Psychology, 62,* 645–650.

Prochaska, J. O., DiClemente, C. C., & Norcross, J. C. (1992). In search of how people change: Applications to addictive behaviors. *American Psychologist, 47,* 1102–1114.

Putallaz, M., & Heflin, A. H. (1990). Parent-child interaction. In S. R. Asher & J. D. Coie (Eds.), *Peer rejection in childhood* (pp. 189–216). New York: Cambridge University Press.

Radke-Yarrow, M., Richters, J., & Wilson, W. E. (1988). Child development in a network of relationships. In R. A. Hinde & J. Stevenson-Hinde (Eds.), *Relationships within families: Mutual influences* (pp. 48–67). New York: Oxford Press.

Retish, P. (1973). Changing the status of poorly-esteemed students through teacher reinforcement. *Journal of Applied Behavior Analysis, 9,* 44–50.

Rhodes, J. E., Contreras, J. M., & Mangelsdorf, S. C. (1994). Natural mentor relationships among Latina adolescent mothers: Psychological adjustment, moderating processes, and the role of early parental acceptance. *American Journal of Community Psychology, 22,* 211–227.

Richard, B. A., & Dodge, K. A. (1982). Social maladjustment and problem solving in school-aged children. *Journal of Consulting and Clinical Psychology, 50,* 226–233.

Richters, J. E., & Cicchetti, D. (1993). Mark Twain meets DSM–III–R: Conduct disorder, development, and the concept of harmful dysfunction. *Development and Psychopathology, 5,* 5–29.

Richters, J. E., & Martinez, P. (1993). The NIMH community violence project: Children's distress symptoms associated with violence exposure. *Psychiatry, 56,* 22–35.

Richters, J. E., & Waters, E. (1991). Attachment and socialization: The positive side of social influence. In M. Lewis & S. Feinman (Eds.), *Social influences and socialization in infancy* (pp. 185–214). New York: Plenum Press.

Roberts M. W. (1982). The effects of warned versus unwarned timeout procedures on child noncompliance. *Child & Family Behavior Therapy, 4,* 37–53.

Roberts, M. W. (1984). An attempt to reduce time-out resistance in young children. *Behavior Therapy, 15,* 210–216.

Roberts, M. W. (1985). Praising child compliance: Reinforcement or ritual? *Journal of Abnormal Child Psychology, 13,* 611–629.

Roberts, M. W. (1988). Enforcing chair timeouts with room timeouts. *Behavior Modification, 12,* 353–370.

Roberts, M., McMahon, R. J., Forehand, R., & Humphreys, L. (1978). The effects of parental instruction-giving on child compliance. *Behavior Therapy, 9,* 793–798.

Roberts, M. W. & Powers, S. W. (1988). The compliance test. *Behavioral Assessment, 10,* 375–398.

Roberts, M. W., & Powers, S. W. (1990). Adjusting chair timeout enforcement procedures for oppositional children. *Behavior Therapy, 21,* 257–271.

Robinson, E. A., Eyberg, S. M., & Ross, A. W. (1980). The standardization of an inventory of child conduct problem behaviors. *Journal of Clinical Child Psychology, 9,* 22–28.

Rogers Wiese, M. R. (1992). A critical review of parent training research. *Psychology in the Schools, 29,* 229–236.

Ruma, P. R., Burke, R. V., & Thompson, R. W. (1996). Group parent training: Is it effective for children of all ages? *Behavior Therapy, 27,* 159–169.

Rutter, M., Tizzard, J., & Whitmore, K. (Eds.). (1970), *Education, health, & behavior.* New York: Wiley.

Safran, J. D. (1990a). Towards a refinement of cognitive therapy in light of interpersonal theory: I. Theory. *Clinical Psychological Review, 10,* 87–105.

Safran, J. D. (1990b). Towards a refinement of cognitive therapy in light of interpersonal theory: II. Practice. *Clinical Psychological Review, 10,* 107–121.

Samenow, S. (1989). *Before it's too late.* New York: Times Books.

Sanders, M. R., & Lawton, J. M. (1993). Discussing assessment findings with families: A guided participation model of information transfer. *Child & Family Behavior Therapy, 15,* 5–35.

Schaefer, C. E., & Breismeister, J. M. (1989). *Handbook of parent training: Parents as co-therapists for children's behavior problems.* New York: Wiley.

Schneider, W. J., Cavell, T. A., Hughes, J. N., & Oxford, M. C. (1999). *Development of the Perceived-Containment Questionnaire.* Paper presented at the Annual Convention of the American Psychological Association, Boston.

Schoenfield, I. S., Shaffer, D., O'Connor, P., & Portnoy, S. (1988). Conduct disorder and cognitive functioning: Testing three causal hypotheses. *Child Development, 59,* 993–1007.

Scott, J. P. (1992). Aggression: Functions and control in social systems. *Aggressive Behavior, 18,* 1–20.

Seilhamer, R. A., & Jacob, T. (1990). Family factors and adjustment of children of alcoholics. In M. Windle & J. S. Searles (Eds.), *Children of alcoholics: Critical perspectives* (pp. 168–186). New York: Guilford Press.

Sensue, M. E. (1981). *Filial therapy follow-up study: Effects on parental and child adjustment.* Unpublished doctoral dissertation, Pennsylvania State University, State College.

Serketich, W. J., & Dumas, J. E. (1996). The effectiveness of behavioral parent training to modify antisocial behavior in children: A meta-analysis. *Behavior Therapy, 27,* 171–186.

Shaw, D. S., & Bell, R. Q. (1993). Developmental theories of parental contributors to antisocial behavior. *Journal of Abnormal Child Psychology, 21,* 493–518.

Shaw, D. F., Winslow, E. B., Owens, E. B., Vondra, J. I., Cohn, J. F., & Bell, R. Q. (1998). The development of early externalizing problems among children from low-income families: A transformational perspective. *Journal of Abnormal Child Psychology, 26,* 95–107.

Sheeber, L. B., & Johnson, J. H. (1994). Evaluation of a temperament-focused, parent training program. *Journal of Clinical Child Psychology, 23,* 249–259.

Shirk, S. R., & Russell, R. L. (1996). *Change processes in child psychotherapy.* New York: Guilford Press.

Simpson, J. A., & Rholes, W. S. (1998). *Attachment theory and close relationships.* New York: Guilford Press.

Simpson, J. A., Rholes, W. S., & Nelligan, J. S. (1992). Support seeking and support giving within couples in an anxiety-provoking situation: The role of attachment styles. *Journal of Personality & Social Psychology, 62,* 434–446.

Simpson, J. A., Rholes, W. S., & Phillips, D. (1996). Conflict in close relationships: An attachment perspective. *Journal of Personality and Social Psychology, 62,* 434–446.

Slaby, R. G., & Guerra, N. G. (1988). Cognitive mediators of aggression in adolescent offenders: 1. Assessment. *Developmental Psychology, 24,* 580–588.

Slep, A. M. S., & O'Leary, S. G. (1998). The effects of maternal attributions on parenting: An experimental analysis. *Journal of Family Psychology, 12,* 234–243.

Snyder, D. K., Cavell, T. A., Heffer, R., & Mangrum, L. (1995). Marital and family assessment. In R. H. Mikesell, D. D. Lusterman, & S. H. McDaniel (Eds.), *Family psychology and systems therapy: A handbook.* Washington, DC: American Psychological Association.

Snyder, J. J. (1977). Reinforcement analysis of interaction in problem and non-problem families. *Journal of Abnormal Psychology, 86,* 528–535.

Snyder, J. J., & Patterson, G. R. (1995). Individual differences in social aggression: A test of a reinforcement model of socialization in the natural environment. *Behavior Therapy, 26,* 371–391.

Speltz, M. (1990). The treatment of preschool problems: An integration of behavioral and attachment concepts. In M. T. Greenberg, D. Cicchetti, & M. Cummings (Eds.), *Attachment in the preschool years: Theory, research, and intervention* (pp. 399–426). Chicago: University of Chicago Press.

Spitzer, A., Webster-Stratton, C., & Hollinsworth, T. (1991). Coping with conduct-problem children: Parents gaining knowledge and control. *Journal of Clinical Child Psychology, 20,* 413–427.

Sroufe, L. A., & Fleeson, J. (1988). The coherence of family relationships. In R. A. Hinde & J. Stevenson-Hinde (Eds.), *Relationships with families: Mutual influences* (pp. 27–47). New York: Oxford University Press.

Sroufe, L. A., Jacobvitz, D., Mangelsdorf, S., DeAngelo, E., & Ward, M. (1985). Generational boundary dissolution between mothers and their preschool children: A relationship systems approach. *Child Development, 56,* 317–325.

Stattin, H., & Magnusson, D. (1989). The role of early aggressive behavior in the frequency, seriousness, and types of later crimes. *Journal of Consulting and Clinical Psychology, 57,* 710–718.

Steinberg, L. (1986). Latchkey children and susceptibility to peer pressure: An ecological analysis. *Developmental Psychology, 22,* 433–439.

Steinberg, M. D., & Dodge, K. A. (1983). Attributional bias in aggressive adolescent boys and girls. *Journal of Social and Clinical Psychology, 1,* 312–321.

Stollack, G. E. (1981). Variations and extensions of filial therapy. *Family Process, 20,* 305–309, 1424–1436.

Stoolmiller, M., Duncan, T., Bank, L., & Patterson, G. R. (1993). Some problems and solutions in the study of change: Significant patterns in client resistance. *Journal of Consulting and Clinical Psychology, 61,* 920–928.

Stover, L., & Guerney, B. G., Jr. (1967). The efficacy of training procedures for mothers in filial therapy. *Psychotherapy: Theory, Research and Practice, 4,* 110–115.

Strassberg, Z. (1997). Levels of analysis in cognitive bases of maternal disciplinary dysfunction. *Journal of Abnormal Child Psychology, 25,* 209–215.

Strassberg, Z., Dodge, K. A., Pettit, G. S., & Bates, J. E. (1994). Spanking in the home and children's subsequent aggression toward kindergarten peers. *Development and Psychopathology, 6,* 445–461.

Strauss, M. A., & Gelles, R. J. (1990). *Physical violence in families.* New Brunswick, NJ: Transaction.

Strupp, H. H. (1996). The tripartite model and the *Consumer Reports* study. *American Psychologist, 51,* 1017–1024.

Sywulak, A. E. (1977). *The effect of filial therapy on parental acceptance and child adjustment.* Unpublished doctoral dissertation, Pennsylvania State University, State College.

Szykula, S. A., Mas, C. H., Turner, C. W., Crowley, J., & Sayger, T. V. (1991). Maternal social support and prosocial mother-child interactions. *Journal of Family Psychology, 5,* 82–92.

Tapscott, M., Frick, P. J., Wootton, J., & Kruh, I. (1996). The intergenerational link to antisocial behavior: Effects of paternal contact. *Journal of Child & Family Studies, 5,* 229–240.

Tolan, P. H., Guerra, N. G., & Kendall, P. C. (1995). Introduction to special section: Prediction and prevention of antisocial behavior in children and adolescents. *Journal of Consulting & Clinical Psychology, 63,* 515–517.

Tremblay, R. E., Pagani-Kurtz, L., Masse, L. C., Vitaro, F., & Pihl, R. O. (1995). A bimodal preventive intervention for disruptive kindergarten boys: Its impact through mid-adolescence. *Journal of Consulting and Clinical Psychology, 63,* 560–568.

Vickerman, R. C., Reed, M. D., & Roberts, M. W. (1997). Maternal intervention in subclinical sibling coercion. *Journal of Applied Development Psychology, 18,* 23–35.

Wahler, R. G. (1969). Oppositional children: A quest for parental reinforcement control. *Journal of Applied Behavioral Analysis, 2,* 159–170.

Wahler, R. G. (1994). Child conduct problems: Disorders in conduct or social continuity? *Journal of Child and Family Studies, 3,* 143–156.

Wahler, R. G. (1997). On the origins of children's compliance and opposition: Family context, reinforcement, and rules. *Journal of Child and Family Studies, 6,* 191–208.

Wahler, R. G., & Bellamy, A. (1997). Generating reciprocity with conduct problem children and their mothers. The effectiveness of compliance teaching and responsive parenting. *Journal of Social and Personal Relationships, 14,* 549–564.

Wahler, R. G., Cartor, P. G., Fleischman, J. & Lambert, W. (1993). The impact of synthesis teaching and parent training with mothers of conduct-disordered children. *Journal of Abnormal Child Psychology, 21,* 425–440.

Wahler, R. G., & Dumas, J. E. (1986). Maintenance factors in coercive mother-child interactions: The compliance and predictability hypotheses. *Journal of Applied Behavior Analysis, 19,* 13–22.

Wahler, R. G., & Dumas, J. E. (1989). Attentional problems in dysfunctional mother-child interactions: An interbehavioral model. *Psychological Bulletin, 105,* 116–130.

Wahler, R. G., & Fox, J. J. (1981). Setting events in applied behavior analysis: Toward a conceptual and methodological expansion. *Journal of Applied Behavior Analysis, 14,* 327–338.

Wahler, R. G., Winkle, G. H., Peterson, R. F., & Morrison, D. C. (1965). Mothers as behavior therapists for their own children. *Behavior Research and Therapy, 3,* 113–124.

Walker, J. L., Lahey, B. B., Hynd, G. W., & Frame, C. L. (1987). Comparison of specific patterns of antisocial behavior in children with conduct disorder with or without coexisting hyperactivity. *Journal of Consulting and Clinical Psychology, 55,* 910–913.

Webster-Stratton, C. (1987). *The parents and children series.* Eugene, OR: Castalia.

Webster-Stratton, C. (1989). Systematic comparison of consumer satisfaction of three cost-effective parent training programs for conduct problem children. *Behavior Therapy, 20,* 103–115.

Webster-Stratton, C. (1990). Long-term follow-up of families with young conduct problem children: From preschool to grade school. *Journal of Clinical Child Psychology, 19,* 144–149.

Webster-Stratton, C. (1994). Advancing videotape parent training: A comparison study. *Journal of Consulting & Clinical Psychology, 62,* 583–593.

Webster-Stratton, C., & Hammond, M. (1990). Predictors of treatment outcome in parent training for families with conduct disordered children. *Behavior Therapy, 21,* 319–337.

Webster-Stratton, C., & Herbert, M. (1994). *Troubled families—problem children.* New York: Wiley.

Webster-Stratton, C., Hollinsworth, T., & Kolpacoff, M. (1989). The long-term effectiveness and clinical significance of three cost-effective training programs for families with conduct-problem children. *Journal of Consulting and Clinical Psychology, 57,* 550–553.

Webster-Stratton, C., Kolpacoff, M., & Hollinsworth, T. (1988). Self-administered videotape therapy for families with conduct-problem children: Comparison with two cost-effective treatments and a control group. *Journal of Consulting and Clinical Psychology, 56,* 558–566.

Webster-Stratton, C., & Spitzer, A. (1996). Parenting a young child with conduct problems: New insights using qualitative methods. In T. H. Ollendick & R. J. Prinz (Eds.), *Advances in clinical child psychology* (Vol. 18; pp. 1–46). New York: Plenum.

Weiss, B., Dodge, K. A., Bates, J. E., & Pettit, G. S. (1992). Some consequences of early harsh discipline: Child aggression and a maladaptive social information processing style. *Child Development, 62,* 1321–1335.

Weisz, J. R., Weiss, B., Donenberg, G. R. (1992). The lab versus the clinic: Effects of child and adolescent psychotherapy. *American Psychologist, 47,* 1578–1585.

Wekerle, C., & Wolfe, D. A. (1996). Child maltreatment. In E. J. Mash, & R. A. Barkley (Eds.), *Child psychopathology* (pp. 492–537). New York: Guilford Press.

Welch, J. C. (1996). *Correlates of interpersonal soothing: "Who can help me feel better?"* Doctoral dissertation, Texas A&M University.

Wells, K. C., Forehand, R., & Griest, D. L. (1980). Generality of treatment effects from treated to untreated behaviors resulting from a parent training program. *Journal of Clinical Child Psychology, 9,* 217–219.

Westerman, M. A. (1990). Coordination of maternal directives with preschoolers' behavior in compliance-problem and healthy dyads. *Developmental Psychology, 26,* 621–630.

Wolin, S. J., Bennett, L. A., & Noonan, D. L. (1979). Family rituals and the recurrence of alcoholism over generations. *American Journal of Psychiatry, 136,* 589–593.

Wootton, J. M., Frick, P. J., Shelton, K. K., & Silverthorn, P. (1997). Ineffective parenting and childhood conduct problems: The moderating role of callous-unemotional traits. *Journal of Consulting and Clinical Psychology, 65,* 301–308.

Worthington, E. L., Jr. (1987). Changes in supervision as counselors and supervisors gain experience: A review. *Professional Psychology: Research and Practice, 18,* 244–250.

Yalom, I. D., Brown, S., & Bloch, S. (1975). The written summary as a group therapy technique. *Archives of General Psychiatry, 32,* 605–619.

Youngstrom, N. (1992, January). Inner-city youth tell of life in "a war zone." *APA Monitor,* pp. 36–37.

Zakriski, A. L., & Coie, J. D. (1996). A comparison of aggressive-rejected and nonaggressive-rejected children's interpretations of self-directed and other-directed rejection. *Child Development, 67,* 1048–1070.

Author Index

Subject Index

About the Author

Timothy A. Cavell, PhD, is an associate professor of clinical psychology at Texas A&M University. He received his doctoral degree from Louisiana State University, and he interned at the Morrison Center for Youth and Families in Portland, Oregon. His research focuses on interventions for aggressive children, the prevention of delinquency and adolescent substance abuse, and the assessment of adolescent social competence. His work has been funded by the National Institute on Drug Abuse, the William C. Hogg Foundation, the Texas Higher Education Coordinating Board, and the Texas A&M University Mini-Grant Program. Dr. Cavell maintains a private practice within a general pediatric clinic. He and his wife have three children who are 10, 7, and 6 years old.